THE INTERNET FOR DUMMIES™

by John R. Levine and Carol Baroudi

Foreword by Paul McCloskey,
Executive Editor, *Federal Computer Week*

IDG BOOKS

IDG Books Worldwide, Inc.
An International Data Group Company

San Mateo, California ♦ Indianapolis, Indiana ♦ Boston, Massachusetts

The Internet For Dummies

Published by
IDG Books Worldwide, Inc.
An International Data Group Company
155 Bovet Road, Suite 310
San Mateo, CA 94402

Library of Congress Catalog Card No.: 93-61073

ISBN: 1-56884-024-1

Printed in the United States of America

10 9 8 7 6 5 4

1B/QV/QU/ZU

Distributed in the United States by IDG Books Worldwide, Inc.

Distributed in Canada by Macmillan of Canada, a Division of Canada Publishing Corporation; by Computer and Technical Books in Miami, Florida, for South America and the Caribbean; by Longman Singapore in Singapore, Malaysia, Thailand, and Korea; by Toppan Co. Ltd. in Japan; by Asia Computerworld in Hong Kong; by Woodslane Pty. Ltd. in Australia and New Zealand; and by Transword Publishers Ltd. in the U.K. and Europe.

For general information on IDG Books in the U.S., including information on discounts and premiums, contact IDG Books at 800-762-2974 or 415-312-0605.

For information on where to purchase IDG Books outside the U.S., contact Christina Turner at 415-312-0633.

For information on translations, contact Marc Jeffrey Mikulich, Foreign Rights Manager, at IDG Books Worldwide; FAX NUMBER 415-358-1260.

For sales inquiries and special prices for bulk quantities, write to the address above or call IDG Books Worldwide at 415-312-0650.

IDG BOOKS is a registered trademark of IDG Books Worldwide, Inc.

About the authors

John Levine was a member of a computer club in high school — before high school students, or even high schools, *had* computers. He came in contact with Theodor H. Nelson, author of *Computer Lib* and inventor of hypertext, who fostered the idea that computers should not be taken seriously and that everyone can and should understand and use computers.

John wrote his first program on an IBM 1130 (a computer roughly as powerful as your typical modern digital wristwatch, only harder to use) in 1967. He became an official system administrator of a networked computer at Yale in 1975. He started working part-time (for a computer company, of course) in 1977, and has been in and out of the computer and network biz ever since. He got his company put on USENET (see Chapter 11) early enough that it appears in a 1982 *Byte* magazine article, which included a map of USENET sites.

He used to spend most of his time writing software, but now he mostly writes books (including *UNIX For Dummies,* published by IDG Books Worldwide) because it's more fun. He also teaches some computer courses and publishes and edits an incredibly technoid magazine called *The Journal of C Language Translation.* He holds a B.A. and a Ph.D in Computer Science from Yale University, but please don't hold that against him.

Carol Baroudi met her first computer in college at Colgate University in 1971. Her first encounter with electronic communication was in the form of *send ttys,* an ancient form of terminal warfare.

She taught programming and helped design a computer science curriculum, but majored in Spanish Literature. For the last ten years she's been writing about computer software, including various electronic mail packages.

She firmly believes that computers should be easy and fun to use but are no substitute for chocolate mousse.

Acknowledgments

The author would like to thank Lydia Spitzer for putting up with me while I wrote this, particularly when I should have been out sailing with her. Sophie, who knows who she is, was patient too, and kept my feet warm.

Many of the tables in *The Internet For Dummies* were adapted from material provided gratis by people on the Internet. The list of countries with Internet connections in Appendix A was written by Professor Larry Landweber. The lists of newsgroups in Chapter 12 were condensed from master lists maintained by David Lawrence. The information on DOS and Windows TCP/IP packages in Chapter 28 was adapted from a list maintained by C. J. Sacksteder at the Pennsylvania State University.

I particularly thank my editors at IDG, Mary Bednarek and Diane Steele, for believing me when I said I was finishing this book, despite considerable evidence to the contrary. And, special thanks to Corbin Collins, who really kept all the bits and pieces of this project running smoothly. Thanks to Geneil Breeze, Becky Whitney, Kristin Cocks, Kezia Endsley, and Tracy Barr for pitching in to tie up loose ends.

Thanks to Stuart Stuple, Jim Moody, and Paul McCloskey for providing some additional perspectives. And, of course, thanks to all the production staff at IDG Books Worldwide in Indianapolis.

The publisher would like to give special thanks to Patrick J. McGovern, without whom this book would not have been possible.

Credits

VP & Publisher
David Solomon

Managing Editor
Mary Bednarek

Acquisitions Editor
Janna Custer

Production Director
Beth Jenkins

Senior Editors
Sandy Blackthorn
Diane Graves Steele

Production Coordinator
Cindy L. Phipps

Acquisitions Assistant
Megg Bonar

Editorial Assistant
Patricia R. Reynolds

Editors
Corbin Collins
Geneil Breeze
Rebecca A. Whitney

Technical Reviewer
Stuart J. Stuple

Production Staff
Tony Augsburger
Valery Bourke
Mary Breidenbach
Drew Moore
Gina Scott

Proofreader
Vickie West

Indexer
Sharon Hilgenberg

Book Design
University Graphics

About IDG Books Worldwide

Welcome to the world of IDG Books Worldwide.

IDG Books Worldwide, Inc., is a subsidiary of International Data Group, the world's largest publisher of computer-related information and the leading global provider of information services on information technology. International Data Group publishes over 195 computer publications in 62 countries. Forty million people read one or more International Data Group publications each month

If you use personal computers, IDG Books is committed to publishing quality books that meet your needs. We rely on our extensive network of publications, including such leading periodicals as *Macworld*, *InfoWorld*, *PC World*, *Computerworld*, *Publish*, *Network World*, and *SunWorld*, to help us make informed and timely decisions in creating useful computer books that meet your needs.

Every IDG book strives to bring extra value and skill-building instructions to the reader. Our books are written by experts, with the backing of IDG periodicals, and with careful thought devoted to issues such as audience, interior design, use of icons, and illustrations. Our editorial staff is a careful mix of high-tech journalists and experienced book people. Our close contact with the makers of computer products helps ensure accuracy and thorough coverage. Our heavy use of personal computers at every step in production means we can deliver books in the most timely manner.

We are delivering books of high quality at competitive prices on topics customers want. At IDG, we believe in quality, and we have been delivering quality for over 25 years. You'll find no better book on a subject than an IDG book.

John Kilcullen
President and CEO
IDG Books Worldwide, Inc.

IDG Books Worldwide, Inc. is a subsidiary of International Data Group. The officers are Patrick J. McGovern, Founder and Board Chairman; Walter Boyd, President. International Data Group's publications include: **ARGENTINA'S** Computerworld Argentina, Infoworld Argentina; **ASIA'S** Computerworld Hong Kong, PC World Hong Kong, Computerworld Southeast Asia, PC World Singapore, Computerworld Malaysia, PC World Malaysia; **AUSTRALIA'S** Computerworld Australia, Australian PC World, Australian Macworld, Network World, Mobile Business Australia, Reseller, IDG Sources; **AUSTRIA'S** Computerwelt Oesterreich, PC Test; **BRAZIL'S** Computerworld, Gamepro, Game Power, Mundo IBM, Mundo Unix, PC World, Super Game; **BELGIUM'S** Data News (CW) **BULGARIA'S** Computerworld Bulgaria, Ediworld, PC & Mac World Bulgaria, Network World Bulgaria; **CANADA'S** CIO Canada, Computerworld Canada, Graduate Computerworld, InfoCanada, Network World Canada; **CHILE'S** Computerworld Chile, Informatica; **COLOMBIA'S** Computerworld Colombia; **CZECH REPUBLIC'S** Computerworld, Elektronika, PC World; **DENMARK'S** CAD/CAM WORLD, Communications World, Computerworld Danmark, LOTUS World, Macintosh Produktkatalog, Macworld Danmark, PC World Danmark, PC World Produktguide, Windows World; **ECUADOR'S** PC World Ecuador; **EGYPT'S** Computerworld (CW) Middle East, PC World Middle East; **FINLAND'S** MikroPC, Tietoviikko, Tietoverkko; **FRANCE'S** Distribuitque, GOLDEN MAC, InfoPC, Languages & Systems, Le Guide du Monde Informatique, Le Monde Informatique, Telecoms & Reseaux; **GERMANY'S** Computerwoche, Computerwoche Focus, Computerwoche Extra, Computerwoche Karriere, Information Management, Macwelt, Netzwelt, PC Welt, PC Woche, Publish, Unit; **GREECE'S** Infoworld, PC Games; **HUNGARY'S** Computerworld SZT, PC World; **INDIA'S** Computers & Communications; **IRELAND'S** Computerscope; **ISRAEL'S** Computerworld Israel, PC World Israel; **ITALY'S** Computerworld Italia, Lotus Magazine, Macworld Italia, Networking Italia, PC Shopping Italy, PC World Italia; **JAPAN'S** Computerworld Today, Information Systems World, Macworld Japan, Nikkei Personal Computing, SunWorld Japan, Windows World; **KENYA'S** East African Computer News; **KOREA'S** Computerworld Korea, Macworld Korea, PC World Korea; **MEXICO'S** Compu Edicion, Compu Manufactura, Computacion/ Punto de Venta, Computerworld Mexico, MacWorld, Mundo Unix, PC World, Windows; **THE NETHERLANDS'** Computer! Totaal, Computable (CW), LAN Magazine, MacWorld, Totaal "Windows"; **NEW ZEALAND'S** Computer Listings, Computerworld New Zealand, New Zealand PC World; **NIGERIA'S** PC World Africa; **NORWAY'S** Computerworld Norge, C/World, Lotusworld Norge, Macworld Norge, Networld, PC World Ekspress, PC World Norge, PC World's Produktguide, Publish& Multimedia World, Student Data, Unix World, Windowsworld; IDG Direct Response; **PANAMA'S** PC World Panama; **PERU'S** Computerworld Peru, PC World; **PEOPLE'S REPUBLIC OF CHINA'S** China Computerworld, China Infoworld, PC World China, Electronics International, Electronic Product World, China Network World; IDG HIGH TECH BEIJING'S New Product World; IDG SHENZHEN'S Computer News Digest; **PHILIPPINES'** Computerworld Philippines, PC Digest (PCW); **POLAND'S** Computerworld Poland, PC World/Komputer; **PORTUGAL'S** Cerebro/PC World, Correio Informatico/ Computerworld, MacIn; **ROMANIA'S** Computerworld, PC World; **RUSSIA'S** Computerworld-Moscow, Mir - PC, Sety; **SLOVENIA'S** Monitor Magazine; **SOUTH AFRICA'S** Computer Mail (CIO),Computing S.A.,Network World S.A.; **SPAIN'S** Amiga World, Computerworld Espana, Communicaciones World, Macworld Espana, NeXTWORLD, Super Juegos Magazine (GamePro), PC World Espana, Publish, Sunworld; **SWEDEN'S** Attack, ComputerSweden, Corporate Computing, Lokala Natverk/LAN, Lotus World, MAC&PC, Macworld, Mikrodatorn, PC World, Publishing & Design (CAP), Datalngenjoren, Maxi Data,Windows World; **SWITZERLAND'S** Computerworld Schweiz, Macworld Schweiz, PC Katalog, PC & Workstation; **TAIWAN'S** Computerworld Taiwan, Global Computer Express, PC World Taiwan; **THAILAND'S** Thai Computerworld; **TURKEY'S** Computerworld Monitor, Macworld Turkiye, PC World Turkiye; **UKRAINE'S** Computerworld; **UNITED KINGDOM'S** Computing /Computerworld, Connexion/Network World, Lotus Magazine, Macworld, Open Computing/Sunworld; **UNITED STATES'** AmigaWorld, Cable in the Classroom, CD Review, CIO, Computerworld, Desktop Video World, DOS Resource Guide, Electronic Entertainment Magazine, Federal Computer Week, Federal Integrator, GamePro, IDG Books, Infoworld, Infoworld Direct, Laser Event, Macworld, Multimedia World, Network World, NeXTWORLD, PC Letter, PC World, PlayRight, Power PC World, Publish, SunWorld, SWATPro, Video Event; **VENEZUELA'S** Computerworld Venezuela, MicroComputerworld Venezuela; **VIETNAM'S** PC World Vietnam

Contents at a Glance

Cartoons at a Glance

By Rich Tennant

page 282

page 131

page 241

page 215

page 297

page 5

page 65

page 16

page 153

Table of Contents

Foreword

A year ago I was the original Internet Dummy.

Although I had been covering technology in one form or another for 10 years as a journalist, I considered most computers to be typewriters on steroids. I just needed a good text editor, about 15 megabytes of storage, and a push-button phone.

Also, I thought most of my office mates who actually did bury their heads in their personal computers were the newsroom equivalents of heating and air conditioning engineers. I had better things to do than marvel about "personal productivity tools" or "spreadsheet performance." Computing in a bubble, I thought.

Then while I was on vacation, a colleague ran some telephone wire into the back of my computer, loaded a communications package, and left me a note about how to launch the operation.

Readers, that note is now framed in my office. Eventually, that telephone wire led to the Internet and to the single most amazing, entertaining, and educational experience of my career.

Quite simply, the Internet has revolutionized the way I interact with the outside world, altered my work habits, and burst the bubble around my PC. It has also challenged my thinking about the future of personal communications technology. And I believe that sooner — rather than later — those changes will be mapped onto society as a whole.

Consider this: My $1,000 PC is now a personal broadcasting station that reaches more people than the CBS affiliate in Washington D.C. I can get more local viewers with a single e-mail posting to the Internet than Sally Jessy Raphael can get in a sweeps month.

Or this: I'm going to send this piece to my editor for about $\frac{1}{60}$ of a cent and $\frac{1}{6}$ of a second. (Memo to the Letter Carriers Union: Invest in night schools, now.)

Or this: When Vice President Al Gore released his proposal for the National Information Infrastructure, his personal vision for the Information Superhighway, it was zapped to my e-mail box that very morning, courtesy of an Internet group I belong to that is interested in such matters. (Hey *Washington Post*! POOF! You're a newsletter!)

I've also had some amazing interactions on the Internet, the implications of which I am still trying to figure out. For instance, a few months ago I was logged on to the Internet's equivalent of a live on-line forum in which two other people were present. Now that's not so unusual, considering the popularity of similar forums running on the dressier, private on-line services. But then one of them handed me a photograph. Actually, it was a little more complicated than that — given the hardware and software being used, I had to execute some commands, download the file, and stomp on it a few times — but that is essentially what happened. Instead of exchanging text messages, we swapped *graphics.*

Although it was a simple transaction, given that I was in Washington, D.C., and the other two people were possibly in Wheaton, Illinois and Durban, South Africa, it was an amazing interaction. Wait until baseball card collectors get ahold of that one.

But that is one of the joys of the Internet. Its constantly evolving set of applications is being driven not so much by software developers but by its users, all crowding around, talking, and trying out new things.

And while the Internet has turned around the way I interact with the outside world, it has also made me more keen about the technology on my end of the wall jack. Those little pieces of software that make my personal computer more of a convenience have a whole new power and meaning when attached to the two million computers on the Internet.

I now run short digital motion pictures on my PC. The software and the graphics are tucked away in their proper places on the Internet. My PC is humming with software — Indiana Jones never saw more icons. My home and office are now wired together. And I no longer discredit the office PC tinkerers; I just urge them to get on the Internet.

I therefore urge you to read John Levine and Carol Baroudi's *The Internet For Dummies.* It will guide you, with patience and a refreshing sense of humor, through the sometimes daunting job of getting going on the Internet. But you *will* be rewarded. And the rest is up to your imagination.

Paul McCloskey
Executive Editor
Federal Computer Week

Introduction

● ●

*W*elcome to *The Internet For Dummies!* There are lots of books available about the Internet, but most of them assume that you have a degree in computer science, would love to learn every strange and useless wart of the Internet, and enjoy memorizing unpronounceable commands and options. We hope this book is different.

Instead, this book describes what you actually do to become an *Internaut* (someone who navigates the Internet with skill) — how to get started, what commands you actually need, and when to give up and go for help. And we describe it in plain old English.

About This Book

This book is designed to be used when you can't figure out what to do next. We don't flatter ourselves that you are interested enough in the Internet to sit down and read the whole thing (although it should be a fine book for the bathroom). When you run into a problem using the Internet ("Hmm . . . I thought I typed a command that would log into another computer, but it didn't respond with any message..."), just dip into the book long enough to solve your problem.

Pertinent sections include:

✔ What the Internet is

✔ Communicating with electronic mail

✔ Using other computers on the Net

✔ Moving files and other data around

✔ Ways to find useful stuff on the Internet

✔ Common mistakes and how to correct them

✔ Where to find services and software to get onto the Internet

How to Use This Book

Use this book as a reference. Look up your topic or command in the Table of Contents or the Index, which refers you to the part of the book in which we describe what to do and perhaps define a few terms (if absolutely necessary).

When you have to type something, it appears in the book like this:

```
cryptic command to type
```

Type it in, just as it appears. Use the same capitalization we do — many systems care very deeply about CAPITAL and small letters. Then press the Enter or Return key. The book tells you what should happen when you give each command and what your options are.

You'll find chapters that list error messages that you may run into as well as common user mistakes. You may want to peruse the latter topic (Chapters 23 and 24) in order to avoid these mistakes before they happen.

Who Are You?

In writing the book, we assumed that

- ✔ You have or would like to have access to the Internet.
- ✔ You want to get some work done with it.
- ✔ Someone has set up your system so that you can use your computer to get to the Internet without running cables, installing satellite dishes, or the like.
- ✔ You are not interested in becoming the world's next great Internet expert.

How This Book Is Organized

This book has six Parts. The Parts stand on their own — you can start reading wherever you like, but you should at least skim Part I first to get acquainted with some unavoidable Internet jargon.

Here are the Parts of the book and what they contain:

Part I: Getting onto the Internet

This Part defines what the Internet is and why it's interesting (at least why I think it's interesting). Also, there's a little chunk of vital Internet terminology and concepts that will help you as you move through the later Parts, and there are discussions about how to get started on the Net no matter what kind of computer setup you have.

Part II: Mail and Gossip

In this Part, you learn how to exchange electronic mail with people down the hall or on other continents and how to use electronic mailing lists to keep in touch with people of like interests. You learn about using *USENET* news to keep in touch even better, and there are even some suggestions for checking out the thousands of topics that USENET addresses.

Part III: Instant Gratification

Here you learn how to log into other computers, how to retrieve useful files from computers around the world, and how to figure out what to do with the files once you've got them.

Part IV: Finding Stuff on the Net

This Part tells you about four extremely cool programs that help you find useful stuff among the millions (no kidding) of computers on the Net.

Part V: The Part of Tens

This Part is a compendium of ready references and useful facts (which implies, we suppose, that the other chapters are full of useless facts, but we hope not).

Part VI: Resource Reference

In this Part, you learn where to find providers of Internet connections, purveyors of useful Internet software — commercial, shareware, and free — and where to learn more.

Icons Used in This Book

This icon lets you know that some particularly nerdy, technoid information is coming up, so that you can skip it if you want (on the other hand, you might want to read it).

This icon indicates that a nifty little shortcut or time-saver is explained.

Watch out below — time to duck and run for cover!

This icon alerts you to particularly juicy information related to locating something or someone on the Net.

What Now?

That's all you need to know to get started. Whenever you hit a snag using the Internet, just look up the problem in the Table of Contents or Index of this book. You'll either have the problem solved in a flash or you'll know whether you need to find some expert help.

Because the Internet has been evolving for over 20 years, largely under the influence of some extremely nerdy people, it was not designed to be particularly easy for normal people to use. So don't feel bad if you have to look up a number of topics before you feel comfortable using the Internet. After all, most computer users never have to face anything as complex as the Internet.

Feedback, Please

Incidentally, in this book, the "I" and "me" refers to Carol Baroudi in Chapters 19, 21, and 22, and John R. Levine everywhere else.

If you want to contact us, please feel free to do so in care of

IDG Books Worldwide
3250 N. Post Road, Suite 140
Indianapolis, IN 46226

Part I
Getting onto the Internet

The 5th Wave   **By Rich Tennant**

"HOW SHOULD I KNOW WHY THEY TOOK IT OFF THE LIST? MAYBE THERE JUST WEREN'T ENOUGH MEMBERS TO SUPPORT AN 'AIREDALES FOR ELVIS' NEWSGROUP."

In this part...

The Internet is an enormous and amazing thing. But it's made up of computers, which means that nothing about it is quite as simple as it should be. First I take a quick look at what the Internet is and where it came from. Then I look at the gruesome details of getting onto the Internet for users of various different kinds of computers.

Chapter 1
What Is the Internet? Why?

What Is the Internet?

The *Internet* — also known as the *Net* — is the world's largest computer *network*, or *net*. "So what?" you're probably saying. "I once saw the world's largest turnip on TV, and it didn't look very interesting — and I bet it didn't taste so great, either." Well, with networks, unlike vegetables, size counts for a lot, because the larger a network is, the more stuff it has to offer.

Actually, the Internet isn't really a network — it's a network of networks, all freely exchanging information. The networks range from the big and formal, like the corporate networks at AT&T, Digital Equipment, and Hewlett-Packard, to the small and informal, like the one in my attic (with a couple of old PCs I bought through the *Want Advertiser*) and everything in between. College and university networks have long been part of the Internet, and now high schools and elementary schools are joining up as well. As of August 1993, over 14,000 networks were in the Internet, with 1,000 new networks per month being added.

A Few Real-Life Stories

You can think of the Internet as being two things: the people who use it and the information that resides in it.

✔ Seventh grade students in San Diego use the Internet to exchange letters and stories with kids in Israel. Partly it's just for fun and to make friends in a foreign country, but a sober academic study reported that when kids have a real audience for their stuff, they write better. (Big surprise.)

> ✔ In some parts of the world, the Internet is the fastest and most reliable way to move information. During the 1991 Soviet coup, a tiny Internet provider called RELCOM, which had a link to Finland and through there to the rest of the Internet world, found itself the only reliable path to get reports in and out of Moscow, because telephones were shut off and newspapers weren't being published. RELCOM members sent out stories that would have been in newspapers, statements from Boris Yeltsin (hand-delivered by friends), and their personal observations from downtown Moscow.

The Internet has more prosaic uses, too. Here are some from my personal experience:

> ✔ One day, my wife wanted to find patterns to make a 1960's-era military shirt. (A friend had an old shirt that he loved from his days in the Army but it was running out of places on which to sew patches.) So I asked the Net to help me. The Net has several running discussions on military topics and one on historical costuming, so I sent out a message asking for help. Within a day, five different people responded by giving me the addresses of pattern makers. Most of them said they'd be happy to offer tips and advice if we ran into trouble.

> ✔ The Internet is its own best source of software. Whenever I hear about a new service (such as the ones described in Chapters 19-22), it usually only takes a few minutes to find software for my computer (a 386 laptop running Windows), download it, and start it up. And nearly all of the software available on the Internet is free.

> ✔ There are local and regional parts of the Internet as well. When I wanted to sell my trusty but tired minivan, a note on the Internet in a local for-sale area found a buyer within two days.

The Internet and You

So the Internet is a network, actually a network of networks, and it really is huge. In fact, nobody knows exactly *how* big it is because it is a collection of separately run smaller computer networks with no single place where all the connections are registered.

At least a million machines are connected to it, and it has many millions of users on every continent (see the sidebar "Every continent?"). *That's* big. One thing we do know is that it's growing like crazy, by something like 10 percent per month. Because there are now at least a million computers on the Net, this means 100,000 new computers monthly!

Another unusual thing about the Internet is that it's probably the most *open* network in the world. Thousands of computers provide facilities that are available to anyone who has Net access. This situation is quite unusual — most networks are very restrictive in what they allow users to do and require specific arrangements and passwords for each service. Although a few pay services exist (and undoubtedly more will be added in the future), the vast majority of Internet services are free for the taking.

The final unusual thing about the Internet is that it is what one might call "socially unstratified." That is, one computer is no better than any other, and no person is any better than any other. Who you are on the Internet depends solely on how you present yourself through your keyboard. If what you say makes you sound like an intelligent, interesting person, that's who you are. It doesn't matter how old you are or what you look like or whether you're a student, a business executive, or a construction worker. Physical disabilities don't matter — I correspond with several people who are blind or deaf. If they hadn't felt like telling me, I'd never have known. There are famous people in the Net community, some favorably and some unfavorably, but they got that way through their own efforts.

What is a computer network, anyway?

If you already know what a computer network is, you can skip this section. But you might want to read it anyway, just to make sure we're using the same words to mean the same thing.

A computer network is, basically, a bunch of computers hooked together somehow. (Here in computerland, we like these crisp, precise definitions.) In concept, it's sort of like a radio or TV network which connects a bunch of radio or TV stations together so that they can share the latest episode of *The Simpsons*.

But don't take the analogy too far. TV networks send the same information to all the stations at the same time (what's called *broadcast* networking, for obvious reasons); in computer networks, each particular message is usually routed to a particular computer. Unlike TV networks, computer networks are invariably two-way, so that when computer A sends a message to computer B, B can send a reply back to A.

Some computer networks consist of a central computer and a bunch of remote stations that report to it (for example, a central airline-reservation computer, with thousands of terminals at airports and travel agencies). Others, including the Internet, are more egalitarian and permit any computer on the network to communicate with any other.

Every continent?

Some skeptical readers, upon reading the claim that the Internet spans every continent, may point out that Antarctica is a continent, even though its population consists largely of penguins, who (as far as we know) are not interested in computer networks. Does the Internet go there? Actually, it does. A few machines at the Scott Base on McMurdo Sound in Antarctica are on the Net, connected by radio link to New Zealand. The base at the South Pole is supposed to have a link to the U.S., but they don't publish their electronic address.

At this writing, the largest Internet-free land mass in the world appears to be Bali, or maybe Java. (Greenland got on the Internet in 1992.)

How Can I Tell If I'm on the Internet Already?

If you have access to a computer or a computer terminal, you may already be on the Internet. Here are some ways to check:

- ✔ If you have an account on an on-line service like CompuServe, GEnie, or MCI Mail, you can use the service's electronic mail system to exchange messages with anyone on the Internet. Some on-line services, notably Delphi, also provide other, more interactive Internet services.

- ✔ If you use a bulletin board system (BBS) that exchanges messages with other BBSs, again you can exchange e-mail with the Internet.

- ✔ If your company has an internal e-mail system, it may also be connected to the Internet. Ask a local mail expert.

- ✔ If your company has a local network, it may be connected directly or indirectly to the Internet, either just for mail or for a wider variety of services. Networks of UNIX workstations usually use the same networking conventions that the Internet does, so that connection is technically easy. Networks of PCs or Macs use different conventions, so a *gateway* is necessary to translate.

How Can I Use the Net?

The Internet's facilities are provided through a large set of different services. There's hardly room to give a complete list here (indeed, a complete list would fill several books larger than this one), but some examples follow to encourage you to keep reading:

✔ **Electronic mail (e-mail):** This is certainly the most widely used service — you can exchange e-mail with millions of people all over the world. And people use e-mail for anything they might use paper mail or the telephone for: gossip, recipes, rumors, love letters, you name it. (I hear that some people even use it for stuff related to work.) Electronic *mailing lists* enable you to join in group discussions and meet people over the Net. *Mail servers* (programs that respond to e-mail messages) let you retrieve all sorts of information. See Chapters 7, 8, and 10 for details.

✔ **On-line conversation:** You can "talk" in real time to other users anywhere on the Net. Although on-line conversation is pretty pointless for someone down the hall, it's great for quick chats with people on other continents, particularly when one party or the other isn't a native English speaker (typing is easier and clearer than talking).

✔ **Information retrieval:** Many computers have files of information that are free for the taking. The files range from U.S. Supreme Court decisions and library card catalogs to digitized pictures (nearly all of them suitable for family audiences) and an enormous variety of software, from games to operating systems. Many of the tools discussed in this book help you make sense of the mountain of information available on the Net and figure out what is available where. As mentioned in the "Introduction," you'll see a "Navigate" icon here and there; this icon points to sections in this book that help you navigate the Net.

✔ **Bulletin boards:** A system called *USENET* is an enormous, distributed, on-line bulletin board with about 40 million characters of messages in over 2000 different topic groups flowing daily. Topics range from nerdy computer stuff to hobbies like cycling and knitting to endless political arguments to just plain silliness. The most widely read USENET group is one that features selected jokes, most of which *are* pretty funny.

✔ **Games and gossip:** A game called *MUD (Multi-User Dungeon)* can easily absorb all your waking hours — in it you can challenge other players who can be anywhere in the world. *Internet Relay Chat (IRC)* is a party line over which you can have more or less interesting conversations with other users all over the place. IRC seems to be mostly frequented by bored college students, but you never know whom you'll encounter.

Where Did the Internet Come From?

The ancestor of the Internet was the *ARPANET*, a project started by the Department of Defense (DOD) in 1969, both as an experiment in reliable networking and to link together DOD and military research contractors, including the large number of universities doing military-funded research. (*ARPA* stands for *Advanced Research Projects Agency*, the branch of Defense in charge of handing out grant money. For enhanced confusion, the agency is now known as *DARPA* — the added *D* is for *Defense*, just in case there was any doubt where the money was coming from.)

The reliable networking part involved *dynamic rerouting.* If one of the network links became disrupted by enemy attack, the traffic on it could automatically be rerouted to other links. Fortunately, the Net rarely has come under enemy attack. But an errant backhoe cutting a cable is just as much of a threat, so it's important for the Net to be backhoe-resistant.

The ARPANET was wildly successful, and every university in the country wanted to sign up. This success meant that the ARPANET started getting hard to manage, particularly with the large and growing number of university sites on it. So it was broken into two parts: *MILNET,* which had the military sites, and the new, smaller ARPANET, which had the nonmilitary sites. The two networks remained connected, however, thanks to a technical scheme called *IP (Internet Protocol),* which enabled traffic to be routed from one net to another as needed. All the networks connected by IP in the Internet speak IP, so they all can exchange messages.

Although there were only two networks at that time, IP was designed to allow for tens of thousands of networks. An unusual fact about the IP design is that every computer on an IP network is, in principle, just as capable as any other, so any machine can communicate with any other machine. (This communication scheme may seem obvious, but at the time most networks consisted of a small number of enormous central computers and a lot of remote *terminals,* which could communicate only with the central systems, not with other terminals.)

Can the Internet really resist enemy attack?

Looks that way. During the Gulf War in 1991, the U.S. military had considerable trouble knocking out the Iraqi command network. It turned out that the Iraqis were using commercially available network routers with standard Internet routing and recovery technology. In other words, dynamic rerouting really worked. It's nice to know that dynamic rerouting works, though perhaps this was not the most opportune way to find out.

Meanwhile, back at the classroom

Starting around 1980, university computing was moving from a small number of large *time-sharing* machines, each of which served hundreds of simultaneous users, to a large number of smaller desktop *workstations* for individual users. Because users had gotten used to the advantages of time-sharing systems, such as shared directories of files and e-mail, they wanted to keep those same facilities on their workstations. (They were perfectly happy to leave behind the disadvantages of time-shared systems. A sage once said, "The best thing about a workstation is that it's no faster in the middle of the night.")

Most of the new workstations ran a variety of *UNIX*, a popular (and, for universities, nearly free) kind of operating software that had been developed at the University of California at Berkeley. The people at Berkeley were big fans of computer networking, so their version of UNIX included all of the software needed to hook up to a network. Workstation manufacturers started to include the necessary network hardware as well, so all you had to do to get a working network was to string the cable to connect the workstations together, something that universities could do for cheap because they could usually get students to do it.

Now, rather than having one or two computers to attach to the ARPANET, a site would have hundreds. What's more, each workstation was considerably faster than an entire 1970s multiuser system, so that one workstation could generate enough network traffic to swamp the ARPANET, which was getting creakier by the minute. Something had to give.

Enter the National Science Foundation

The next event was that the *National Science Foundation (NSF)* decided to set up five *supercomputer* centers for research use. (A supercomputer is a really fast computer with a hefty price, like $10 million apiece.) The NSF figured that it would fund a few supercomputers, let researchers from all over the country use the ARPANET to send their programs to be supercomputed, and then send the results back.

The plan to use the ARPANET didn't work out for a variety of reasons, some technical, some political. So the NSF, never shy about establishing a new political empire, built its own much faster network to connect the supercomputing centers: the *NSFNET*. Then it arranged to set up a bunch of regional networks to connect the users in each region, with the NSFNET connecting all the regional networks.

The NSFNET worked like a charm. In fact, by 1990 so much business had moved from the ARPANET to the NSFNET that, after nearly 20 years, the ARPANET had outlived its usefulness and was shut down. The supercomputer centers that the NSFNET was supposed to support turned out to be not very successful: some of the supercomputers didn't work, and the ones that did were so expensive to use that most potential customers decided a few high-performance workstations would serve their needs just as well. Fortunately, by the time it became clear that the supercomputers were on the way out, the NSFNET had become so entrenched in the Internet that it lives on without its original purpose.

The NSFNET only permits traffic related to research and education, so independent, commercial IP network services have appeared that can be used for other kinds of traffic. The commercial networks connect to the regional networks just like the NSFNET does, and provide direct connections for customers. See Chapter 27 for a list of these services.

Outside the United States, IP networks have appeared in many countries, either sponsored by the local telephone company (which is usually also the local post office) or run by independent national or regional providers. Nearly all of them are connected directly or indirectly to some U.S. network, meaning that they all can exchange traffic with each other.

The national network

In 1991, then-senator Al Gore decided that for the United States to continue to be a competitive, with-it, first-world kind of country, we should have really great computing and networks. He sponsored the High-Performance Computing Act of 1991, which is supposed to hook up all researchers, universities, primary schools, government agencies — you name it — into one big happy and very fast (100 times faster than the primary Internet links are now) network called the *National Research and Education Network*, or *NREN*.

Considerable political wrangling has since ensued, as lots of different organizations have attempted to belly up to the trough in order to get part of the very lucrative business of building this network. At the moment, the main concrete progress toward the NREN is that the NSFNET is now officially the interim NREN. Doubtless, the NREN will be built eventually; equally doubtless, it will take longer and cost more than anyone cares to admit.

What this means for you is debatable. Many people find the prospect of a network brought to them by the same people who run the post office and Amtrak to be underwhelming, and it is certainly true that fast commercial networks, which are already under construction, will appear long before the NREN actually arrives. On the other hand, if you are in an impoverished part of the educational establishment, such as a public elementary school, the NREN is supposed to hook you up to the same resources as the big guys — and the reports trickling in from the field say that getting Internet access in the K-12 world is pretty exciting.

OK, Really, How Do I Get Onto the Internet?

You've looked all over the place — you've got no network cables, at least none that connect to the outside world. No networked mail services, no shared bulletin boards, just a computer and a modem at the office or at home. Now what?

One approach, let's call it the "geek" or "deranged" approach, is to run network cables (held in place by duct tape, of course) all over your house, climb up on the roof, put up radio antennas, and fill up the attic with humming boxes full of Routers and Subnets and Packet Driver NDIS Shims and heaven knows what else. This approach can be made to work (in fact, I've actually done it), but if you were the kind of geek who liked to do that sort of thing, you probably wouldn't be reading this book.

The other approach, the "normal" approach, is to use your computer and modem and dial into an Internet service where the geeks have already set things up for you. You run a normal terminal program on your computer, something like Crosstalk or Procomm or Macterminal, and then use your modem to call in the same way you'd call into Compuserve or your local computer bulletin board. I've done that, at the beach. (Hey, I was on vacation, and I was out of duct tape.) For more details on modem wrangling, consult Tina Rathbone's *Modems For Dummies,* published by IDG Books Worldwide.

There are lots of Internet services you can use, with more appearing every month. See Chapter 27, "Public Internet Service Providers," for a long list of them. If there's a Freenet in your city (they're listed on pages 311 through 314), try that first, since it's free, gives you a taste of what the Internet has to offer, and is interesting in its own right.

Failing that, see whether there's a commercial provider in your own city (they're listed on pages 302 through 310) and check them out. You'll probably find that if you use the Internet at all, you'll be on-line for long periods of time, so it's nice if both the service itself and the voice help line are a local phone call away.

If there's no local provider, try Delphi (listed on page 302) which provides Internet service nationally. Delphi usually will give you five free introductory hours on-line so that you can see how you like it.

While we're talking about public Internet services, here's the answer to the most often asked question by new public Internet service users. One of the most popular Internet services is FTP, which lets you retrieve files of useful stuff such as games, programs, pictures, and databases, from all over the Internet (see Chapters 16, 17, and 18). But once you've retrieved the files, they're on the Internet service's computer. How do you get them from the service's computer to *your* computer where they'll be useful? The answer is simple (well, fairly simple); you download them. Details of downloading vary, unfortunately, from one system to another, but the general sequence of events is as follows:

- Find a downloading scheme that both your terminal program and the service support, such as Kermit, Ymodem, or Zmodem.

- Type the command to the service to tell it to prepare to download a file or group of files.

- Give the command (usually something like Alt-PgDn) to your terminal program to tell it to start collecting the files from the service.

- Wait awhile while the download happens.

For more info on downloading, see *Modems For Dummies.* You may have to call the service's help line to find out exactly how to make it download stuff, since no two systems seem to use the same downloading commands.

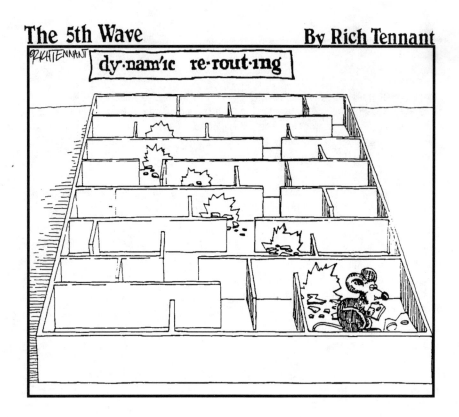

Chapter 2
Names, Numbers, and Rules

• •

In This Chapter

▶ What's in a number?

▶ What's in a name?

▶ How much do I care about these names and numbers?

▶ Names around the world

▶ Rules and regulations

• •

*W*ell, OK, so the Internet has over a million computers attached to it. How do you find the one you want? There are two ways (nobody said this was going to be simple). Each machine on the Net is identified by a number and a name. First, I look at the numbers, and then at the names.

Executive Summary

The way that the numbers and names are assigned on the Internet is, unavoidably, fairly technical. So here's the short version, in case you'd rather save the full version for later.

✔ Each machine on the Net (called a *host* in Internet-ese) has a number assigned to identify it to other hosts, sort of like a phone number. The numbers are in four parts, like 123.45.67.89. You should know the host number of the computer you use most, but otherwise can forget about the numbers.

✔ Most hosts also have names, which are a lot easier to remember than numbers are. The names have multiple parts separated by dots, for example *chico.iecc.com,* the name of my computer. Some hosts have more than one name, but it doesn't matter which of them you use.

✔ There are complicated rules that control how names and numbers are assigned. But because you're not likely to be doing any of the assigning, you don't really need to know what they are.

✔ Each network in the Internet has rules about what kinds of traffic it allows. You should know the rules that apply to the network(s) you use to avoid getting the network managers mad at you.

What's in a Number?

Any computer of any kind, from the smallest to the largest, that is attached to the Internet is called a *host* (which must make us users parasites — *yuck*). Some hosts are giant mainframes or supercomputers providing services to thousands of users, some are little workstations or PCs with one user, and some are specialized computers, like *routers* which connect one network to another or *terminal servers* which let dumb terminals (or PCs running Procomm, Crosstalk, or the like) dial in and connect to other hosts. But from the Internet's point of view, they're all hosts.

Each machine is assigned a *host number*, which is sort of like a phone number. Being computers, the kind of numbers hosts like are 32-bit binary numbers. For example, my computer's number is

```
10001100101110100101000100000001
```

Hmmm. That's not very memorable. To make the number slightly easier to remember, it's broken up into four 8-bit groups, and then each group is translated into a decimal equivalent. So, my computer's number turns into

```
140.186.81.1
```

which isn't a whole lot better, but it's at least possible for humans to remember for a minute or two.

TIP

How much should I care about these numbers?

By and large, you can get by without knowing any host numbers because in most cases you use the much more memorable host names described later in this chapter. Occasionally, however, the naming scheme breaks down. In such a case, having written down the following two numbers is helpful:

✔ The number of the computer you use

✔ The number of some other nearby computer to which you have access

The reason to know the second number is that if you can contact the second computer by number but not by name, you can reasonably conclude that the naming scheme has failed. If you can't contact it either way, it's more likely that the network, or at least your network connection, has failed, quite possibly because you inadvertently kicked a cable loose. Oops.

Networks have numbers, too?

I'm afraid so. Consider, for a moment, your phone number, which is something like 202-653-1800. In the phone number, the first six digits designate where the phone exchange is — in this case, Washington, D.C. The last four digits are a particular phone in that exchange — in this case, the master clock at the U.S. Naval Observatory.

Internet *host numbers* are also divided into two parts: the first part is the network number (remember, the Internet is composed of a lot of different but interconnected networks), and the second part, the *local* part, is a host number on that particular network. In the case of my computer, 140.186.81.1 means network number 140.186, and local host number (on that network) 81.1. Sometimes, for added confusion, people write out network numbers in four parts by adding zeros, like 140.186.0.0.

Because some networks have a lot more hosts on them than others, networks are divided into three sizes: large, medium, and small. In large networks (*Class A*), the first of the four numbers is the network number, and the last three are the local part. In medium networks (*Class B*), the first two numbers are the network number, and the last two are the local part. In small networks (*Class C*), the first three numbers are the network number, and the last is the local part.

The first of the four numbers tells you what class the network is. Table 2-1 is a little table summarizing classes and sizes.

Table 2-1	**Network Numbers and Sizes**		
Class	*First Number*	*Length of Net Number*	*Maximum Number of Hosts*
A	1-126	1	16,387,064
B	128-191	2	64,516
C	192-223	3	254

Great big organizations (or at least organizations that have a whole lot of computers) tend to have Class A networks. For example, IBM has network 9, and AT&T has network 12, so host number 9.12.34.56 would be at IBM, and 12.98.76.54 would be at AT&T. Medium-sized organizations, including most universities, have Class B networks. Rutgers University has network 128.6, and Goldman Sachs (an investment broker that presumably uses a lot of computers to keep track of all the money it handles) has network 138.8. Class C networks are used by small organizations and sometimes small parts of large organizations. Network 192.65.175, for example, is used by a single IBM research lab. (Why don't they use the general IBM network number? Who knows.)

Some host and network numbers are reserved for special purposes. In particular, any number with a component of 0 or 255 (two numbers with great mystical significance to computers) is special and can't be used as an actual host number. (This is a slight exaggeration, but it's close enough for most purposes.)

Subnets, supernets, super-duper nets, . . .

This discussion is extremely technoid. Don't say I didn't warn you.

Frequently, an organization that has a single network number wants to set up its computers internally on multiple networks. For example, all the computers in a single department are usually attached together on a single network, with some sort of connection linking department networks together. (Both administrative and technical reasons exist for this arrangement, but I won't bore you with them.) But adhering to the way the Internet was originally set up would mean that an outfit with 25 internal networks would have to get 25 different network numbers for them.

This was bad news for several reasons. It meant that every time a company set up a new internal network, it had to apply for a new network number. Even worse, the rest of the Internet world had to put that network number in their tables so that they knew how to route messages to it.

Clearly, something had to be done. That something is called a *subnet*. All that means is that one network can be divided into pieces called subnets by treating part of what would normally be the host number as part of the network number. For example, in network 140.186, the third number in the host number is the subnet number, so for machine 140.186.81.1 (the one on which this book is being typed) the subnet number is 140.186.81, and the host number is 1. This enables plenty of local networks to be installed (currently we use only 90 of the 254 possible subnets), and as far as

the outside world is concerned, there's still only the single network 140.186 to worry about.

In practice, all but the smallest networks are subnetted. Also in practice, you almost never have to worry about subnets. When your computer is first attached to the net, the guru who installs it has to set its *subnet mask* to correctly reflect the current subnetting conventions. If the mask is wrong you may have strange problems, like being able to communicate with half your company's departments (such as the even-numbered ones but not the odd-numbered ones).

A few organizations have an opposite problem. They have too many computers for a Class C network (more than 254) but nowhere near enough to justify a Class B. Or, a growing company may expect to have too many machines for a Class B network (more than 64,000) but can't get a Class A network number because there are so few of them that you can't get one any more. In this case, the organization can get a block of adjacent network numbers and treat part of the network number as a host number, a process called *supernetting.*

(The supernetted number is then invariably subnetted, an extra wart that we won't even start to consider.) Supernetting is currently uncommon but will become more widely used as more companies put a lot of computers on the Internet. Like subnetting, you don't have to worry about it unless someone screws up your system's configuration.

Multiple multiple numbers numbers

The final added confusion in host numbering is that some hosts have more than one number. The reason for this is actually quite simple: some hosts are on more than one network, so they need a host number on each of the networks to which they are attached. If you need to contact a machine with multiple host numbers, it doesn't matter which of the numbers you use.

What's in a Name?

Normal people use names, not numbers, so in a rare bow to normality, Internet hosts are usually referred to by name, not number. For example, the machine we have heretofore referred to as 140.186.81.1 is named *chico*. In the earliest days of the ARPANET, machines had simple one-part names, and there was a master list of names. The machine at Harvard was called *HARVARD*, and so forth. But with a million machines on the Net, it'd be kind of hard to come up with different names for all of them.

To avoid a crisis of naming creativity, the solution was to go to multipart names, a scheme grandly known as the *Domain Name System* or *DNS*. Host names are a string of words (or at least word-like things) separated by dots. In the multipart regime, chico's real name is CHICO.IECC.COM. (The naming scheme was evidently invented by people WHO LIKE TO SHOUT EVERYTHING IN CAPITAL LETTERS. Fortunately, the lowercase in host names is always taken to be equivalent to uppercase, and henceforth we will avoid shouting and put the names in lowercase.)

Zones, domains, and all that

You have to decode an Internet name from right to left. This may seem perverse, but it turns out in practice to be more convenient than the other way around, for the same reason that we put surnames after first names. (In England, where they drive on the left, they write host names from left to right. Typical.)

The rightmost part of a name is called its *zone*. If we examine chico's full name, the rightmost part is *com*, which means that this is a *commercial* site (in the com zone), as opposed to educational, military, or some other kinds of zones I mention later in this chapter.

The next part of chico's name, *iecc*, is the name of the company, I.E.C.C. (Yes, it's sometimes pronounced "yecch" — I should have picked a better name.) The part to the left of the company name is the particular machine within the company. Mine happens to be a rather small company with only six computers, so chico's friends, milton, astrud, and xuxa, are known as *milton.iecc.com*, *astrud.iecc.com*, and *xuxa.iecc.com*.

There actually is a logic to the naming scheme I used. They're named after my favorite Brazilian pop stars. Chico is Chico Buarque, who's quite political. Milton is Milton Nascimento, who's more lyrical and melodic. And Xuxa is Xuxa, who's sort of a cross between Madonna and Mr. Rogers. Astrud (Astrud "Girl from Ipanema" Gilberto) is the link between my net and the rest of the Internet.

The host naming system is quite egalitarian. In it, iecc.com, a company with two employees, is right up there with *ibm.com*, a company with several hundred thousand employees. Larger organizations usually further subdivide machine names by site or department, so that a typical machine in the Computer Science Department at Yale University is called *bulldog.cs.yale.edu*. Each organization can set up its names any way it wants to, though in practice names with more than five components are rare, not to mention hard to remember and type.

If you type a simple host name with no dots, your local computer should assume that the rest of the name is the same as the computer that you're currently using. So, if I'm logged into milton and want to contact chico, I can simply refer to chico and it assumes that I mean chico.iecc.com.

The Twilight Zone?

Name zones divide into two general categories: the three-letter kind and the two-letter kind. The three-letter zones are set up by kind of organization. We've seen *com* for *commercial*. Table 2-2 lists the rest of them.

Is there a complete list of host names anywhere?

No. In principle it should be possible to go through all of the various systems where names are registered and enumerate them all. People used to try to do that, partly out of nosiness, and partly out of an interest in collecting network statistics. They gave up when the Net had grown to the point that the collection program ran for over a week and still hadn't finished.

Table 2-2	Three-Letter Zone Names
Zone	**Meaning**
com	Commercial organizations
edu	Educational institutions
gov	Government bodies and departments
int	International organizations (mostly NATO at the moment)
mil	Military sites
net	Networking organizations
org	Anything else that doesn't fit elsewhere, such as professional societies

Within the United States, most Internet sites have names in one of the three-letter zones. Elsewhere, it's more common to use geographic names, which are discussed next.

Where's Vanuatu?

Two-letter zone names are geographically organized. Each zone corresponds to a country or Other Recognized Political Entity. There's an official international standard list of two-letter country codes, which is used almost but not quite unmodified as the list of two-letter zones. The country code for Canada is CA, so a site at York University in Canada is called *nexus.yorku.ca*. The network administrators in each country can assign names as they see fit. Some countries have organization-level subdivisions; for example, a site at a university in Australia is called *sait.edu.au*. Others assign names more haphazardly.

In the United States, relatively few computers have names in the geographic U.S. zone, which is organized by city and state. Because I.E.C.C. is in Cambridge, Massachusetts, chico.iecc.com used to be known as *iecc.cambridge.ma.us*. (I hadn't named it chico yet, because at the time it was the only computer I had.) In the United States, the choice of geographic or organizational names is pretty arbitrary. If you have one or two machines, it's easier to get a geographic name. If you have more than that, it's easier to get an organizational name, which lets you administer names within your organization yourself. (See Chapter 6 for some gruesome details of how names are registered.)

Table 2-3 lists some of the more common geographic zone names. There's a full table of geographic zones in Appendix A.

Table 2-3	Some Two-Letter Zone Names
Zone	*Country*
AU	Australia
AT	Austria (Republic of)
BE	Belgium (Kingdom of)
CA	Canada
CZ	Czech Republic
DK	Denmark (Kingdom of)
FI	Finland (Republic of)
FR	France (French Republic)
DE	Germany (Federal Republic of)
IN	India (Republic of)
IE	Ireland
IL	Israel (State of)
IT	Italy (Italian Republic)
JP	Japan
NL	Netherlands (Kingdom of the)
NO	Norway (Kingdom of)
RU	Russian Federation
SU	Former Soviet Union (officially obsolete but still in use)
ES	Spain (Kingdom of)
SE	Sweden (Kingdom of)
CH	Switzerland (Swiss Confederation)
TW	Taiwan, Province of China
UK	United Kingdom (official code is GB)
US	United States (United States of America)

Do you need a number to get a name?

No. It is quite possible to register a site as a *Mail Exchange* or *MX* site, meaning that it's not really on the Net but you can send electronic mail to it. Many sites on other networks, including all sites on the hobbyist network, have MX names. For sending mail, you can treat an MX name the same way as any other name.

No other Internet services work for MX machines, though. If you try to reach them any other way, either the attempt will fail or you will reach a machine on the Net that forwards mail for them. Most on-line and e-mail services including CompuServe, MCI Mail, AT&T Mail, and Prodigy are also MX'ed into the Internet. See Chapter 9 for more info.

Some other random zones

There are a few other zones and pseudozones that you might run into. Even though the ARPANET has been officially dead for several years, a few sites still, for historical reasons, have names ending in *arpa*. And as for machines on the UUCP and BITNET networks, you will occasionally see names ending in *uucp* and *bitnet*. These aren't real zones, and hence names using them aren't really valid host names, but a lot of systems have arranged to treat these names as special cases and route mail to them anyway. Any BITNET or UUCP site can arrange to get itself a real host name, so *bitnet* and *uucp* names are heading for well-deserved oblivion.

Rules of Conduct

Various parts of the Internet have some fairly firm rules of conduct. Depending on what part of the Net you are attached to, the rules may be more or less strict. The most restrictive rules are for the NSFNET (summarized in the following sidebar), which prohibits all commercial activity. As of late 1993, most educational institutions in the United States were attached directly or indirectly to the NSFNET, although at that point the plan was to move nearly all of them to commercial networks.

Regional networks have less restrictive policies, and commercial networks are less restrictive still. All reserve the right to boot you off for malicious or destructive conduct. Be aware of the rules that apply to your site and be prepared to honor them.

Also keep in mind that even if you are on a less restrictive network, if you use a more restrictive one — for example logging on a machine at an educational institution via the NSFNET — you are subject to the most restrictive rules of any net that you use.

The NSFNET backbone services acceptable use policy

The NSFNET supports research and education, primarily for schools and research institutions, but also for commercial firms when they do the same sorts of things. Here's a summary of the policy:

- ✔ It's OK to use it to communicate with people on foreign networks.

- ✔ It's OK to use it for "professional development," scheduling academing conferences, society meetings, and the like.

- ✔ It's OK to use it for applying for and administering grants. (Not surprising, since the NSF is the biggest grantmaker around.)

- ✔ New product announcements are OK; advertisements aren't.

- ✔ For-profit uses are forbidden except when they support a permitted use above.

- ✔ Extensive use for private or personal business is forbidden.

Chapter 3
Starting Off, If You're a DOS User

In This Chapter

▶ DOS vs. the Internet

▶ Too many ways to get hooked up

▶ Why PCs have trouble receiving e-mail

DOS vs. the Internet

On larger computers, hooking up to the Internet is a relatively straightforward task. You pay an unconscionable amount of money to your software vendor, they send you the network software that goes with your system, your hired expert installs it, and after no more than six months or so of arguing with tech support and finger-pointing, your hookup works.

With DOS-based PCs, however, life is not so simple. Dozens of different Internet-compatible network packages are available, ranging from flaky (and sometimes shaky) shareware to slick commercial stuff (and, of course, vice versa). Even worse, you can hook up your PC to the Internet in about four fundamentally different ways.

I presume that you have better things to do than to install your own Internet software and have a local expert utter the magic incantations needed to install the network software. (Well, even if you *don't* have better things to do, there's no way I could give instructions for more than one or two of those packages, and you just *know* neither one would be the package that you use.)

So in this chapter, I look at the different ways that you can hook up a PC to the Internet and the advantages and disadvantages of each way. Chapter 28 has a list of most of the currently available PC packages for hooking up to the Internet. Your best bet is to use one for which there is a local expert who can help you get set up.

These software packages for hooking up to the Internet are based on the *TCP/IP protocol*, which is techspeak for the system networks use to communicate with each other. You'll learn most of what you need to know about TCP/IP in Chapter 6, so if you're interested in the lingo, turn to that chapter for some background.

Through a Gateway Dimly

The first question is whether your PC has a *native* connection to the Internet or whether it goes through some other type of network. If it has a native connection, your PC actually runs network software that handles the TCP/IP network protocols that the Internet uses.

The alternative is that your PC is running another kind of network software (most often Novell's Netware) and is attached to a gateway system that speaks Netware on one side and TCP/IP on the other. To add to the confusion, it's also possible to load up both TCP/IP *and* some other kind of network software on the same PC and run them on the same physical network cables at the same time.

The pros and cons are the following:

- ✔ If you already have a large Netware network, your system manager can load up a single Netware gateway that all the other PCs on the network can use. If each PC will be running TCP/IP itself, your network manager has to load TCP/IP on each PC, which is a lot more work.

- ✔ TCP/IP works better in *heterogeneous networks* — that is, networks made up of lots of different kinds of computers. As far as TCP/IP is concerned, the only difference between a $10 million Cray supercomputer and a $900 PC is that the Cray is a little faster. Novell Netware is great on networks of PCs and less great on other kinds of computers, because Netware at this point works on far fewer kinds of computers than TCP/IP does.

- ✔ Depending on the particular gateway you use, you may not be able to do everything through a Netware gateway that you can do through native TCP/IP.

SLIPping an Ethereal Token

Let's assume that your PC runs TCP/IP by itself and not via another kind of network. The next question is: how is it connected to the rest of the net? The three major choices are *Ethernet, Token Ring,* and *serial lines* (the last using schemes I discuss later in this chapter, which are called *SLIP* and *PPP*).

Through the ether

The most common way to hook PCs to networks is with Ethernet, a kind of network which is fast and cheap, but limited to a total distance of under a mile. (For larger networks, a person can hook several Ethernet networks together, but that's a complication we can ignore.)

Fire at the wall

Even if your PC runs native TCP/IP software, if you're in a large organization that has (not altogether unreasonable) concerns about confidential company secrets leaking out via the Internet, a *firewall* system placed between the company network and the outside world may limit outside access to the internal network.

The firewall is connected both to the internal network and to the external network, so any traffic between the two has to go through the firewall. Special programming on the firewall limits what kind of connections can be made between the inside and outside and who can make them.

In practice, this means that you can use any Internet service that is available within the company, but for outside services you're limited by what can pass through the firewall system. Most of the standard outside services, such as logging into remote computers, copying files from one computer to another, should be available, although the procedures may be somewhat more complicated than what's described here.

Often, you have to log into the firewall system first, and from there get to the outside. It's usually impossible for anyone outside the company to get access to systems or services on the inside network (that's what the firewall is for). Except for the most paranoid of organizations, electronic mail flows unimpeded in both directions.

Finally, keep in mind that you probably have to get authorization to use the firewall system before you can use *any* outside service other than mail services.

The three main varieties of Ethernet are known as *thicknet, thinnet* (or *cheapernet*), and *twisted pair*. Your classic Ethernet is ½-inch thick yellow cable (that you rarely see because it's all hidden in the wall or ceiling), shown in Figure 3-1. Your computer is connected to the Ethernet by a different kind of cable known as a *drop cable,* which is about the same size as Ethernet but is usually gray. The business end of the drop cable attaches to your computer via a plug with 15 pins and a clever little slide latch.

If your computer uses thicknet and it suddenly develops network forgetfulness, the most likely problem is that the clever little latch has let go. Plug it back in and see if you can slide the latch more firmly.

Figure 3-1:
Thick
Ethernet
cabling
(thicknet).

Figure 3-2:
Thin
Ethernet
cabling
(thinnet or
cheapernet).

Classic thick Ethernet was intended for organizations that plan years ahead and arrange to expensively prewire all their offices for network connections. Real organizations aren't usually like that. They have a few PCs and want to wire them up without ripping all the walls apart. They need thinnet (cheapernet). Thinnet is thin, flexible, and black (see Figure 3-2). It resembles cable television cable (although it's not quite the same). The connection to the computer is a little T-shaped connector that plugs directly into a matching connector on the back of the computer.

Cheapernet is quite unforgiving. In particular, the tee connector must be plugged directly into the computer. You can't put the tee on the floor and run a connecting cable to the computer, not even an inch-long stub, because it just won't work. You should also remember that if you break the cable, everyone's connection to the network stops working. (It may seem reasonable to think that computers on the same side of the break could continue to talk to each other, but they can't. If you want to know why not, just corner someone who has a degree in electrical engineering and ask.)

The third kind of Ethernet cabling is twisted-pair, which is the same kind of wiring that telephones use (see Figure 3-3). Most offices have tons of spare phone wire in the walls already, and even if they don't, it's by far the cheapest kind of wire to string. So, twisted-pair Ethernet is pretty much the only kind used in new installations. A wire that looks a lot like a phone wire with the familiar phone jack (see Figure 3-4) plugs into the back of your computer. Each computer has its own separate wire back to a central connection box called a *hub* — which is usually stashed in a closet somewhere — so if you unplug your computer, you won't affect anyone else's. As long as you don't physically mangle the wire, twisted pair is pretty foolproof.

Figure 3-3:
Twisted pair
Ethernet
cabling.

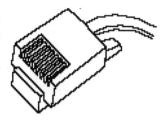

Figure 3-4:
Twisted pair
jack (just
like a phone
jack).

A token of our esteem

A few years back, IBM decided that because every other computer manufacturer in the world was using Ethernet, it would avoid the heartache of excessive compatibility by coming up with its own network called *Token Ring*. Furious technical debates raged on the relative merits of Ethernet and Token Ring, which we can summarize by saying that the differences are 95 percent political. Token Ring uses a clever rectangular connector which has the advantage over many versions of Ethernet in that it only comes unplugged when you want it to.

SLIP sliding away

One place where the Internet's TCP/IP network protocol definitely wins over other brands of networks is at the low end. All you actually need to set up a TCP/IP connection is the lowly serial port that your PC already has. It's not as fast as an Ethernet connection — but it's not as expensive either. You can run a wire directly to another computer nearby, or you can use a modem and a phone line and dial a computer somewhere else.

One extra complication of using a serial connection is that there are two incompatible software schemes used. One is called *SLIP (Serial Line IP)* and the other is *PPP (Point-to-Point Protocol)*. Which one you use depends on what kind of system you're connecting to — you use what they use.

If you're using a modem and a phone line, you want to use the fastest modem you can get. The standard cheap 2400 bps (bits per second) modems seem pretty fast when you're dialed up to an on-line service like Compuserve, but these modems are painfully slow on the Internet. Faster 9600 and 14,400 bps modems are now available and are quite adequate. (Modem weenies call these last two kinds V.32 and V.32*bis*, where *bis* is French for "and a half." Ask for them by name at your computer store, and they'll think you're an expert.)

SLIP really works and can make your computer a full-fledged player on the Internet. For example, I wrote this chapter holed up in a cottage on a sandbar at the New Jersey shore, using a laptop computer with my modem dialed in via SLIP to an Internet-connected system on the mainland that let me do anything on the Net — like retrieving data from computers in Australia — that I can do back at my office plugged into the Ethernet. Just a little slower.

Getting SLIP or PPP configured correctly is a pain in the neck that involves phone numbers, login names, passwords, and everything else required to log into a remote system over the phone, *on top of* the usual network configuration problems. Before you take your computer to the beach, try plugging it into a spare phone line at the office and dialing in to make sure that its SLIP configuration is working. Then, when you find that it's not, you have your office network guru on hand to figure out what's wrong.

Is Windows Really a Lot Cooler Than DOS?

I'm still undecided about Windows in general, but when it comes to TCP/IP, Windows wins hands down over DOS for two reasons. The first is aesthetic. Most DOS TCP/IP applications are straightforward ports of the UNIX originals — which means that they use a line-at-a-time interface, like the DOS command language or, perish the thought, EDLIN, the old DOS text editor. (Actually, *nothing's* as bad as EDLIN.) If you want to know more about the UNIX background for the Internet, see Chapter 4 for plenty of details.

Windows network applications, on the other hand, have all the spiffy bells and whistles that you expect from all Windows applications. In many cases, this makes them a lot easier to use. For example, when you're using FTP — the program that copies files from one computer to another — most Windows versions let you pick the files to copy by clicking on filenames in a list in a window, whereas the DOS versions make you type in the filenames yourself.

The other reason that Windows works better is that it allows *multitasking,* which is computerese for *running several programs at once.* Under Windows, you can have several network applications running at one time in different windows. You can even have terminal sessions in different windows that are logged into several computers *at the same time,* while you simply click among them. A few DOS versions of TCP/IP (such as the shareware program Ka9q) offer multitasking, but none as conveniently as Windows does.

See Chapter 28 for a list of DOS and Windows TCP/IP packages, both free and commercial.

At Your Service, Not

In one important way, DOS computers are not really full-blown members of the Internet. Every Internet application uses the *client/server* model, in which part of the application, the *client,* runs on your computer, and the other part, the *server,* runs on a remote computer that has the resources you want to use.

(Client/server is the hot new thing in mainframe computing, but the Internet and its predecessors have been using the concept since at least 1969. They didn't know how advanced they were — they just wanted to get the job done.)

To be frank, PCs make fine clients but rather inferior servers. DOS and Windows are simply not the best environments for servers. For example, let's say that you want to make some resource available on the Internet, such as a bunch of files for people to retrieve. You put them all in a common place and then start a server program that waits for client programs to contact it and ask it to do something. But because DOS only runs one program at a time, if you ᵤᵢ t the server program, the PC can't do anything else.

Sometimes that's OK — a single dedicated computer is a pretty cheap way to provide a service when compared to some of the alternatives — but it's *not* real great if it's the same PC you need to use to get your work done. Even under Windows, which is designed to allow multiple programs to run at once, servers don't work all that well — largely because most non-network programs tend to hog the computer when you run them and don't give the server any time to serve its clients.

Note: The following discussion of mail trouble applies *only* to users of *native* Internet mail (sometimes known as *SMTP* mail). If you have a different mail system — that is, one that uses a gateway to the Internet — then from the point of view of other Internet systems all your mail is sent and received by the gateway, and the following doesn't apply.

"But," you say, "I don't *need* to publish files. I just want to use resources elsewhere on the Internet. I don't need to run any servers." That's almost but not quite true. The biggest problem with not having servers occurs when you receive electronic mail. Internet e-mail considers the *sender* to be the client, the *recipient* the server.

Here's the scenario and its complications:

- The sender's machine tries to contact the recipient's machine to deliver a message.

- If the recipient's machine doesn't have a mail server running, the sender's machine tries a few more times but eventually gives up.

- If your mail program doesn't happen to be running at the moment the sender tries to send you something, the message may not get delivered.

- Reality: If you have correspondents in different time zones, they may well send you mail in the middle of the night when your computer is turned off.

Fortunately, a workaround exists for this problem. Your system manager can (and probably already has) arranged to have your mail received on a larger computer that runs 24 hours a day. When you want to read your mail, your mail program contacts that computer and downloads any waiting mail. The usual downloading scheme is known as *Post Office Protocol,* or *POP* (of which a bunch of versions exist, the current ones being *POP2* and *POP3*).

With any luck, all this works automatically, but it's worth remembering that, although POP is common on PCs, it's not the way the rest of the Net handles its mail. In particular, it means that the machine that sends your mail (your PC) is different from the one that receives your mail (the larger one), a situation that has been known to foul up some automated mail robots (see Chapter 10). If that turns out to be a problem for you, your system manager can probably fiddle with the mail setup so that your mail *appears* to be sent and received by the same system.

WINSOCK? Like at an airport?

No, WINSOCK is short for Windows Sockets. It's like this: Every DOS version of TCP/IP actually consists of two parts. One part is the application programs you use to access various services over the Internet. The other part is a common library of network functions that all the network applications use. In each case, the vendor documented the functions in the library so that third parties could write applications of their own that worked with the vendor's TCP/IP package.

Unfortunately, each vendor's functions are slightly different in the details, even though functionally they do the same thing, so applications that work with one won't work with another. Some of the vendors boast that they have compatibility libraries for four or five other vendors so that programs that expect to use the other vendors' libraries will work. (It's like the situation with electrical appliances in Europe: the power is all the same, but the plugs are all different. So if you bring an English sewing machine to France, you can't use it unless you can find an adapter plug.)

In 1991, all the network vendors were gearing up to produce Windows TCP/IP packages. One day, a bunch of them got together at a trade show and thrashed out a common, standard set of functions for Windows TCP/IP applications based on the Sockets library that most versions of UNIX use. Every TCP/IP vendor (even Microsoft, which has a TCP/IP version for Windows NT) quickly agreed to support this Windows Sockets library, or WINSOCK.

In practice, this means that once a few compatibility bugs are shaken out (which should happen by early 1994), any Windows TCP/IP application you find that uses WINSOCK, whether commercial, shareware, or free, should work with any Windows TCP/IP networking package. In the annals of software development, this degree of a priori compatibility is virtually unprecedented, so let's hope that it's a harbinger of things to come.

Chapter 4
Starting Off, If You're a UNIX User

• •

In This Chapter

▶ UNIX network facilities

▶ UNIX-specific facilities

▶ Networked files

▶ Electronic mail

▶ The yellow plague

• •

*M*ost UNIX systems come with Internet software either as part of the standard package or as an add-on from the same vendor who supplies the UNIX operating system. For those who don't, or who do but aren't directly connected to the Internet, all UNIX systems come with an old but serviceable package called *UUCP*. UUCP uses ordinary modems and phone lines to handle e-mail and network news (see Chapter 9 for more info).

Your Usual UNIX Network Stuff

If you're using a UNIX workstation, it definitely includes Internet software. The main question is whether you're attached to the Internet directly, indirectly, or (horror of horrors) not at all. To be sure that you have Internet software loaded, try typing this command:

```
telnet localhost
```

You should get a login prompt shortly (in a few seconds) from your own computer. Log in as yourself and then log out. So far, so good. If it says something like `telnet: not found`, you're using one of the few remaining UNIX systems with no network software. Bummer. (You still may be able to send and receive e-mail by way of UUCP.)

You can also check for the trappings of networking: is there a network cable attached to the back of your computer? (See Chapter 3 for a rundown of popular network cable types.) When you print something, does it appear on a printer attached to a different computer? That's a sure sign that a network is active. Can you send electronic mail to people on other computers? Again, that's a sure sign.

Help! I'm Trapped in a Local Network!

Even assuming that your network software is all tuned up and your computer is attached to a network (usually with an Ethernet cable hanging out the back), the question remains whether it's attached to the Net or just to some local machines. This important detail has nothing to do with the setup of your computer, but rather whether the local network to which your computer is attached is in turn attached to the Internet.

Probably the easiest way to check is to see whether you can contact well-known Internet sites. Try to *telnet* (log in as a terminal) to *rs.internic.net*, the Network Information Center for the domestic part of the Internet, by typing this line:

```
telnet rs.internic.net
```

If it says Connected and you see messages from the NIC telling you what's available, you win — you're on the Net. (Type **exit** to make the NIC disconnect.)

If not, either your network isn't directly attached to the Internet or you have some other connection problem — you will have to ask a local guru for advice. Again, even if your network isn't attached directly to the Internet, you may still be able to exchange mail with people on the Net.

For Your Convenience, We've Done Everything Twice

UNIX supports the two most traditional Internet services: telnet, for logging in to a remote host, and FTP, for copying files to and from a remote host. The UNIX network facilities were written by a bunch of college students, however, and they couldn't leave well enough alone. They invented a second set of similar (but different) programs with names beginning with *r* that are primarily useful only between UNIX systems.

  ✔ *rlogin* is almost but not quite like telnet

  ✔ *rsh* runs one command at a time on remote machines

  ✔ *rcp* sort of resembles FTP

Each of these *r* programs has its own advantages and is worth learning about. The main advantage they all share is that you can arrange things on machines on which you have accounts so that you can log in from one to another and copy stuff among them without having to enter your username and password every time you want to do something.

We discuss the *r* commands in the same chapters with their generic non-UNIX equivalents. You can find rlogin and rsh in Chapter 14 and rcp in Chapter 16.

My Files Are Where?

Another network feature particularly common to UNIX systems is *NFS (Network File System),* originally released by Sun Microsystems but now commonly available from most UNIX vendors. NFS lets you treat disk files and directories that are present on one computer as though they were on another computer. In particular, this means that many of the files that seem to be on your computer may actually be on a machine down the hall. This situation normally doesn't make much practical difference unless the network or the other computer breaks, and then your computer comes to a screeching halt in much the same way as it would if you unplugged a disk drive attached directly to the computer.

Fortunately, NFS picks up pretty reliably where it left off when the network or other computer is fixed. A legendary tale is often told of a program on a workstation that waited patiently while the computer with its NFS files broke and was taken apart and shipped back to the vendor. A replacement system soon arrived, so the new server was assembled, reloaded from the backup tapes, and restarted. Then the program, which by then had been waiting for about six months, continued.

Stupid NFS Tricks

Although NFS originally was written for UNIX systems, versions of NFS also exist for lots of other kinds of computers ranging from Macs and PCs to IBM mainframes. These versions allow for flexible file-sharing. While this book was written, for example, the files with the text and graphics resided on a UNIX system, but the MS-DOS and Windows examples were run on a networked PC. Then the screen shots were saved, by way of NFS, in files back on the UNIX host.

The connector *is* the network, unfortunately

If you try all this stuff and still get no network response, a surprisingly common problem is that your workstation has come unplugged from the network. The three kinds of Ethernet cable are known as *thicknet, thinnet,* and *unshielded twisted pair (UTP).* You can see pictures of these cable types in Chapter 3.

The original thicknet uses a cable about as big around as one of your fingers. The connector at the end of the cable attaches to the computer by way of a large, flat connector that has a clever slide latch. The latch's only disadvantage is that it doesn't work very well. It often comes loose and the plug falls out. If this is your problem, just plug the cable back in.

Thinnet (also known as *cheapernet* because the cable is indeed much cheaper than thick Ethernet) is a much thinner cable — the same size as cable TV cable. It uses what are known in the network biz as *BNC connectors,* which twist and latch quite reliably. The main problem with thinnet is that if several computers are attached by thinnet cable, the cable must physically come all the way to the computer where there is a T-shaped connector with the BNC jack. With this setup, there usually are two cables — one to the computer and one from the computer.

Because this arrangement looks untidy, some people try to clean things up by putting a section of cable between the T and the computer. For boring reasons that have to do with the laws of physics, doing so introduces so much electrical noise into the network that *all* communication can come to a screeching halt. So don't do that.

If your computer happens to be the last one on its cable, one cable will lead to the usual T connector, which is plugged into the back of the computer, and a little *terminator* plug will be on the other end of the T. That's OK.

A few sites have a clever setup with a special cable from the wall to the computer that combines both the *to* and *from* cables in one physical cable leading to a BNC plug with the T hidden in molded plastic. That setup is OK too (and very tidy), although it's so expensive that it's not widely used.

UTP uses plain telephone wire and a connector similar to but larger than a telephone plug that actually *works,* so you're less likely to run into trouble with it. Because phone wire is so much cheaper and easier to use than are thicknet or thinnet, you may reasonably ask why they didn't use it in the first place. Those who designed Ethernet didn't realize that it would work. Oh well.

If you are one of the few sites that has a *Token Ring network,* you may be interested in knowing that Token Ring networks use a sturdy connector that isn't likely to give you any trouble unless you kick it hard. If the token connector comes out, you must reboot your computer after plugging it back in, because the computer must perform a special initialization sequence to get back *on the ring.*

If you use a bunch of different kinds of computers, NFS is often the only workable way to hook them all together because it runs on a much wider variety of computers than does any other file-sharing system.

NFS is based on a pair of standard Internet communication protocols called *UDP/IP.* (Chapter 6 explains what these protocols are, but it's not important now.) If your machine uses NFS, therefore, you can in principle use NFS files that are anywhere on the Internet, as long as the host where the files live grants you permission to access them.

If your computer and the one where the files live are connected by a fast enough network, you can use files many miles away just as though they were local. Remote network links are usually considerably (often about 100 times) slower than local networks are, which means that you can get the impression of a very s-l-o-o-o-w disk.

For use as regular file storage, slow remote NFS is hopeless unless you are a total masochist. As a way to browse and retrieve files from an archive, however, NFS can be OK. Many systems that have large file archives allow anyone to access their disks by way of NFS (for reading, not for writing — they're not totally stupid). Because public archive systems can have hundreds of directories and thousands of files, mounting a remote system's disk by way of NFS lets you use familiar directory and file commands to look at them.

Yes, it takes a while to list directories, read files, and so on, but it would take a while whether you used NFS or FTP (the standard remote-file program, described in Chapter 16). When you find a file or group of files you like, copy to a faster disk if you plan to use them much.

On most UNIX systems, mounting remote NFS systems requires help from the system administrator, so you have to ask for help.

Playing Post Office

All UNIX systems come with at least a rudimentary mail system, and most have pretty good mailers. You can at least mail stuff to other users on your local system and those on the local network. If you're on the Internet, you can send mail to any other user on the Internet. Even if you're not directly on the Net, you may still be able to send and receive mail to and from other systems by way of other intermediary systems.

Several large Internet sites, such as UUNET and PSI, provide network mail connectivity for hundreds (if not thousands) of dial-in systems, and many smaller systems provide mail forwarding on a more or less formal basis. (See Chapter 27 for a list of some of these systems.)

The easiest way to tell whether you can send and receive Internet e-mail is to try it (see Chapter 7 for details).

Because so many different mailers are on UNIX systems, it is hard to give general-purpose directions that will work on any of them. Our examples use *elm,* which is probably the most widely used UNIX mailer (it works, and it's free). If you use another mail system, such as *mail* or *mh,* you have to inquire locally for instructions. Fortunately, almost all the UNIX mailers use the same mailbox format, so no matter which mailer various people use, the mail still gets through.

The Yellow Plague

The final network concept UNIX users need to know about is the *Network Information System (NIS).* NIS used to be called *Yellow Pages* until someone pointed out that the name is a trademark of the local phone company in some countries. Many NIS commands still begin with the letters *yp,* however.

When a company or department has a bunch of workstations, the most convenient way to set them up is to have them all share files by way of NFS and to give all users accounts on all machines so that they act like a large shared system. (This setup mimics the central time-sharing systems that were popular in the 1970s, which now are generally considered hopelessly obsolete. Hmmm.)

The practical aspects of keeping all the workstations' administrative information in sync, however, was a nightmare. Each system has a password file that lists valid users, a mail names file that lists mail users and mailing lists, and a set of *mount points* (directories in which remote files can be referenced). In a cluster of 50 workstations, when the system manager added a new user, that user had to be added to 50 password files, 50 mail files, and so on, and the chances of getting everything right was close to nil. System administrators were tearing out what little hair they had left.

NIS solves much of this problem by putting nearly all the administrative data in one place controlled by NIS, and all the workstations consult NIS rather than their private files. When a new user arrives, the administrator has to add only the user to the shared NIS database, which instantly makes all the workstations available to the new user.

This capability is great in principle, and in practice it works pretty well. Occasionally, however, the NIS databases can get out of sync. (After the administrator updates the master files, a clumsy set of commands is necessary in order to regenerate the NIS database, and it's easy to make a mistake.) When the NIS gets out of sync, it can cause some extremely peculiar results. Also, the design of NIS makes it possible to create some embarrassing security holes — a minor annoyance if the computers are accessible to only a small group of trustworthy users but potentially disastrous if any of the millions of users on the Internet can break in.

NIS and Mail

One thing NIS does is to centralize e-mail sorting. Each user's electronic mailbox resides on a *home* machine. It usually is the same machine generally used for day-to-day work, but it doesn't have to be. NIS centralizes the mail-addressing database, so even though a user has accounts on every machine in the group (courtesy of NIS), mail is automatically routed to the mailbox on the user's home machine. No matter which machine a user happens to be using, she can read mail from her mailbox and send mail to both users in the group and elsewhere.

This capability can cause some peculiar-looking mail addresses in mail that comes from users on NIS systems. Suppose that a company has 26 worksta-tions, named in alphabetical order. For example, you would start with *aaron.yoyodyne.com*, then go to *bertha.yoyodyne.com* . . . and on through the alphabet until you finally get to *zelda.yoyodyne.com*. Depending on which machine a user happens to be sitting in front of, the return address on e-mail messages may be *lauren@aaron.yoyodyne.com, lauren@bertha.yoyodyne.com,* or any of the others.

If you are responding to mail from a user in this type of group, how do you know which machine to send it to? The answer, fortunately, is that it doesn't matter. Send it to any of them. If the machine you choose happens not to be the user's home machine, it automatically forwards the mail to the home machine. This extra forwarding step adds about an extra half-second to the time it takes to deliver a mail message but is otherwise invisible. (If having your e-mail arrive half a second late is an issue, you have bigger problems than NIS.)

SLIP sliding away

Ideally, you want your computer attached to the Net by the fastest and most reliable connection available. Realistically, you take what you can get. Sometimes the best you can get is a regular ol' dial-up modem. The Internet community fortunately has had plenty of impoverished users, and plenty of support for networking is available on a shoestring.

The two main techniques for working by way of a dial-up phone link are called *SLIP (Serial Line Internet Protocol)* and *PPP (Point-to-Point Protocol).* (You can forget these names.) In the fanciest SLIP and PPP setups, your computer automatically dials its Net neighbor and logs in whenever there is network traffic to send, and then it hangs up after a minute or two of inactivity. More typically, though, you have to do the logging in yourself by using programs with names like *slattach.*

Little consistency exists in the way SLIP and PPP are started up; guru assistance is often needed. Don't forget to say thank you when you receive assistance, because SLIP and PPP are fragile enough that expert help is almost always needed from time to time.

You may wonder what the difference is between SLIP and PPP. Technically, a considerable difference exists: SLIP is a *network layer protocol* and PPP is a *link level protocol.* There are two practical differences: PPP is a little faster, and PPP can handle other kinds of networks, such as DECnet. If you're at a low-budget site doing one or the other, though, be grateful that you have *any* kind of network.

Chapter 5
Starting Off, for Everyone Else

· ·

In This Chapter

▶ Macs and the Net

▶ VMS systems

▶ Third-party access services

· ·

A Few Words about Macintoshes

How hard could it be to get a Mac onto the Net? Everyone knows that Macs have great networking; just plug them in and they work. That's true as long as the only things you want to network to are other Macs. Getting Macs on the Internet is kind of a pain, partly because the built-in networking actually tends to get in the way.

First things first

Normally, when you plug Macs together, they communicate using a built-in scheme called *AppleTalk*. So long as all you have are Macs, and they're all physically close enough to connect using standard Apple-type cable, AppleTalk works great. Over longer distances AppleTalk doesn't work as well, and on most non-Mac machines it doesn't work at all. But for a long time, AppleTalk was pretty much all that Apple Computer supported for Mac networking.

A few years back, Apple finally admitted that the Internet's *TCP/IP* (the Internet's usual protocol — see Chapter 6 for more info on TCP/IP) was here to stay. (The original plan was for the entire rest of the world to convert to AppleTalk. Nice try, fellas.) So they wrote some standard low-level TCP/IP support that nearly all Mac Internet software now uses.

The support code is generally known as *MacTCP*, although its official product name is now *TCP/IP Connection for Macintosh* (see Chapter 28). The current version of MacTCP is 2.0.2, which is supposed to fix some serious problems in version 2.0.

Older versions of MacTCP were sometimes bundled with network applications; that's no longer the case — you should bite the bullet and get an up-to-date copy, even if you have to pay for it.

Installing MacTCP is a little tricky; unless you are in the mood for a serious Mac Hack Attack, get a local Mac expert to do it and at the same time arrange for the network wiring.

MacTCP does two things for you: It appears as a Mac control panel that gives you some ability to adjust what it's doing, and it has some standardized internal libraries that network applications use so that multiple network applications can run without clobbering each other. In System 7, the applications can even run simultaneously.

What if I have to install this stuff myself?

The Internet itself offers some excellent advice about connecting your Mac to the Net. If you already have Net access, a MacTCP primer is available from FTP or Gopher (see Chapters 16 and 20) from site *spider.math.ilstu.edu,* under the name */pub/mac/mac-tcp.txt.*

A four-part Mac communications *Frequently Asked Questions* note is posted monthly on the USENET group *comp.sys.mac.comm.* It is available by way of FTP from *sumex-aim.stanford.edu* as *info-mac/report/comp-sys-mac-comm-faq.txt.* This note talks about all sorts of Mac communications, but the third part is mostly about TCP/IP networking.

And for a complete discussion of Macintosh networking, see *Macworld Networking Handbook* (Dave Kosiur and Nancy E.H. Jones, IDG Books Worldwide, 1992).

Hey, my MacTCP is locked!

If your Mac has been set up by someone else, you may find that you cannot make any changes on your MacTCP control panel because it's locked. That's probably good news because it means that whoever set it up took the trouble to set and lock your MacTCP options.

The only way to unlock the control panel is with an administrator's version of MacTCP. If you have a problem, rather than try to steal the disk and fiddle with it yourself, find the administrator who set the lock and ask that person (politely, as always) to make any network changes you need.

Note that you have to unlock only to change network parameters. You do *not* have to unlock to use — or even to install — network applications.

Down the wire

Three network wiring options are available for your Mac:

- **LocalTalk** or **PhoneNet:** These puppies use thin cable and small connectors.
- **Ethernet:** This option uses thick cable, thin cable-TV-like cable, or phone wire (see the discussions of Ethernet wiring in Chapter 3; Macs have the same Ethernet options as PCs).
- **Token Ring:** This system uses thin cable and big, square connectors.

All three wiring options have their advantages and disadvantages, but the choice is usually obvious: You have to have whatever kind of network the other computers around you use so that you can talk to them.

If you have a LocalTalk network, most of the other computers on the network will also be Macs, and you need a gateway box to connect you to the outside Internet TCP/IP world. If you have Ethernet or Token Ring, you can be on the same network with all sorts of other computers. You may or may not need a gateway box.

Talking the talk

There are unfortunately far too many different ways to set up your Macintosh network. The reason is that there are two different network *protocols,* which are software conventions for communicating among computers, and three different kinds of network hardware.

The two most important protocols are as follows:

- Internet's TCP/IP
- Apple's AppleTalk

The three kinds of hardware are as follows:

- LocalTalk (or Phonenet, which for purposes of this discussion works in the same way)
- Ethernet (any of the three varieties)
- Token Ring

A Mac can handle AppleTalk on LocalTalk, Ethernet, or Token Ring. It can also handle TCP/IP on Ethernet or Token Ring. OK so far? (If not, never mind — with luck, you won't need to know about this subject.)

AppleTalk has the advantage when you're using a Mac that it's well-integrated into the rest of the Mac system. As soon as you turn on an AppleTalk connection, your Mac can *see* all the other AppleTalk resources on the net, such as printers, Mac file servers, and Novell AppleShare servers. AppleTalk can run on any of the kinds of hardware just mentioned. When your Mac sends AppleTalk via an Ethernet, that's known as *Ethertalk*. When it sends AppleTalk via a Token Ring, that's *Tokentalk*.

TCP/IP has the advantage in that many other kinds of computers can handle it, including every computer on the Internet. When your Mac sends TCP/IP over an Ethernet or Token Ring, it's known as TCP/IP. (No cutesy names are needed on the Internet.) There's no provision for native TCP/IP on LocalTalk.

If you want your Mac to communicate with the Internet, therefore, your Mac *must* speak TCP/IP. But when your Mac sends out a packet of Internet TCP/IP data, it can do it in two different ways:

   ✔ Wrap a layer of AppleTalk around it and send it out as an AppleTalk packet with the TCP/IP hidden inside (called *encapsulated* TCP/IP)

   ✔ Send it out as a regular *native* TCP/IP packet

In the former case, only other Macs that are running MacTCP and a few compatible gateway systems can understand it. In the latter case, any other TCP/IP system can immediately understand it.

In short, if your net uses Ethernet or Token Ring, you should set up your Mac to use native TCP/IP. (You set it that way on the MacTCP control panel.) This setup gives you maximum access to other TCP/IP systems, both Mac and non-Mac.

On the other hand, if you are using LocalTalk, you have to use encapsulated TCP/IP; if you want to connect to the outside Internet world, you need a gateway box that unwraps the encapsulated data and sends it along to the outside. Many different gateway boxes are available, including Shiva's FastPath, Cayman Systems' Gatorbox, Webster Computer Corporation's Multiport Gateway, and Compatible Systems' EtherRoute/TCP.

Incidentally, it is possible to send native TCP/IP and AppleTalk over the same cable — it often makes sense to communicate with other nearby Macs using AppleTalk, and with the outside world using TCP/IP, both running at the same time on your Mac.

Whaddaya mean, I'm not dynamic?

One exciting aspect of Mac TCP/IP networking (in the sense that it unavoidably generates excitement even though people would rather remain calm) is *address assignment.* Every computer on the Internet has a four-part numeric address similar to 127.85.46.9, which identifies it to other computers on the Net.

Each Internet network is assigned a range of addresses for the computers on that network. The normal way to assign addresses to individual computers is to go around to each computer in the office and slap a sticker with an address on the computer. This process is called *static addressing* because the address stays with the computer permanently (or as permanently as anything in the computer biz can be).

If your Macs communicate with each other by using AppleTalk and are hooked to the outside world by using a gateway box, they use an alternative numbering scheme known as *dynamic addressing.* Rather than permanently assign an address to each Mac, the gateway box is given a pool of Internet addresses. Every time one of the Macs contacts the gateway box to get in touch with the outside world, the box assigns the Mac a free address from the pool. When the Mac is finished with its Internet application, the address goes back into the pool.

Dynamic addressing has a couple of advantages:

- ✔ There's no need for a system administrator to wander around the office with stickers and to have to come up with a new sticker every time someone gets a new Mac.

- ✔ You can get away with having fewer addresses than you have Macs.

Because the Internet is in the midst of a numbering crisis, if you have a thousand Macs in your organization, getting a thousand addresses is a major bureaucratic hassle. On the other hand, it's much easier to get 250 addresses (the size chunk the Internet powers that be like to hand out). If you don't expect more than a quarter of your Macs to be using the Internet at one time, you can get by with 250 addresses for 1,000 Macs.

This formula applies equally on a smaller scale. If your organization has a bunch of departments, it probably will take its 250 addresses and divide them into eight subnets with 30 addresses each (a few addresses get lost to roundoff and other reasons). So you may have a 50-Mac network with 30 addresses — same principle.

Dynamic addressing has one main disadvantage: The outside world cannot find any particular Mac. If you want to have a server that other people can use (a folder of public or semipublic files, for example), the Mac doing the serving must have a static address so that people on the ouside can find it. It's possible to have mixed setups in which most Macs use dynamic addresses but some have fixed static addresses, so the servers can have static addresses and everyone else uses dynamic addresses.

Your network guru should have set up your addressing already, so in general you do not have to worry. If you want to provide some network service to friends on the outside, however, be sure that your server has a static address.

Now that I have it, what do I do with it?

After you have MacTCP going, you can run a bunch of applications on top of it, which gives you access to all the network services discussed in this book (see Chapter 28 for sources). Some popular applications include the ones in this list:

- ✔ **NCSA Telnet:** The most popular version of *telnet,* which is the application that lets you log into other computers. This application is popular for two unbeatable reasons: It works well, and it's free. It also includes *FTP* (file transfer protocol), the application that copies files from one computer to another, and both an FTP client that allows you to copy files to and from other computers and an FTP server that (if you turn it on) lets other people copy files to and from your computer.

  NCSA Telnet happens to be one of the few Mac TCP/IP applications that doesn't require MacTCP, although it works with MacTCP if it's there. If you have a single Mac and a modem, NCSA may be all you need in order to get on the Net. See Chapter 28 for more information.

- ✔ **COMET:** Another version of telnet, from Cornell. It includes an IBM 3270-style telnet, which you need in order to communicate with many IBM mainframes.

- ✔ **SU-Mac/IP:** A full-featured package from Stanford with telnet, FTP, printing, and other goodies. It's available only to educational institutions.

- ✔ **Eudora:** This is a full-featured mail-sending and receiving program. Versions through mid-1993 were free; now it's a commercial program from Qualcomm.

- ✔ **Newswatcher:** This is a USENET news-reading program developed by Apple but available for free.

Unstacking the DEC

One of the most popular kinds of minicomputers on the Internet circuit is the Digital VAX. You can run one of three different operating systems on a VAX:

- ✔ VMS
- ✔ Ultrix
- ✔ OSF/1

The latter two systems are versions of UNIX, so you can find out about how to work with them in Chapter 4. VMS is different, so let's talk about it a little here.

TIP

Help, I've Bin Hexed!

In the opinion of users of most other kinds of computers in the world, Macintoshes use strange kinds of files. Each Mac file contains two parts, called the *data fork* and the *resource fork*. The data fork contains the plain data of the file (text if it's a document and the actual image if it's a GIF picture); the resource fork stores stuff related to the data such as international settings, the page you were last editing, and voice annotations, Mac executable files consist almost entirely of resources.

Other kinds of computers don't handle these two-part files, so a bunch of ad hoc conventions have been developed (which folks in the computer biz call *hacks* or *gross hacks*). These conventions pack up Mac files so that they can be stored and transferred by other, inferior kinds of computers. The two main hacks are listed here:

✔ **MacBinary:** Simply takes the two parts of the files and (here's another technical computer term) *gloms* them together with a little bit of other info, such as the file's true name (most computers cannot handle names like *Second draft of my novel*), file type, and creation date. MacBinary then makes a simple one-part file that any computer can handle. If you see a file in an online archive whose name ends in *.bin,* it's a MacBinary.

✔ **BinHex:** Does the same thing as MacBinary and takes it one step further to produce a version of a file that is disguised as printable text characters. The reason it does this is that if you want to pass a file around as e-mail or as USENET news (see Chapters 7 and 11), the file must look like text because that's all that mail and news handle. If you see a file whose name ends in *.hqx,* it's BinHex-ed. BinHex messages are easy to recognize, because they all start with the following line:

(This file must be converted with BinHex 4.0)

Several versions of BinHex have been created over the years, but the one that everyone uses is 4.0.

Lots of programs turn files into MacBinary or BinHex and back. Some of the network applications do it automatically, or you can use a standalone program such as StuffIt instead.

A discussion of the intricacies of Mac file-wrangling are beyond the scope of this book, so check out some of Mac books from IDG Books Worldwide for the complete lowdown. Here are a few to get you started: *Macs For Dummies* (1992) by David Pogue; *Macworld Macintosh SECRETS* (1993) by David Pogue and Joseph Schorr; and *Macworld Complete Mac Handbook Plus CD* (1993) by Jim Heid.

By and large, the VMS TCP/IP Internet network facilities are modeled after the UNIX ones. (Indeed, wherever possible, they borrowed the UNIX code and adapted it.) But VMS is different for a couple of reasons:

✔ There is no single dominant version of TCP/IP for VMS. About five versions exist, all from different vendors, and all provide slightly different services. Whoever runs your VMS machine will have chosen one of them already, so you have what you have. They all work perfectly well but have slightly different warts.

✔ VMS has its own native network (DECnet) and its own file-management system (RMS). In many places (notably mail), VMS assumes that when you talk about a network, you mean DECnet, and you have to say specifically that, no, you mean the Internet instead.

Mail peculiarities

Most VMS shops use DEC's standard mail package or something compatible with it, or else the All-In-1 office-automation package. Normal mail addresses are taken to be DECnet addresses, so you have to say something special to mean Internet addresses. In DEC Mail, you usually say something like this:

```
MX%"elvis@ntw.org"
```

MX is a common, free, Internet mail gateway. Some people use IN% rather than MX%. (You have to contact a local expert to find out the exact incantation to use.)

If you're using a VMS system within Digital's own Easynet network, all Internet mail is routed through the DECnet host called *DECWRL*. To send to the Internet from a system on Easynet, you say the following:

```
nm%DECWRL::"elvis@ntw.org"
```

If you're using All-In-1, the address looks something like this:

```
elvis@ntw.org @Internet
```

Again, details vary depending on how your local network is set up, so you have to ask a local expert. While you're asking, ask what your Internet e-mail address is because there are various ways to turn a DECnet address into an Internet address.

File peculiarities

The people who designed the Internet's FTP file-transfer program did not have VMS and in particular RMS in mind. (In fairness, FTP predates RMS by several years.) If you have a file full of plain ol' text, you can transfer it without trouble by using FTP. If, on the other hand, you have a nontext file of some sort, you're in minor trouble.

Don't bother to read the remainder of this VMS section until after you have read Chapters 16 and 17 (they discuss FTP). The information is here because it's about VMS.

If you want to transfer RMS files by using FTP, you have two basic choices:

✔ If the machine you're transferring to or from is also running VMS, with any luck they both have FTP programs that have been upgraded to know about RMS. Try saying **STRU VMS** or checking your FTP program's documentation for a command to transfer VMS-structured files. If such a command exists and it works when you try it (the other end must cooperate in order for it to work), you're all set and you can transfer any kind of file you want without trouble.

✔ The alternative is to hide the RMS file in a plain file and then transfer the plain file and unhide it on the other end. The usual hiding technique is to use the command **VMS BACKUP** to create a small backup file that contains your file (or files — there can be more than one) or else use **ZIP** to create an archive. Given a choice, ZIP probably will create a smaller (and therefore faster to copy) transfer file.

X Marks the Spot

One kind of computer terminal that has become popular in recent years is the *X terminal*, which is basically a stripped-down workstation running a single program, X Windows. X terminals invariably have a network connection to other nearby computers, so you log into one or more of those computers to get your work done. But since the Internet is an egalitarian network, if the network to which your X terminal is connected is attached to the Internet, you can (in principle, see next "Tip") use X-compatible programs on any Internet host in the world.

Your typical X terminal has a windowed telnet (see Chapter 14) application built in which you use to log into a nearby computer. For anything beyond that initial long session, you use programs which open their own windows on your screen. Typically, you'll start a couple of xterm windows logged into nearby computers.

Many Internet services, such as Archie, Gopher, and WAIS (Chapters 19-21) have X versions called, creatively, *xarchie*, *xgopher* and *xwais*. You can use them and have their windows automatically appear on your terminal. Just be sure that you set your DISPLAY environment variable (or the equivalent on non-UNIX systems) to point at your screen. If your terminal is called *x15.ntw.org*, for example, you type one of the following lines in a telnet or xterm window before starting another X application:

```
setenv DISPLAY x15.ntw.org:0        (C shell)

DISPLAY=x15.ntw.org:0 ; export DISPLAY (Bourne or Korn shell)
```

The **:0** is necessary to indicate that your terminal is supposed to use the first screen on your display. (Yes, I know that your display only has one screen, but computers, because they're stupid, don't know that.)

You also have to tell your X terminal that it's OK to allow X client applications on other computers to draw their windows on your screen. The details of that process vary by model of X terminal, but generally you have to add to the list of hosts allowed to use your screen the name of the computer on which the X application is running (probably the one you have telnetted to in the first place).

Although you usually run X client programs only on nearby computers, in principle X applications anywhere in the Internet can draw their windows on your screen so that you can use them directly, even if they're running on a computer in, say, Slovenia. In practice, though, the connection to the other computer had better be very fast or else the application will be so sluggish that you won't want to use it.

I've run X clients in Wisconsin with windows on my screen in Massachusetts, using a medium speed link and it worked, but I wouldn't want to use it every day because i-t w-a-s a-w-f-u-l-l-y s-l-l-o-o-o-w-w-w. (Perhaps if I'd had a more relaxed California frame of mind rather than an overwrought Easterner's, or if I'd worked while immersed in a vat of molasses so that I couldn't move my fingers or any other part of my body very fast, it would have been OK.)

If You've Gotten This Far, I Have No Idea What Kind of Computer You Have

Most computers connected directly to the Internet have network applications modeled after the UNIX versions, that in turn were modeled after the DEC-20 originals, written more than 20 years ago. The commands described for FTP, telnet, and so on, therefore, will work because the programmers who wrote your version of the programs were lazy and used the same commands they were already used to using. Even if your versions use a window system or are otherwise souped up, you can probably recognize the originals underneath. For example, window versions of the FTP application tend to have menus and buttons with choices that, amazingly enough, match almost exactly the commands in the command-oriented original.

As far as physical network connections go, pretty much the same set of choices exist for nearly all computers these days.

✔ If a local network connects computers in the same building, it almost certainly is some version of Ethernet or a Token Ring.

✔ If you have a very forward-thinking and resource-rich employer, you may use an extremely fast network called *FDDI,* but it's just like the Ethernet or Token Ring, only faster.

✔ If you have a single computer, its connection to the outside is likely to be some kind of modem and a phone line, either dial-up or a dedicated line to a network hub.

✔ If you're using a supercomputer or giant mainframe, it may have some sort of super-exotic, fiber optic, broadband network gizmo. In that case, however, guards would probably arrest you if you tried to fiddle with the network connection, so it hardly matters which kind it is.

✔ The other possibility is that your computer doesn't have a network connection or software, just a modem and a terminal emulator. In that case, you can probably log in as a terminal to a time-shared system that does have an Internet connection. In that case, it's the system you log in to rather than the computer you're using as a terminal that determines which kind of software you have.

Chapter 6
How Does the Internet Work?

In This Chapter

▶ Packet switching

▶ How networks are hooked together

▶ An unbelievable amount of nerdy terminology

This chapter contains gruesome details about how the Internet actually sends data from one place to another. You can skip this entire chapter if you want. But don't, because I think it's interesting. And besides, I've been telling you since Chapter 1 that this chapter tells you all about the famous TCP/IP, so you wouldn't want to waste it.

Why the Post Office Isn't Like the Phone Company

What the Internet does, basically, is transmit data from one computer to another. How hard could that be? Well, it's not that hard, but it is fairly complicated.

The most familiar examples of information transfer in real life are the post office and the phone company. If you want to contact someone by telephone, you pick up the phone and dial the number. The phone company then arranges an electrical circuit from your phone to the phone that you're calling. You and the other person gossip until you're done (or if it's a modem call, your computer and the other computer gossip until *they're* done) and then you hang up, at which point the phone company releases the circuit. Then you can call someone else. At any particular moment, you can only have one call in progress over a particular phone line. (Yeah, there's three-way calling, but that doesn't count.) This scheme is called *circuit switching* because a circuit is set up for the duration of the conversation. Well, the Internet doesn't work this way, so forget it. (Don't entirely forget it; we'll come back to simulated circuit switching later.)

The other model is the post office. If you want to mail a package to someone, you write the recipient's address and your return address on it and mail it. The U.S. Postal Service doesn't have dedicated trucks from every post office to every other post office (they may be inefficient but they're not *that* inefficient). Instead, the package is routed from your local post office to a central post office, where it's then loaded onto a truck or a train headed in the right general direction and repeatedly passed from office to office until it gets to the recipient's post office, at which point the letter carrier delivers it to the door along with the rest of the day's mail.

This is a lot closer to how the Internet works. Each time a host wants to send a message to another host, either the recipient is on a network to which the first host is directly connected, in which case it can send the message directly, or else it's not. In that case the sender sends the message to a host that can forward it. The forwarding host, which presumably is attached to at least one other network, in turn delivers the message directly if it can or passes it to yet another forwarding host. It's quite common for a message to pass through a dozen or more forwarders on its way from one part of the Net to another.

You're probably wondering: *What kind of cretin would think the post office is a better model than the phone company?*

Don't be led astray by the analogy. The main complaints that people have about the post office are that it's slow and that it loses stuff. The Internet occasionally has both of these problems, but they're not as much of an issue as they are with paper mail. In the middle of a busy day, the Net can indeed slow down, though the time a message takes to be delivered is still measured in seconds. Losing stuff turns out not to be a problem in practice, for reasons discussed later in this chapter.

All the World's a Packet

Now let's take our postal analogy a step further. Let's say that you have a close friend in the island nation of Papua New Guinea, to whom you want to send a copy of the manuscript for your new and very long book. (There aren't many bookstores in New Guinea.) Unfortunately, the manuscript weighs 15 pounds, and the limit on packages to Papua New Guinea, is 1 pound. So you divide the manuscript into 15 pieces and on each package you write something like *PART 3 OF 15* and send them off. When the packages eventually arrive, probably not in the right order, your friend takes all the pieces, puts them back in order, and reads them.

The various networks on the Internet work pretty much the same way: They pass data around in chunks called *packets,* each of which carries the addresses of its sender and its receiver (those host numbers I talked about in Chapter 2). The maximum size of a packet varies from network to network, but is usually a few thousand *octets* (Internet-speak for *bytes* or *characters*). A typical size is 1536 octets, which for some long-forgotten reason is the limit on an Ethernet network. Messages that are too large for a single packet have to be sent as several packets.

One advantage the Internet has over the post office is that when Internet software breaks a large package of data into smaller pieces, putting the pieces back together is no problem; when the post office delivers something in small pieces, you are generally out of luck.

Defining the Internet

The set of conventions used to pass packets from one host to another is known as the *Internet Protocol* or *IP*. (Catchy, huh? Actually, the network is named after the protocol, not the other way around.) The Internet, quite simply, is the collection of networks that pass packets to each other using IP.

It's entirely possible to set up a network that uses IP but that isn't actually connected to the Internet. A lot of networks were set up that way in companies that wanted to take advantage of IP (which comes free with every UNIX workstation) but that weren't connected at all to the outside world or were connected only by a dial-up mail connection. In the last year or two, a lot of these disconnected networks have become attached to the Internet because the advantages of being on the Net have increased and because new commercial Internet vendors have made the cost of connection about a tenth of what it used to be.

A lot of other protocols are used in connection with IP. The two best known are *Transport Control Protocol (TCP)* and *User Datagram Protocol (UDP)*. TCP is so widely used that many people refer to *TCP/IP*, the combination of TCP and IP used by most Internet applications.

I'll Build a Gateway to Paradise

Three kinds of *things* (for lack of a better term) pass packets from one network to another: *bridges, routers,* and *gateways.* Here's a quick rundown of the differences among them so that you can hold your own at nerd cocktail parties.

Bridges

A *bridge* connects two networks in a way that makes them appear to be a single, larger network. Bridges most commonly are used to connect two Ethernet networks. The bridge looks at all the packets flying by on each of the networks and when it sees a packet on one network destined for a host on the other, the bridge copies it over.

Ethernet host numbers, which are different from Internet host numbers, are assigned by the serial number of the Ethernet card rather than by network number, so the bridge has to build a table listing which hosts are on which network, based on the return addresses on all the packets flying by on each network. It's a miracle that it works at all.

The good thing about bridges is that they work transparently — the hosts whose packets are being bridged aren't aware that a bridge is involved, and a single bridge can handle a whole bunch of different kinds of network traffic (like Novell and Banyan as well as IP) at the same time. The disadvantages of bridges are that they can only connect two networks of the same type and that bridging fast networks which are not physically close together is very difficult.

Routers

A *router* connects two or more IP (that's the Internet Protocol) networks. The hosts on the networks have to be aware that a router is involved, but that's no problem for IP networks because one of the rules of IP is that all hosts have to be able to talk to routers.

- ✔ A good thing about routers is that they can attach physically different networks, such as a fast, local Ethernet to a slower, long-haul phone line.
- ✔ A bad thing about routers is that they are slower than bridges because it requires more calculation to figure out how to route packets than it does to bridge them, particularly when the networks are of different speeds.

A fast network can deliver packets a lot faster than a slow network can take them away, causing network constipation, so the router has be able to tell the sending host to talk slower.

Another problem is that routers are protocol-specific — that is, the way a host talks to an IP router is different from the way it talks to, say, a Novell or DECnet router. This problem is now addressed by the router equivalent of a Ginsu knife that slices and dices every which way and knows about routing every kind of network known to humankind. These days, all commercial routers can handle multiple protocols, usually at extra cost for each added protocol. Incidentally, this kind of router is usually pronounced *ROOter,* because a *ROWter* is something you use in a woodworking shop.

Gateways

A *gateway* splices two different kinds of protocols together. If, for example, your network talks IP, and someone else's network talks Novell or DECnet or SNA or something else, a gateway converts traffic from one set of protocols to another. Gateways are not only protocol-specific, they are also application-specific, because the way you convert electronic mail from one network to the other is quite different from the way that you convert a remote terminal session.

Routers: the good, the bad, and the really bad

One of the hot topics among Internet weenies these days is *Routing Policy*. The Internet is for the most part *redundantly connected* — that is, getting from one network to another can be accomplished in several ways. In the good old days, finding a route was relatively easy because the main goal was to find the fastest route to each known network. Only a handful of networks were around, so the routers (hosts that pass packets from one network to another) simply compared notes to figure out which one had the shortest route to where. If you wanted to be really fancy and if you had two equally fast routes to somewhere, you could monitor the amount of traffic on each route and send packets by the less busy route.

Things are no longer so simple. For starters, the number of networks of which a router has to be aware is no longer a handful (unless you have extraordinarily large hands). Over 10,000 different networks are attached to the Internet, and more are added weekly. Furthermore, the speeds of communication lines have increased much more quickly than have the speeds of computers used for routing, enough so that special hardware is clearly going to be needed to keep up with the networks that will be installed in the next few years.

Another issue is that there are now political as well as technical distinctions among networks. Some networks, such as the NSFNET, can only handle noncommercial traffic, whereas others can handle any type. This means that some traffic can't be routed the most direct way, if the traffic isn't appropriate for one of the networks on that route.

Another wart on the face of routing is that many organizations have *firewall* routers that only pass certain kinds of traffic. Typically, firewall routers allow incoming electronic mail but not incoming remote terminal sessions or file transfers in an effort to keep out ill-mannered users looking for security holes (and if you have a large enough internal network, a hole will certainly be found somewhere).

Lots of technical papers are published about advanced new routing schemes, policies, or whatever. Fortunately, you as a user can completely ignore the issue because as long as routers eventually get your packets to the right place, it doesn't really matter how they do it.

Mix-and-match terms

These terms are not cast in stone. The term *gateway* has often been used for what we here call a *router*, and there are things called *brouters* that act like something halfway between a bridge and a router. Also, keep in mind that all the differences among bridges, routers, and gateways are based on software, so in some cases it's quite possible to make the same pieces of hardware into a bridge, router, or gateway, depending on the software in use.

TCP: the Rocket-Powered Mailman

I've established that the Internet works just like the post office, in that it delivers unrelated hunks of data (packets) one at a time. So what do you do if you want to "have a conversation," such as logging into a remote computer? Back to the postal analogy. Let's say that you're a chess player. Normal chess is played face-to-face with each player immediately responding to the other. Abnormal chess is sometimes played by mail with each player mailing moves to the other. Such games can take months to complete. But what if your mail were delivered by someone with rocket shoes who zipped each move to the other player within a fraction of a second? That would be a lot more like normal chess.

TCP (Transport Control Protocol) is that rocket-powered mailman. TCP provides what looks like a dedicated connection from one computer to another. Any data you send to the other computer is guaranteed to be delivered, in the same order it was sent, just as though a dedicated circuit were connected from one end to the other (the details of this process are explained in the next section). In fact, what TCP provides isn't really a circuit, it's just a lot of IP packets, so what TCP provides is called a *virtual circuit.* But it's real enough for most purposes, which is why nearly every Internet application uses it.

TCP has to add quite a lot of glop to each packet to do its magic, which makes TCP somewhat slower than the raw IP. A considerably less fancy protocol called *UDP (User Datagram Protocol)* doesn't make any promises about reliability, making do with whatever IP gives it, for the benefit of applications that want to roll their own reliability features, or that can live with the flakiness. (In most cases, IP delivers upwards of 99 percent of all packets correctly, even without TCP's help.)

Certify That Packet!

Make no mistake, the Internet shares with the U.S. Postal Service some inherent unreliability. The Postal Service has two schemes for ensuring that something is delivered: registered mail and return receipts. If you're mailing something of great intrinsic value, such as an original 45 RPM record of Bill Haley and the Comets' "Rock Around the Clock," you send it registered. When you mail something registered, the clerk at the post office immediately puts it in a locked drawer. Each time the package is moved from one place to another, it's carefully logged and signed for all the way until the recipient signs for it. Registered mail is quite reliable but slow because of all of the logging and signing. (Yeah, these days any sane person uses overnight express, but it turns out to be handled a lot like superfast registered mail: electronically scanning the bar code on the package label logs the package's progress. But I digress.)

The other scheme is used for certified letters that don't have any intrinsic physical value but contain an important message, typically a letter from your insurance company saying that they've cancelled your insurance. These letters are sorted and handled normally until they are delivered, at which point the recipient signs a card that is mailed back to the sender. If the sender doesn't get the card back in a reasonable amount of time, he or she sends the letter again.

Different computer networks use either of these schemes. *X.25* networks (used in many commercial networks like Tymnet and Sprintnet) use the registered model, with each packet carefully accounted for. There's even a protocol called X.75 that is used to hand packets from one network to another very reliably. X.25 works OK, but it's slow for the same reason that registered mail is slow — there's all of that logging and checking at each stage.

TCP/IP is much more like certified mail. As IP routes each packet through the network, it does what it can to deliver it, but if some problem arises or if the packet is garbled on a communication line, tough luck — IP just throws away the packet. TCP numbers each packet, and the TCP software on the two communicating hosts (but not on any intermediate hosts) track the packet numbers: each tells the other what it has received and what it hasn't and resends anything that got lost.

This approach has two advantages over the X.25 approach. One is that the end-to-end approach is faster and fundamentally more reliable because it doesn't depend on all the intermediate hosts (between the sender and the recipients) doing everything correctly. The other is that it enables networks to be built much more cheaply because routers can be much dumber. A router for TCP/IP need only understand IP, not TCP or any other higher level protocol.

This means that for a small network, you can build a perfectly adequate router out of a small computer and a few network cards. For example, all the Internet traffic to and from the network here at I.E.C.C. passes through a router built out of an old clone 286 PC, which cost only $300. Works fine.

Any Port in a Storm

The final topic in this survey of Internet Geek-speak is *ports*. In postal terms, port numbers are sort of like apartment numbers. Let's say that you want to communicate with a particular host. OK, you look up its host number and you send it some packets. But we have two problems here. One is that a typical host has lots of programs running that can be having simultaneous conversations with lots of other hosts, so you have to find some way to keep the different conversations separate. The other problem is that when contacting a host, you need some way of telling it what sort of conversation you'd like to have. Do you want to send some electronic mail? Transfer files? Log in?

Ports solve both of these problems. Every program on a host that is engaged in a TCP or UDP conversation is assigned a *port number* to identify that conversation. Furthermore, a large set of low port numbers is reserved (sort of like low-numbered license plates) for particular well-known services. For example, if you want to log into a host using the standard telnet service, you contact port 23 because that's where the telnet server is.

Connections to *client programs* — programs that use remote services — are assigned arbitrary port numbers that are only used to distinguish one connection from another. Servers, on the other hand, use well-known port numbers so that the clients can find them. Several hundred well-known (well-known to Internet programming geeks, at least) port numbers are assigned. Hosts are under no obligation to support them all, just to use the correct number for those that they support. Some of the well-known numbers are pretty stupid, like port 1025 for network blackjack games; others are very specialized, like port 188 for an implementation of the MUMPS database language. But they're there if you need them.

Usually you don't have to worry about port numbers, but there are a few cases when it's handy to know about them. When you want to use a conversational service on another computer, the usual technique is to use the telnet program to connect to port 23 on the remote computer and log in as a normal user. (See Chapter 14 for all the gory details.) But there are some services provided on other ports.

For example, a computer in Michigan offers a geography server (described in Chapter 15) that lets you look up any place name or ZIP code in the U.S. If you telnet to that computer on the standard port 23, you get an invitation to log in as a regular user. This isn't very useful, since you don't have any passwords for that computer. (If it makes you feel better, neither do I.) But if you telnet to port 3000 on the same computer, you're connected directly to the geography server. When you need to use a port other than the standard one to contact any service, that's noted in the service's description.

Actually, two separate sets of port numbers exist: one for TCP and one for UDP. But all of the well-known port numbers are assigned identically for both. For example, TCP port 23 is telnet, so UDP port 23 is also telnet for inattentive users who don't mind if some of their data gets lost.

ISO protocols: trust us, they'll be great

The *International Organization for Standardization* (inexplicably known as *ISO*) has for many years been developing a set of communication protocols that is in many areas supposed to replace TCP/IP eventually. ISO is an enormous international consortium of standardization groups, so it probably will not come as a big surprise to hear that they move ahead at a rate that suggests that they are stapled to a rather arthritic snail.

A bunch of ISO standards are supposed to define various network protocols (I mentioned X.25 already) but they are in most cases slow, complex, and not well debugged (much like the group that is defining them), so nobody uses even the ones that exist unless they are forced to for political reasons. If someone tells you to forget all this unofficial and unsanctioned TCP/IP nonsense because ISO protocols will replace them all, nod politely and pay no attention.

In fairness, the ISO's electronic mail protocols have achieved moderate success. The mail transfer standard is called X.400 and is used in many places as a gateway protocol between mail systems. (You can find out about sending mail to X.400 addresses in Chapter 9.) X.400 is in some ways better than Internet mail because you can use addresses similar to those you'd use for real postal mail, rather than often arbitrary login names as is more common with Internet mail. The standard for name-lookup service, X.500, is late and slow but looks to be widely adopted because the Internet has nothing like it. However, mail is the *only* place where ISO is getting much attention — their standards for file transfer and other applications seem to be dead on arrival.

Part II
Mail and Gossip

The 5th Wave   By Rich Tennant

"NO SIR, THIS ISN'T A DATING SERVICE. THEY INTRODUCE PEOPLE THROUGH A COMPUTER SO THEY CAN TALK TO EACH OTHER IN PERSON. WE INTRODUCE PEOPLE IN PERSON SO THEY CAN TALK TO EACH OTHER THROUGH A COMPUTER."

In this part...

Rumors, gossip, jokes, recipes, bad jokes, tourist travel tips, and really bad jokes (as if there aren't enough in here already): these are only a few of the things you can read and write about with electronic mail and news. Read on to find out how.

Chapter 7
Basics of Electronic Mail

In This Chapter

▶ Mail addresses

▶ Sending mail

▶ Receiving mail

▶ Mail etiquette

*E*lectronic mail is without a doubt the most widely-used Internet service. Every system (other than *dedicated router hosts* and the like) supports some sort of mail service, meaning that no matter what kind of computer you're using, if it's on the Internet you can send and receive mail.

Mail, much more than any other Internet service, is connected to a lot of non-Internet systems, which means that you can exchange mail with a lot of people not on the Internet as well as with all the people who are on it (see Chapter 8 for details).

Mailboxes Here, Mailboxes There

Before you do much mailing, you need to figure out your electronic mail address so that you can tell it to people who want to get in touch with you. And you need to figure out some of their addresses so you can write to them. (I suppose that if you have no friends or plan only to send anonymous hate mail, you can skip this section.)

Internet mail addresses have two parts, separated by @ (the *at* sign). The part before the @ is the *mailbox,* which is (roughly speaking) your personal name, and the part after is the *domain,* usually the name of the computer you use. Sometimes the domain used is the group that contains all the local computers. For example, if you're with the Nuke the Whales Foundation, your computer might be called *shamu.ntw.org,* but the mail domain might be just *ntw.org.* This lets the local mail system take care of getting your mail to the correct computer within the group, which is particularly handy if people switch computers a lot — it avoids having to tell the rest of the world every time you move from one cubicle to another.

What's My Address?

The mailbox is usually your *username* (the name you use to log into your computer, assuming that you're using a computer that needs a login), so your address may be *king@ntw.org*. Domain names are traditionally represented in uppercase (as in *NTW.ORG*), and mailbox names in lowercase or mixed case (as in *king*). But case never actually matters in domains and rarely matters in mailbox names. Therefore, to make it easy on your eyes, most of the domain and mailbox names in this book are given in lowercase. If you're sending a message to another user in your domain (same machine or group of machines), you can leave out the domain part altogether when you type the address.

If you're using a machine like a PC or a Mac that doesn't handle multiple users, you still have a mailbox name, but the way you set that name varies from system to system. In some cases, you set it when you start up the computer; in other cases, you log in when you start the mail program. If your incoming mail is stored on a mail server (see the sidebar "Are PCs real computers, mailwise?") you'd better use the same mailbox name on your PC as you have on the server if you ever want to get any answers to your outgoing mail.

A practical problem arises in figuring out e-mail addresses because how usernames are assigned is not consistent. Some usernames include first names, last names, initials, first name and last initial, first initial and last name, or anything else, including completely *made up* names. Over the years, for example, I've had the usernames *john, johnl, jrl, jlevine, jlevine3* (must have been at least three *jlevines* there), and even *q0246*.

Back when far fewer e-mail users were around, and most users of any particular system knew each other directly, it wasn't all that hard to figure out who had what username. These days, it's becoming much more of a problem, so a lot of organizations are creating consistent mailbox names for all users, most often by using the user's first and last names with a dot between them. In such a scheme, your mailbox name may be something like *elvis.presley@ntw.org*, even though your username is something else. (If your name isn't Elvis Presley, adjust this example suitably. On the other hand, if your name *is* Elvis Presley, please contact me immediately. I know some people who are looking for you.)

Mailing to the outside world

One of the best things about Internet mail is that it is surprisingly well connected to all sorts of other mail systems. In most cases, the connection is seamless enough that you send mail to off-Net users in exactly the same way that you send it to users directly on the Net. In other cases, you have to type the address using strange punctuation (like ! and * and %) but in every other way you send and receive mail the same as always. See Chapters 8 and 9 for more on addressing magic.

Are PCs real computers, mailwise?

Usually, no, unfortunately. Internet mail is passed around using something called *SMTP* for *Simple Mail Transfer Protocol* (presumably named by some programmers with a sense of humor, because it's only simple compared to, say, refinancing the national debt). SMTP was designed on the presumption that all of the machines on the Net are prepared to receive mail pretty much all the time. When one host has a piece of mail to deliver, it immediately contacts the destination host using SMTP and delivers the message. (One of the nice things about Internet mail is that a message is normally delivered within a minute or two after you send it.)

This means that most systems always have an SMTP *daemon* (a program, usually named *smail* or *sendmail,* that lurks in the background, waiting for work to do) hanging around, waiting for the virtual phone to ring with incoming mail. If the destination machine doesn't respond, the sender's machine puts the message in a safe place and tries again every few hours, on the assumption that the destination machine will be working again soon. If the message can't be delivered after three days or so, the sending machine gives up.

This model of mail handling is a definite non-starter in the DOS world. DOS, not being a real operating system (I'm not being snide here, it's just a fact), only runs one program at a time. So, when someone wants to send you some mail, chances are that your machine is running Virtual Valerie or some other business productivity-type application rather than a mail program. Therefore, the chances of your mail program and a sending mail program getting together for SMTP are roughly zero.

This problem can be finessed in one of three ways:

- If you have a workstation or a multiuser system nearby, you can let it handle all of your mail, and log into it as needed using telnet (see Chapter 14).

- On a network with a lot of PCs, many organizations run a PC-networked mail system, like cc:Mail or Microsoft Mail, which keeps all of the mailboxes on a mail-server PC, and then use an extra-cost gateway feature to pass stuff between the PC mail system and Internet SMTP mail. In that case, you send and receive messages in the usual way with your mail system, using some strange punctuation to tell it to pass messages to the Internet. You have to ask a local mail expert for advice.

- For dedicated PC Internet users, it's possible to have your mail stored on a UNIX workstation (or, in principle, on any other machine that can handle mail daemons, although in practice they're all UNIX boxes). When you want to check your mail, you run a program that uses *POP2* or *POP3* (which stand for *Post Office Protocol,* second and third attempts, respectively, to get it right) to retrieve your new mail from the machine that's been holding it. Then use a local PC mail reader on the newly arrived mail.

Other than the extra step to pick up your mail, POP mail readers act pretty much like any other mail readers. For outgoing mail, some POP mail readers pass it back to the mail host to have it sent from there; others use SMTP directly. Again, ask a local expert whether you're set up for POP. Depending on the mail program on your PC, using POP can be a pain in the neck, because sometimes you have to use arcane commands to retrieve your new mail from the POP server. Unless you have a PC mail program that automates all this (most of the Windows mail programs do) or you have a text editor on your PC that you just adore (for writing new messages), it's usually just as easy and a lot less hassle to use the first technique: log into the mail host and read your mail there.

Having several names for the same mailbox is no problem, so the new, longer, consistent usernames are invariably created in addition to, rather than instead of, the traditional short nicknames.

If you don't know what your e-mail address is, a good approach is to send yourself a message, using your login name as the mailbox name. Then examine the return address on the message. See Chapter 9 for more suggestions on finding e-mail addresses.

Mailers, Mailers, Everywhere . . .

So now you know what your address is, or else you've decided that you don't care. Either way, it's time for some hand-to-hand combat with your e-mail system.

At least a dozen different *mailers,* e-mail reading and writing programs that people use on the Internet, are available for UNIX workstations alone, and many more exist for other kinds of computers that are attached directly and indirectly to the Net. The examples here are three representative mailers chosen by the highly scientific method of seeing what's already installed on my local computer.

 ✔ **Berkeley mail:** Called *mail* (or sometimes *Mail* or *mailx*), it is the basic mailer that comes with most UNIX systems. Like most people, we call it *Berkeley mail* because it was written (if that's the right word for such a pile of hacks) at the University of California at Berkeley.

 ✔ **xmail:** This is a graphical front end for Berkeley mail that runs on the *X Windows system.* (Readers familiar with *The Wizard of Oz* can think of xmail as the fire-breathing wizard that Dorothy and friends found in the Emerald City, and Berkeley mail as the man behind the curtain.)

 ✔ **elm:** The third mailer is a rather nice mail program with a full-screen terminal interface. Like a lot of the best Internet software, elm was written and is actively maintained entirely by volunteers. The original author of elm works for Hewlett-Packard, and HP workstations all come with elm as the standard mail program.

Ahoy, there

Sending mail is easy. You run your mail program, typing the address you want to send mail to:

```
mail king@ntw.org
```

The traditional UNIX mail program operates under the traditional UNIX *no-news-is-good-news rule,* so at this point, unless there is some problem starting the mail program, it says nothing. Depending on how the mail is configured (it has about 14 zillion options, most of them useless), it may ask you for a subject line. If it does, give it one, as in the following example (if it doesn't, you can give it one anyway, but we get to that later):

```
mail king@ntw.org
Subject: Hound dogs
```

Now you type your message. It can say anything you want and it can be as long as you want. Here's a short example:

```
mail king@ntw.org
Subject: Hound dogs
When you said that I ain't nothing but a hound dog, did you mean
a greyhound, a basset hound, or some other kind of hound?
Signed,
A Curious Admirer
```

Now you're done. You can end your message in one of two ways (UNIX is always like this — you get used to it after a while). In most versions of mail, you can type a dot by itself on a line to say that you're done. If it works, mail responds with EOT (for End Of Text). If a dot doesn't work, you can employ the usual Ctrl-D that UNIX always lets you use to mark the end of input. *Note:* Be careful not to type it more than once or you're likely to log yourself out. That's all you need to do. The message is delivered or, if not, you get back a cryptic response from the mail system explaining why it didn't deliver it.

By the way, about the Subject: line: If mail doesn't ask you for a subject, and you want to add one, while you're typing in your message type a line with a ~ (tilde), the letter s (for Subject), and the subject itself, as in the following:

```
~sHound dogs
```

This sort of thing is called a *tilde escape* and about two dozen of them exist, most of them not very useful.

If you are fortunate enough to use elm, it is considerably easier to send a message. You start in nearly the same way, except that you run elm instead of mail.

```
elm king@ntw.org
```

A screen pops up and waits for you to enter a subject.

```
                                Send only mode [ELM 2.3 PL11] To: king@ntw.com
  Subject:
```

After you put in the subject, elm may ask for `Copies to:`, which for the moment you can ignore (press Enter to skip it). Then elm automatically runs the standard local text editor, which, with any luck, you already know how to use. (If not, see *UNIX For Dummies,* John Levine and Margaret Levine Young, IDG Books Worldwide, 1993).

Type in the message using any old editor features you want. After you're done and have saved the file (a temporary file, created by elm, for your message), elm comes back with a little menu:

```
And now: s
    Choose e)dit message, !)shell, h)eaders, c)opy file, s)end,
or f)orget.
```

The elm program suggests that you press s to send the message. Resist, for the moment, the urge to try out all of those swell options, and press s to send it. The elm program responds with a cheery `Mail sent!` message, and you're all set.

If you're using xmail, life is considerably more complicated. First you have to start xmail, either by typing **xmail** to the UNIX shell or by some other allegedly user-friendly way set up by your local system administrator. After it starts, xmail shows up in a window like the one in Figure 7-1.

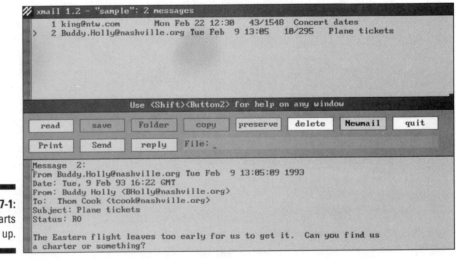

Figure 7-1:
xmail starts
up.

If you look carefully at Figure 7-1, you notice that one of the dozen buttons in the middle of the window is labeled Send. When you click on the Send button, xmail pops up a new window running a text editor (probably *vi,* the usual UNIX text editor).

"Hey, wait!" you may be saying. "What about the subject line? Who the heck am I sending this to?" For some reason, xmail does everything backwards: first you type the message and then you address it (whoever wrote xmail probably puts on socks after shoes, too). Play along with the gag. Write your message, save the file (it makes a temporary file for your message), and leave the editor.

After you leave the editor, xmail pops up yet another window that looks like the one in Figure 7-2.

Figure 7-2:
xmail asks
for the
subject and
address.

To:
Subject:
Cc:
Bcc:
Autograph   Deliver

Type the e-mail address of the person you want to send the letter to and press Enter to get to the second line. Type the subject. Then click Deliver, and xmail sends the message. You may surmise from this example that xmail was designed more to make life easy for the man behind the curtain than to make it useful for mere users. Well, yes, but it's too late to do much about it now.

What if I have some other kind of computer?

Part of the charm of the Internet is that there are hundreds of different kinds of incompatible computers attached to it, all working slightly differently. Sending e-mail always involves more or less the same steps, but the details are never the same. If you're on a PC, depending on which of the dozens of different PC mail programs you're using, you may have to run a separate program after the mail program to upload outgoing messages to a *mail hub.*

If you're using a non-Internet mail system with a gateway, you may have to use some strange syntax to tell it that you're using Internet mail. For example, on Digital VMS systems, you usually have to use a mail address like this one:

```
INTERNET::"king@ntw.org"
```

(That's *usually,* not always, because several different Internet software packages are available for VMS, and several different ways to set up the mail system exist. See Chapter 9 for a list of mail-addressing schemes.)

TIP

My mailer is better than yours

Particularly on UNIX systems, dozens of different mail programs are available, with names like *pine, MH, mush,* and *zmail.* Each of them has different advantages and disadvantages. Some, such as pine, are easier for new users to use. Others, such as MH, are more flexible for heavy-duty users. (Serious e-mail users can easily get over 100 messages per day — I get about 80, counting all the mailing lists I'm on.)

Something *every* e-mail program has is people who will tell you why it is the best mailer in the entire universe and that you'd be a fool to use anything else. Be polite to these people because they can get violent if provoked. For plain day-to-day use, there isn't that much difference among mail programs. Use the mail program that everyone else uses, because that makes it easier to pick up on local mail tricks and to find someone who can help you when you get stuck.

As mentioned previously, if you're running a PC network that doesn't use the Internet's native *TCP/IP* networking (see Chapter 6 for more on TCP/IP), zillions of ways are available to send Internet mail. Again, you have to ask a local expert for more on those other zillions.

Mail Call!

If you start sending e-mail (and in most cases even if you don't), you'll start receiving it. The arrival of e-mail, which is always exciting, even when you get 50 messages a day, is often heralded by a hint from your computer. If you use a system with multiple windows on the screen (like a Mac or a Windows-like graphical environment), the flag on the mailer icon may flip up, looking something like Figure 7-3.

Figure 7-3:
Mail icons, before and after a message arrives.

On some computers, arriving mail is announced by a sound from the computer's speaker, ranging from a quiet *boop* to (nerd alert here) trumpet flourishes and the like. Stick with the boop — your neighbors will thank you.

When you think you may have e-mail, run your favorite mail program. You should see a list of new messages, sort of like the one shown by elm in Figure 7-4.

```
              Folder is 'chuckie' with 2 messages [ELM 2.3 PL11]

        1   Feb 22 Elvis Presley      (13)    Re: hound dogs
        2   Feb 9  Buddy Holly        (10)    Plane tickets




           !=pipe, !=shell, ?=help, <n>=set current to n, /=search pattern
      a)lias, C)opy, c)hange folder, d)elete, e)dit, f)orward, g)roup reply, m)ail,
        n)ext, o)ptions, p)rint, q)uit, r)eply, s)ave, t)ag, u)ndelete, or e(x)it
      Command: []
```

Figure 7-4:
elm lists
newly
arrived
messages.

TIP

If you have a totally antique mail program, it may immediately show you the first message. If this happens to you, demand something better. Budget limits are no excuse: some of the nicest mail programs, such as elm and pine, are free for the taking.

Assuming you have a *real* mail program, you usually read messages by moving the cursor to the message of interest (it starts by putting the cursor on the first new message, usually a good choice) and pressing Enter to view the message, as in Figure 7-5.

If you're using a line-oriented program like Berkeley mail, it shows the messages by assigning a number to each one. Type the number of the message you want to see. In xmail, click the line with the message you want and then click the Read button. If you're using some other mail program, you have to do something similar (consult a local expert).

```
Message 1/2  From Elvis Presley                    Feb 22 '93 at 4:46 pm gmt
                        Re: hound dogs

Actually it was an Abyssinian Kudu hound, 'cuz that's what my daddy's
hound dog was.

Eternally,
EP
```

Figure 7-5:
Reading a
newly
arrived
message.

```
Command ('i' to return to index):
```

After you've seen the message, you can do a bunch of different things with it (much the same as with paper mail). Here are your usual choices:

- ✔ Discard it
- ✔ Reply to it
- ✔ Forward it to other people
- ✔ File it

Unlike paper mail, you can do any or all of these things to any message. The details vary (sorry to waffle, but if we put in the details of every option to every mail program, this book would be as long as a big city phone book — and about as readable). In general, you press r to reply, f to forward, s to save, and so forth. If you don't tell your mailer what to do to a message, the message either stays in your mailbox for later perusal or sometimes gets saved to a file called *mbox*.

If your mailer automatically saves messages in mbox, be sure to go through your mbox every week or so, or it will become enormous and unmanageable. See Chapter 8 for more hints on filing and forwarding messages.

A Few Words from the Etiquette Ladies

Sadly, the great Etiquette Ladies like Emily Post and Amy Vanderbilt died before the invention of e-mail. But here is what they might have suggested about what to say and, more importantly, what *not* to say in electronic mail.

E-mail is a funny hybrid, something between a phone call (or voice mail) and a letter. On the one hand, it's quick and usually informal; on the other hand, it's written rather than spoken, so you don't see any facial expressions or hear tones of voice.

E-mail always seems ruder than it's supposed to

This means:

- ✔ When you send a message, watch your tone of voice.

- ✔ If someone sends you an incredibly obnoxious and offensive message, as likely as not it is a mistake or a joke gone awry. In particular, be on the lookout for failed sarcasm.

Flame off!

Pointless and excessive outrage in electronic mail is so common, it has a name of its own: *flaming*. Don't flame. It makes you look like a jerk.

When you get a message so offensive that you just *have* to reply, stick it back in your electronic in-box for a while and wait until after lunch. Then, don't flame back. The sender probably didn't realize how the message would look. In about 20 years of using electronic mail, I can testify that I've never, ever regretted *not* sending an angry message. (But I have regretted sending a few. Ouch.)

When you're sending mail, keep in mind that someone reading it will have no idea of what you *intended* to say — just what you actually *did* say. Subtle sarcasm and irony are almost impossible to use in e-mail and usually come across as annoying or dumb instead. (If you are an extremely superb writer, you can disregard this advice, but don't say you weren't warned.)

Sometimes it helps to put in a : -) (called a *smiley*), which means *this is a joke*. (Try leaning way over to the left, if you don't see why it's a smile.) In some communities, notably CompuServe, ⟨g⟩ or ⟨grin⟩ serves the same purpose. Here's a typical example:

```
People who don't believe that we are all part of a warm, caring
community who love and support each other are no better than
rabid dogs and should be hunted down and shot. :-)
```

Smileys sometimes help, but if a joke needs a smiley, maybe it wasn't worth making. It may sound like all your e-mail is supposed to be totally humorless. It's not that bad, but until you have the hang of it, limit the humor. You'll be glad you did.

How private is e-mail?

Fairly, but not totally. Any recipient of your mail might forward it to other people. Some mail addresses are really mailing lists that redistribute messages to many other people. In one famous case, a mistaken mail address sent a message to tens of thousands of readers. It started out, "Darling, at last we have a way to send messages that is completely private . . ."

The usual rule of thumb is to not send anything that you wouldn't want to see posted next to the water cooler, or perhaps scribbled next to a pay phone. The latest e-mail systems are starting to include encryption features that make the privacy situation somewhat better, so that anyone who doesn't know the keyword used to scramble a message can't decode it. There's no standard for encrypted mail yet, so you have to ask locally whether any e-mail encryption is available and, if so, what set of recipients can arrange to read it.

BTW, what does IMHO mean? RTFM!

E-mail users are often lazy typists, and a lot of abbreviations are common. Here are some of the most widely used:

Abbreviation	What It Means
BTW	By The Way
IMHO	In My Humble Opinion
RSN	Real Soon Now (vaporware)
RTFM	Read The_____ Manual—you could and should have looked it up yourself
TIA	Thanks In Advance
TLA	Three-Letter Acronym

One of the most widely used encryption programs, both in the U.S. and abroad, is called *PGP* (for *Pretty Good Privacy*). PGP is good enough to deter all but the most determined and sophisticated snoop. (The National Security Agency doubtless has no trouble cracking it, but if the NSA wants to read your mail, you've got more complicated problems than I want to consider.) PGP is available free on the Net; your system administrator should be able to download and install it within an hour or two.

Another possibility to keep in the back of your mind is that it is technically not very hard to forge e-mail return addresses, so if you get a totally off-the-wall message from someone that seems out of character for that person, somebody else may have forged it as a prank. (No, I'm not going to tell you how to forge e-mail. How dumb do you think I am?)

Hey, Mr. Postmaster

Every Internet host that can send or receive mail has a special mail address called *Postmaster* that is guaranteed to get a message to the person responsible for that host. If you send mail to someone and get back strange failure messages, you might try sending a message to the Postmaster. For example, if *king@ntw.org* returns an error from *ntw.org*, you might try a polite question to *postmaster@ntw.org.* The Postmaster is usually an overworked volunteer system administrator, so it is considered poor form to ask a Postmaster for favors much greater than *does so-and-so have a mailbox on this system?*

Chapter 8
More Mail Tricks

• •

In This Chapter

▶ Forwarding and filing mail

▶ Gateways to mail systems around the world

▶ Exchanging mail with robots and fax machines

• •

*O*K, now you know how to send and receive mail. Now it's time for some tips and tricks to make you into a real mail aficionado.

Mail as Hot and Cold Potatoes

After you get a piece of electronic mail, there are about three things you can do with it:

✔ Throw it away (maybe even before you read it, if you don't like the subject line)

✔ Save it for posterity

✔ Pass it along to someone else

Throwing away mail is easy enough that you probably figured out how to do it already: just delete it in the mail program. If you are using a decent mail program that shows you a screen of the subject lines, you can often throw away the really boring stuff without even reading it, just like with paper junk mail.

Hot potatoes

You can forward e-mail along to someone else. Forwarding is one of the nicest things about electronic mail and at the same time it's one of the worst things. It's good because you can easily pass messages along to people who need to know about them. It's bad because you (well, not you personally but, um, people around you, that's it) can just as easily send out floods of messages to recipients who would just as soon not hear yet another press release from the local Ministry of Truth. So, you have to think a little about whether you will enhance someone's quality of life by forwarding a message to him or her. (If you don't care about the quality of life, pick some other criterion.)

Truth in forwarding

Two ways are available (computers never leave well enough alone) to forward stuff: *remailing* and *forwarding*. Remailing is the electronic version of scribbling another address on the outside of the envelope and dropping it back in the mailbox. Unlike paper mail, you can read e-mail without having to tear open the envelope (but these analogies are never perfect). Remailing makes sense when the letter is really for someone else. Remailing is sometimes also called *bouncing*, because the R key is already used to Reply to messages, so it's B for Bounce.

What's usually called *forwarding* a message involves wrapping the message in a new message of your own, sort of like sticking Post-It notes all over it. Usually, forwarding a message copies the original contents and precedes each line with > (the greater-than character). Replying to a message can work in much the same way, with the original message quoted the same way except that you're writing back to the person who wrote the message in the first place, as in the following reply:

```
>Is there a lot of demand for fruit pizza?
>
In answer to your question, I checked with our
research department and found that the favorite pizza
toppings in the 18-34 age group are pepperoni, sausage,
ham, pineapple, olives, peppers, mushrooms, hamburger,
and broccoli. I specifically asked about prunes and
they said that there was no statistically significant
reponse about them.
```

You then get to edit the message. Generally, it's a good idea to get rid of uninteresting parts. All the glop in the message header is frequently included in the forwarded message and almost none of it is comprehensible, much less interesting, so get rid of it.

The tricky part is editing down the actual text. If the message is short, a screenful or so, you should probably leave it alone. If it's really long, and only part of it is relevant, you should cut it down to the interesting part as a courtesy to the reader. I can tell you from experience that people pay a lot more attention to a concise, one-line e-mail message than they do to 12 pages of quoted stuff followed by a two-line question.

Sometimes it makes sense to edit down material even further, particularly to emphasize one specific part. Of course, when you do so, be sure not to edit to the point where you put words in the original author's mouth or garble the sense of the message, as in the following reply:

```
>In answer to your question, I checked with our
>research department and found that the favorite pizza
>toppings ... and
>they said that there was no statistically significant
>reponse about them.
```

That's an excellent way to make new enemies. Sometimes it makes sense to paraphrase a little bit — in that case put the paraphrased part in square brackets, like this:

```
>[When asked about prunes on pizza, research]
>said that there was no statistically significant
>reponse about them.
```

People disagree about whether paraphrasing in order to shorten quotes is a good idea. On the one hand, if you do it well, it saves everyone time. On the other hand, if you do it badly and someone takes offense, you're in for a week of accusations and apologies that'll wipe out whatever time you may have saved. The decision's up to you.

Cold potatoes

Saving e-mail for later reference is like putting potatoes in the fridge for later (don't knock it if you haven't tried it — day-old boiled potatoes are yummy with enough butter or sour cream). Lots of your e-mail is worth saving, just like lots of your paper mail is worth saving. (Of course, lots of it *isn't*, but we already covered that.)

You can save e-mail in a few different ways:

✔ Save it in mailboxes full of messages

✔ Save it in regular files

✔ Print it out and put it in a file cabinet with paper mail

The easiest method usually is to stick messages in a mailbox (a mailbox is usually no more than a file full of messages with some sort of separator between them). Most mail programs by default have a bad habit of saving all your incoming messages in a file named something like *mbox,* except for the ones you delete. This plan might have made sense back in the Paleozoic era, when on a really busy day you might get five messages. Now it makes about as much sense as handling your paper mail by stuffing it all into your desk drawer. If you let your mailer save messages in this manner, your mbox file will grow like the giant blob in that old sci-fi movie until it devours all storage in sight. This is generally not considered Effective Disk Space Management, so don't let it happen to you.

File or discard things yourself. Disabling the automatic-filing feature is usually possible by twiddling a configuration parameter somewhere. Consult your local e-mail guru. If you're really desperate, you might try reading the manual, although too many manuals these days merely assert that the program is user-friendly and, therefore, intuitively obvious. Ho, ho. Find a guru. (Take along a few chocolate chip cookies. It can't hurt. It would be fitting to use the two-fifty recipe, if you have it handy.)

Two general approaches are used in mail filing: by sender and by topic. Whether you use one or the other or both is mostly a matter of taste. Often, mail programs help you file stuff by the sender's name, so if your friend Fred has the username *fred@something.or.other,* with a keystroke or two your mailer will automatically file messages from Fred in a mailbox called *fred.* Of course, if some crazed system administrator has given him the username *z92lh8t@something.or.other,* the automatic naming can leave something to be desired, so make up names of your own.

For filing by topic, it's entirely up to you to come up with the mailbox names. The hardest part is coming up with memorable names. If you're not careful, you'll end up with four mailboxes with slightly different names, each with a quarter of the messages on a particular topic. Try to come up with names that are really obvious, and don't abbreviate. If the topic is *accounting,* call the mailbox *accounting,* because if you abbreviate, you'll never remember whether it's called *acctng, acct, acntng,* or any of a dozen other short abbreviations.

UNIX systems enable you to assign several names to a single file by using *links.* This offers a solution to the slightly-different-name problem. If you can't remember which of four names to use for a project's mailbox, make one mailbox and link it to all four names. That way you get the same mailbox no matter which name you use.

A related issue is where mailboxes live. Most mail programs have a favorite directory for mailboxes, usually called something creative like *Mail.* That's usually as good a place as any to put your mailboxes. Sometimes, though, it makes more sense to put the mailbox for messages about a project in the same directory as other files for that project. Again, with UNIX you can use links so the mailbox is both in the Mail directory and in the project directory.

TIP

Chain letters: Arrrrrgggghhh!

One of the most obnoxious things you can do with e-mail is to pass around chain letters. Because all mail programs have forwarding commands, with only a few keystrokes you can take a chain letter and send it along to hundreds of other people. Don't do it. Chain letters are cute for about two seconds and then they're just annoying.

A few chain letters just keep coming around and around, despite our best efforts to stamp them out. Learn to recognize them now and avoid embarrassment later. Here are some of the hangers-on:

Dying boy wants greeting cards: (Sometimes it's business cards.) Not anymore, he doesn't. Several years ago, an English boy named Craig Shergold was hospitalized with what was thought to be an inoperable brain tumor. Craig wanted to set the world record for most greeting cards. Word got out, and Craig received millions and millions of cards and eventually got into the Guinness Book of World Records. When it turned out that maybe the tumor *wasn't* inoperable, U.S. TV billionaire John Kluge paid for Craig to fly to the United States for an operation, which was successful. So, Craig is OK now and definitely doesn't want any more cards. (You can read all about this story on page 24 of the July 29, 1990, edition of the *New York Times*.) Guinness is so sick and tired of the whole business that it closed the category — no more records for the most cards will be accepted. If you want to help dying children, give the two dollars that a card and stamp would have cost to a children's welfare organization like UNICEF.

The modem tax rumor: In 1987, the Federal Communications Commission (FCC) briefly floated a proposal for a technical change to the rules governing the way on-line services, like CompuServe and GEnie, are billed for their phone connections. Implementing the proposal would have had the effect of raising the prices these services charge. Customers of on-line services made their opposition clear immediately and loudly, members of Congress made concerned inquiries, and the proposal was dropped — permanently. Unfortunately, undated alarmist notices about the proposal have

circulated around bulletin boards ever since. If you see yet another modem tax scare, demand the FCC's current docket number, because the FCC — being a government bureaucracy — can't blow its nose without making announcements, accepting comments, and so forth. So, no docket means no action, which means it's the same old rumor that you should ignore.

Make big bucks with a chain letter: Usually, these letters are signed by "Dave Rhodes," contain lots of testimonials from people who are now rolling in dough, and tell you to send $5 or so to the name at the top of the list, put your name at the bottom, and send the message to a zillion other suckers. Some even say "this isn't a chain letter" (you're supposedly helping to compile a mailing list or something, your 100 percent guaranteed tip-off that it *is* a chain letter). Don't even think about it. These chain letters are extremely illegal, and besides, they don't even work. (Why send any money? Why not just add your name and send it on?) Think of them as *gullibility viruses.* Just ignore them, or perhaps send a polite note to the sender's postmaster to encourage him or her to tell users not to send any more chain letters.

The "two fifty" cookie recipe: According to this one, someone was eating chocolate chip cookies somewhere (Mrs. Fields and Neiman-Marcus are frequently cited) and asked if she (it was always a she) could have the recipe. "Sure," came the answer, "that'll be two-fifty, charged to your credit card." "OK." When the credit card statement came, it turned out to be two hundred and fifty *dollars,* not two dollars and fifty cents. So in retribution, the message concludes with the putative Mrs. Fields and/or Neiman-Marcus recipe, sent to you for free. The story is pure hooey: Mrs. Fields doesn't give out her recipes, for money or otherwise; Neiman's has never even served chocolate chip cookies. The recipe, which varies somewhat from one version to the next, makes perfectly OK cookies, but I don't think it's any better than the one on the back of the bag of chips.

Filing in files

If you're lucky, mailboxes are editable files. On UNIX systems, for example, they're usually plain text files in which each message is preceded by a line like this one:

```
From johnl Wed Apr 21 18:39:18 1993
```

If this seems like a pretty lame separator, that's because it is. This format was dreamed up in about two minutes by somebody who wrote an early mail program, and we've been stuck with it ever since.

An alternative format separates messages with lines containing four Ctrl-A characters, which can look strange on the screen but are easy enough to handle in an editor where they usually look something like ^A^A^A^A, or some smiley faces like this:

```
☺☺☺☺
```

On other systems, though, mailboxes are filled with impenetrable binary junk that makes them impossible to edit. In that case, if you want to use the contents of a message in another file, it may make sense to copy messages into plain text files, one per file, so that you can edit them.

Paper???

Well, sure. If most of your files on a topic are on pieces of paper in a folder in a file cabinet, and you have a few mail messages, you might as well print the messages out and put them in the folder so all the stuff is in the same place.

Yes, this is unbelievably retro, but it works. In the Land of the Future, you'll scan everything into your computers and it'll all be stored in Object-Oriented Hypertextual Databases (add more buzzwords to taste). In the Land of the Present, however, we all have big, old, paper files that aren't going away anytime soon, so we may as well make the best of them.

Hey, Mr. Robot

Not every mail address has an actual person behind it. Some are mailing lists (which we'll talk about in the next chapter) and some are *robots*. Mail robots have become very popular as a way to query databases and retrieve files because it's a lot easier to set up a connection that handles electronic mail than it is to set up one that handles the more standard file transfer. You send a message to the robot (usually referred to as a *mail server*), it takes some action based on the contents of your message, and it sends back a response. For example, if you send a message to *Clinton-Info@Campaign92.Org*, you get back a response telling you how to sign up to get speeches, press releases, and so forth. (Yes, the campaign is over, but the press releases continue.)

The most common use for mail servers is to put yourself on and off *mailing lists,* which we explore in gruesome detail in the next chapter. They're also used to retrieve files from archive sites (see Chapter 16 for details).

Sound! Pictures! Action!

Most e-mail contains plain old typewriter-style text. It's perfectly readable, but let's face it — that's *boring*. And if there's one thing computer geeks can't stand, it's boredom. So, as soon as their computers could handle anything better, they promptly set about improving e-mail to handle all sorts of other stuff. The result is called *MIME*. (If you care, which you don't, it stands for *Multipurpose Internet Mail Extensions*. Whoopee.)

Just the fax, ma'am

One question that comes up a lot is whether there is an e-mail-to-fax gateway on the Net. Quite a few of them exist, actually, but few are open for public use because no provision exists for charging back the cost of the phone calls. An alternative is to use a commercial service like MCI Mail or AT&T Mail, both of which have gateways to the Net, in which you mail a message to your account on one of those systems and then forward it on to a fax address.

If you want to send a lot of faxes, for a few hundred dollars you (or more likely a local techie who is more interested in getting the software right) can get a fax modem, plug it into your computer, and send the faxes yourself. With most e-mail systems, setting things up so that e-mail messages are passed to the fax modem is reasonably straightforward (as much as configuring e-mail software is ever straightforward).

Incoming faxes are more of a problem because although it is really easy to turn a text message into a fax, it is not at all easy to turn a fax back into text. (For example, what if it contains pictures or handwriting?) A frequent compromise is to put faxes in files that you can look at with an image-display program and to e-mail you a message telling you that there's a fax file to look at.

As of mid-1993, a volunteer Internet fax-relay network was forming on the Internet. The best way to find out about it is probably via the USENET group *comp.dcom.fax*. See Chapters 11 and 12.

MIME is a convention for including stuff other than plain text in e-mail messages. There is a long list of the kinds of stuff, ranging from slightly formatted text using characters (like *emphasis* for *emphasis*) up through color pictures, full-motion video, and high-fidelity sound. The MIME group had enough sense to realize that not everyone has a computer that can handle all the fancy high-end stuff; so a single MIME message can contain alternative forms of the same thing, like beautifully formatted, typeset text for people with fancy video screens and plain text for people on simple terminals. MIME also handles nested messages, so a single MIME message might actually contain a document and a couple of illustrations that go with it.

MIME is supposed to be a *four-wheel-drive mail system,* meaning that MIME messages can be delivered over all sorts of hostile and unhelpful mail links. They do this by disguising the MIME contents as plain old text. (At least it looks to the computer like text. To me, it looks more like QW&IIdfhfFX97/$@.) You can recognize a MIME message by looking for special mail headers that look something like this:

```
MIME-version: 1.0
Content-type: TEXT/PLAIN; CHARSET=US-ASCII
Content-transfer-encoding: 7BIT
```

The first line says that the message is using version 1.0 of the MIME standard (the only version defined to date). The second line says that this particular message contains plain old text. The third line says that the text is represented in the message as, get this: text. (Computers are so dim that even this isn't obvious to them.) Different kinds of messages use different Content-type headers. At this point, they all use the same Content-transfer-encoding.

- ✔ If you are using a mail program that is *MIME-compliant,* as the jargon goes, you know you have a MIME message because as you're reading your mail, all of a sudden a window pops up with a picture or formatted text, or perhaps your computer starts singing the message to you (and you thought singing telegrams were a thing of the past).

- ✔ If your mail program doesn't know about MIME and you get a MIME-ized message, it shows up as a large message in your mailbox. If it contains text, about half of the kinds of tarted up text are readable as is, give or take some ugly punctuation. The sound and pictures, on the other hand, are totally hopeless because they are just binary digitized versions of the images and not any sort of text approximation.

- ✔ If you get a picture or sound MIME message, and your mailer doesn't automatically handle it, clunky but usable methods may exist for saving the message to a file and extracting the contents with separate programs. Consult your local e-mail guru for help.

Your Own Personal Mail Manager

After you start sending e-mail, you will probably find that you are receiving quite a lot of it, particularly if you put yourself on some mailing lists (see Chapter 10). Your incoming mail shortly becomes a trickle, then a stream, then a torrent, and pretty soon you can't walk past your keyboard without getting soaking wet (metaphorically speaking).

Fortunately, most mail systems provide ways for you to manage the flow and avoid ruining your clothes (enough of this metaphor, already). If most of your messages come from mailing lists, you should check to see if the lists are available as *USENET* news instead (see Chapter 11). USENET news-reading programs generally enable you to look through the messages and find the ones of interest a lot quicker than your mail program does, and to automatically sort the messages so that you can quickly read or ignore an entire thread of messages on a particular topic.

Even for mailing lists that don't have a USENET equivalent, if you're using a reasonably capable system (like a UNIX workstation) and have a cooperative system manager, it turns out to be easy to arrange the mail plumbing (oops, that metaphor just won't go away) to make particularly chatty mailing lists look like USENET news.

Finally, there is mail-sorting software. Depending on the enthusiasm of your system administrator and whether you can round up a volunteer willing to give you 20 minutes or so of programming help, you may have a mail-sorting program available that can automate a lot of the more mundane mail handling. For example, if you get a lot of messages from a boring mailing list, you can have it stuff them all in a separate mailbox that you can read when things are slow. If your computer has a speaker, you can arrange for various boops and beeps to alert you to different kinds of mail, based on who sent it or what the topic is.

The most common UNIX mail-sorting program is called *delivermail,* which is available for free to anyone who wants it, although it takes a couple of hours for a system administrator to compile and install it. (It's in the *comp.sources.unix* archive at *ftp.uu.net* — see Chapter 18.) After it's installed, each user can have a *delivery script,* which is a command file interpreted by the usual UNIX shell, the command language.

Note: This is where you need the programming help. Someone who is familiar with shell scripts can easily write you a delivery script that looks for sender names and subject line keywords and dispatches mail appropriately. (It helps to have chocolate chip cookies on hand to encourage your shell programmer to help you out.)

All this automatic sorting nonsense may seem like overkill, and if you only get five or ten messages a day, it is. But after the mail really gets flowing, you find that dealing with your mail is taking a lot more of your time than it used to. So keep those automated tools in mind — if not for now, then for later.

Hail to the Chief

The White House, long a technological backwater, has finally crept into the computer age. (Legend has it that when President Eisenhower retired to Gettysburg in 1961, he picked up the phone, heard a dial tone, and had no idea what to do, because in the preceding 20 years when he'd been a general, a college president, and U.S. President, he'd never used a dial phone.) You can now send e-mail to the President and Vice President of the United States. Their addresses are

- president@whitehouse.gov
- vice.president@whitehouse.gov

At the moment, e-mail messages are printed out and handled like paper mail, although they plan to fix that as soon as they can. (Don't hold your breath, though, waiting for Bill and Al to read them personally. The mail is still handled by the staff.) Your message should include your return address (paper mail — because they mail you a response) and should be reasonably formal, like normal correspondence. Feel free to use this sample letter as a model:

```
Gentle Reader
123 Mockingbird Lane
Anytown USA 96943

Dear Mr. President:

I have just finished reading
The Internet For Dummies. It is
the most important book ever
written. Every American, in-
cluding Socks, must have a copy
right away. I beg you to buy
and distribute them immedi-
ately, as a matter of the
greatest national urgency.
Raise my taxes if you need to —
it's worth it.

     Sincerely,

     G. Reader
```

Chapter 9
Finding Electronic Mail Addresses

. . . .

In This Chapter

▶ How to find an address
▶ On-line directories
▶ Lots and lots of mail systems

. . . .

Where in Cyberspace Is Everyone?

As you've probably figured out, one teensy detail is keeping you from sending e-mail to all your friends: you don't know their addresses. In this chapter, you learn lots of different ways to look for addresses. But we'll save you the trouble of reading the rest of the chapter by starting out with the easiest, most reliable way to find out people's e-mail addresses:

Call them on the phone and ask them.

Pretty low-tech, huh? For some reason, this seems to be the absolute last thing people want to do (see sidebar "Top ten reasons not to call someone to get an e-mail address"). But try it first. If you know or can find out the phone number, it's a lot easier than any of the other methods.

Whaddaya mean, you don't know your own address?

It happens a lot—usually it's because a friend is using a proprietary e-mail system that has a gateway to the outside world which provides instructions for how to send messages to the outside but no hint on how outsiders send stuff in. Fortunately, the solution is usually easy: tell your friend to send you a message. All messages have return addresses, and all but the absolute cruddiest of mail gateways put on a usable return address. Don't be surprised if the address has a lot of strange punctuation. After a few gateways, you always seem to end up with things like:

"blurch::John.C.Calhoun"%farp@slimemail.com

But usually if you type the strange address back in, it works, so don't worry about it.

They won't mind if you give them the finger

NAVIGATE

One of the most useful commands, if you generally know where someone receives mail, is *finger*. On most UNIX systems, you can use finger to find out who is logged in right now and to ask about particular users. If you run finger without asking for any particular user, you get a list of who's logged in now, something like the following:

Login Office	Name	TTY	Idle	When
root	0000-Admin(0000)	co	12:	Wed 16:04
johnl	John R. Levine	vt	1d	Wed 16:03
johnl	John R. Levine	p0		Wed 16:10
johnl	John R. Levine	p1	1	Wed 16:10
johnl	John R. Levine	p2	13:	Wed 16:10
johnl	John R. Levine	p3	8:04	Wed 16:49
johnl	John R. Levine	p4		Sat 19:45

Top ten reasons not to call someone to get an e-mail address

✔ Want to surprise long-lost friend.

✔ Want to surprise long-lost *ex*-friend who owes you a lot of money and thinks he's given you the slip.

✔ You and/or friend don't speak English. (Actually happens, because many Internauts are outside the U.S.)

✔ You and/or friend don't speak at all. (Actually happens — networks offer a uniquely friendly place for most people with handicaps because nobody knows or cares about the handicaps.)

✔ It's 3 a.m. and you need to send a message right now or you'll never get to sleep.

✔ You don't know the phone number and, due to an unfortunate childhood experience, you have a deathly fear of calling directory assistance.

✔ Phone only takes quarters; nobody around can break your $100 bill.

✔ Company installed a new phone system, nobody has figured out how to use it, and no matter what you dial you always end up with Dial-a-Prayer.

✔ Inadvertently spilled entire can of soda into phone; can't wait for it to dry out to make the call.

✔ You called yesterday, didn't write down the answer, and forgot it. Oops.

This is a pretty typical response for a workstation. If the user is running a windowing system and has a bunch of windows open on the screen, each window shows up as a separate *pseudoterminal*. This doesn't mean that the user has six terminals with six keyboards arranged like a pipe organ; it's just a messy screen. The Idle column shows, for each terminal (or window), how long it's been since somebody typed something — a useful number if you're trying to see whether anyone is actually there. It's normally displayed in hours and minutes (or days if there's a *d*).

You can also finger a particular person. For example, because John's username is johnl, if you type

```
finger johnl
```

you get back something like the following:

```
Login name: johnl        In real life: John R. Levine
Directory: /usr/johnl    Shell: /bin/sh
On since Jun 30 16:03:13 on vt01      1 day 9 hours Idle Time
Project: Working on "The Internet For Dummies"
Plan:
Write many books, become famous.
```

The exact format of the response varies a lot from one system to another, because fiddling with the finger program is a bad habit of many UNIX system hackers. (In this case, you'd actually get six copies of the response, one for each window, but we thought we'd save the paper.)

Finger also, with some limitations, can match approximate names. If you type

```
finger john
```

it finds all the people whose real names (according to the system password file) are *John something* or *something John*.

Project that plan! (or is it plan that project?)

On UNIX systems, the response to the finger command comes back with a *project* and a *plan*. You, too, can have a project and a plan so that you look like a well-informed, seasoned network user (appearances are everything).

Your project is a file called *.project* (yes, it starts with a dot), and your plan is a file called *.plan* (it starts with a dot, too). You can put anything in them you want. The finger command only shows the first line of the project but all of the plan. Try not to go overboard. Ten lines or so is all people are willing to see, and even that's stretching it if it's not really, *really* clever.

Fingering far-off friends for fun

The shrewd reader has probably noticed that so far we've discussed fingering only people on one's own machine, which isn't very interesting. What makes finger useful is that it can finger other machines equally well. If you type

```
finger @ntw.org
```

it shows you who's logged in at ntw.com, assuming that it allows incoming finger requests (most but not all sites do). You can also ask about a particular person. For example, if you type

```
finger elvis@ntw.org
```

you get back the same response as if a local user had typed *finger elvis*. If you know a user's name, you can usually use finger to figure out his or her e-mail address, which is generally the same as the username. If, say, you finger *chester@glorp.org* and get back

```
User    Full name              What- Idle TTY -Console Location-
chet    Chester A. Arthur      csh   7:17 rb   ncd16 (X display 0)
```

you can be pretty sure that the mail address is *chet@glorp.org*.

The industrial-strength finger

Some places, universities in particular, have attached their finger programs to organizational directories. For example, if you finger *bu.edu* (Boston University), you get the following response:

```
[bu.edu]
    Boston University Electronic Directory (finger access)
This directory contains listings for Students, Faculty,
Staff and University Departments. At present, most informa-
tion about students is not accessible off-campus or via
finger on bu.edu. The primary directory interface is ph; if
this is not available, finger accepts <user>@bu.edu where
<user> can be a login name or FirstName-LastName (note dash
'-' not space). Also note that <user> can include standard
Unix shell patterns.
...
```

So, you can try fingering *Jane-Smith@bu.edu* and the like to find the address. Other universities with similar directories include MIT and Yale. It's worth a try — the worst that can happen is that it'll say not found.

Hey, Ms. Postmaster

Sometimes you have a pretty good idea what machine someone uses, but you don't know the name. In that case, you can try writing to the postmaster. Every *domain,* the part of the address after @ (the at sign), that can receive Internet mail has the e-mail address *postmaster,* which contacts someone responsible for that machine. So if you're pretty sure your friend uses *moby.ntw.org,* you might try asking (politely, of course) *postmaster@moby.ntw.org* what the address is. (We assume that, for some reason, you can't just call your friend and ask what the e-mail address is.)

Most postmasters are overworked system administrators who don't mind an occasional polite question, but you shouldn't expect any big favors. Also, keep in mind that the larger the mail domain, the less likely it is that the postmaster knows all the users personally. Don't write to *Postmaster@ibm.com* to try to find someone's e-mail address at IBM. (Fortunately, IBM has a *whois server* — see next section, "Who 'zat?".)

Postmaster is also the appropriate place to write when you're having trouble with mail to or from a site. If your messages to someone are coming back with a cryptic error message that suggests the mail system is fouled up, or if you're receiving a flood of mechanically generated junk mail from a deranged automatic mail server (see Chapter 10), the postmaster at the relevant site is the one to write to.

Who 'zat?

Quite a long time ago (at least, a long time ago in the *network* frame of mind — 15 or 20 years) some of the network managers started keeping directories of network people. The command that lets you look up people in these directories is called *whois.* Some systems have a whois command, so in principle you can type

```
whois Smith
```

and it should contact the whois database and tell you about all the people named Smith. In practice, however, it isn't quite that simple. For one thing, around the end of 1992, the main system that keeps the Internet whois database moved, and most whois commands haven't yet been updated to reflect that move. The standard server that most whois programs contact now holds only the names of people who work for the Department of Defense. Fortunately, you can tell the whois program to use a particular server, as in

```
finger -h whois.internic.net Smith
```

because the civilian Internet service is now at *whois.internic.net.* The *-h* stands for *host,* as in the host where the server is.

OK, how do I find people at IBM?

I thought you'd never ask. IBM has a mail server that lets you look up people's names. Send a message to *nic@vnet.ibm.com* containing a line like

whois Watson, T

It lists any users with e-mail addresses whose names match. Although nearly all IBM employees have internal e-mail addresses, only a fraction can receive mail from the outside, and you can see only those addresses. (Makes sense, no point in telling you about mail addresses you can't use.)

Many other companies have a straightforward addressing system that gives everyone at the company an alias like *Firstname.Lastname*. This works at AT&T, so mailing to

Theodore.Vail@att.com

finds someone pretty reliably. This also works at Sun Microsystems (*sun.com*). It's always worth a try, since the worst that can happen is that you get your message back as undeliverable. If several people have the same name, you usually get a mechanical response telling you how to figure out which of them you want and what the correct address is.

For systems that don't have the whois command, you can usually use *telnet* (see Chapter 14) instead. You can telnet to whois.internic.net; then at the prompt, type **whois whoever**. For European Net people, try typing **whois.ripe.net**. A large list of whois servers is in a file that you can *FTP* (see Chapter 16) from *sipb.mit.edu*, filename */pub/whois/whois-servers.list*.

Compatible Mail System — a Contradiction?

A zillion different networks are spliced into the Internet in one way or another. With a lot of them, you can barely tell that it's a different network. For example, a lot of individual UNIX systems pass mail around using *UUCP* (which stands for *UNIX to UNIX CoPy*), an ancient but sturdy dial-up scheme. Most of them have arranged to register standard Internet addresses, so you can send mail to them the same way you send mail to any other Internet mailbox.

But a lot of proprietary mail systems are out there, and many of them are in fact connected to the Internet. However, most of the connections seem to have been assembled with spit and baling wire, so you have to type something strange to get the mail through. In the section "A Parade of Mail Systems" later in this chapter, you should find the necessary strange stuff you need for this task.

X.400: we're from the government and we're here to help you

After the Internet had been around for several years, and e-mail had been flowing for far longer than that, the international organization in charge of standards for telephones and stuff like that, known then as the *CCITT* (a French acronym for the International Telephone Committee), decided that they were going to get into the e-mail business, too.

You might think that the obvious thing to do would be to adopt the existing standards, as they'd been shown to be reliable and robust. (Well, silly you — that just goes to show *you'll* never get very far as an international telecommunications standards developer.) They decided to come up with *X.400,* something all new, all singing, all dancing, and much, much more complex — as befits the grandeur of the international telecommunications Establishment. In all fairness, X.400 does handle a few things that Internet mail (known as *RFC822,* after the document that describes it) doesn't, or at least didn't until recently. But X.400 is so complicated that it has taken nearly ten years from the publication of the first version for it to become at all common.

An X.400 address isn't just a name and a domain: it's a whole bunch of attributes. The official specification goes on for dozens, if not hundreds, of pages, but I'll spare you the detail (which would have been fascinating if I'd had the space, you can be sure) and report on the bare minimum. The attributes that are usually of interest and the codes used to represent them are the following:

- **Surname (S):** the recipient's last name
- **Given name (G):** the recipient's first name
- **Initials (I):** first or middle initial(s)
- **Generational qualifier (GQ or Q):** Jr., III, and so on (these folks think of everything)
- **Administration Domain Name (ADMD or A):** more or less the name of the mail system
- **Private Domain Name (PRMD or P):** more or less the name of a private system gatewayed into a public ADMD
- **Organization (O):** the organization with which the recipient is affiliated, which may or may not have anything to do with the ADMD or PRMD
- **Country (C):** a two-letter country code (see Appendix A)
- **Domain Defined Attribute (DD or DDA):** any magic code that identifies the recipient, such as username or account number

You encode these attributes in an address, using / (a slash) to separate them and writing each attribute as the code, an equal sign, and the value. Is that clear? No? (Can't imagine why.)

Here's a concrete example: Let's say that your friend uses Sprint's Sprintmail service (formerly known as Telemail, the ADMD), which has an X.400 connection to the Internet. Your friend's name is Samuel Tilden, he's in the United States, and he's with Tammany Hall. His attributes would be

- ✔ **G:** Samuel
- ✔ **S:** Tilden
- ✔ **O:** TammanyHall
- ✔ **C:** US

So the address would be

```
/G=Samuel/S=Tilden/O=TammanyHall/C=US/ADMD=TELEMAIL/@sprint.com
```

because the Internet domain for the gateway is *sprint.com*. Note that a slash appears at the beginning of the address and just before the @. The order of the slash-separated chunks doesn't matter.

Exactly which attributes you need for a particular address varies all over the place. Some domains only connect to a single country and ADMD, so you don't use those attributes with those domains. Others (such as Sprintmail) connect to many, so you need both. It's a mess. You need to find out for each X.400 system which attributes it needs. In theory, redundant attributes shouldn't hurt, but in practice, who knows?

One minor simplification applies to the hopefully common case in which the only attribute needed is the recipient's actual name. If the user's name is Rutherford B. Hayes, the full attribute form is

```
/G=Rutherford/I=B/S=Hayes/
```

But instead you can write

```
Rutherford.B.Hayes
```

Pretty advanced, eh? You can leave out the given name or the initial if you want. You can hope that most X.400 addresses can be written this way, but you are probably doomed to disappointment.

In most cases, the easiest way to figure out someone's X.400 address is to have your recipient send you a message and see what the `From:` line says. Failing that, you have to experiment.

X.500: we're from the government and we're back

An official *white pages* directory service model called *X.500* is brought to us by the same people who brought us X.400. X.500 organizes its data like a shelf full of phone books (or in a large X.500 system, like a library of shelves organized by country). For any particular person, you have to tell X.500 which book or books to look in. **Note:** It looks like X.500 will actually be used all over the place for two reasons. One reason is that it is somewhat more usable than X.400, and the other reason is that no other competing candidates exist. (I'll give you one guess as to which is the more important reason.)

At this point in time, most X.500 services are *interactive,* which means that you log into them and type your request. Generally, you enter the parts you know, such as the names of the person and the organization, and it shows you the account names that match. All the interactive systems have some sort of help, so if you're stuck, try pressing ? or typing **help**.

The most common X.500 service is called *fred* (which stands for *FRont End to Directories*). You can try it out by telnetting (see Chapter 14) to *wp.psi.com* or *wp1.psi.com* and logging in as *fred*. If you just type someone's name, fred tries to look it up in the local directory of people who work at PSI, the Internet network provider that offers the demonstration fred service. Most likely, the person you are looking for isn't at PSI, so you need to tell fred where to look. The easiest thing to do, if you think your friend is at an organization that starts with, say, the letter F, is to type

```
whois John Smith -org f*
```

Fred then goes through each of the matching organizations and asks you whether you want to look in their phone book. Press Y or N, depending. In theory, you should be able to type

```
whois John Smith -org * -geo @c=US
```

to have it look in all of the directories for companies in the United States. But in practice, the fred program is still kind of buggy and tends to die when you make complex queries.

Know what?

One more address-finding system that's worth trying is *knowbot*. You telnet (see Chapter 14) to it by typing

```
telnet nri.reston.va.us 185
```

(The *185* means you want to log into the knowbot server rather than the usual login prompt.) It then displays a prompt. Just type the person's name and wait, sometimes for as long as several minutes, as it looks through a whole bunch of directories and tells you what it finds. Knowbot has access to some directories not otherwise easily accessible, including the one for MCI Mail, so it's worth checking. In my experience, though, it sometimes misses things — for example, I have an MCI Mail account, but for some reason Knowbot can't find me there.

A Parade of Mail Systems

Here is a short (well, *pretty* short) list of major mail and on-line systems that are connected to the Internet and how to send mail to people on that system.

America Online

An AOL user's username is usually his or her full name. To send mail to a user named Aaron Burr, type

```
aaronburr@aol.com
```

Note: Some AOL users have chosen mail names unrelated to their actual names; for them, you'll have to pick up the phone and call them.

Applelink

Applelink users typically use their last name as their usernames:

```
reinhold@applelink.apple.com
```

AT&T Mail

AT&T Mail users have arbitrary usernames. To send mail to a user whose username is *blivet*, type

```
blivet@attmail.com
```

BITNET

BITNET is a network of mostly IBM mainframes. Each system name is eight characters long or less. System names often contain the letters *VM*, the name of the operating system used on most BITNET sites. Usernames are arbitrary, but are usually also eight characters or less. Many BITNET sites also have Internet mail domain names, so you can send mail to them in the regular Internet way.

If the mailer you use is well configured, it probably has a BITNET support setup to handle BITNET systems not directly on the Internet. So you can send mail to, say, *JSMITH* at *XYZVM3* by typing

```
jsmith@xyzvm3.bitnet
```

Failing that, you have to address mail directly to a BITNET gateway. Here are addresses using two gateways that tolerate outsiders' mail:

```
jsmith%xyzvm3.bitnet@mitvma.mit.edu
jsmith%xyzvm3.bitnet@cunyvm.cuny.edu
```

These two gateways are provided by MIT and the City University of New York (CUNY), respectively, as a courtesy to the Net community.

BIX

BIX is a commercial system formerly run by *Byte* magazine and now run by General Videotext. Usernames are arbitrary short strings. To mail to user *xxxxx*, type

```
xxxxx@bix.com
```

CompuServe

CompuServe is a large on-line service. (Is there anyone who doesn't know that?) For ancient, historical reasons, CompuServe usernames are pairs of *octal* (base eight) numbers, usually starting with the digit 7. If a user's number is 712345,6701, the address is

```
712345.6701@compuserve.com
```

Note: the address uses a *period,* not a *comma,* because Internet addresses can't contain commas.

Delphi

Delphi is an on-line service from General Videotext, the same people who run BIX, although the services are separate (Delphi was recently sold to Rupert Murdoch, the media baron). Delphi usernames are arbitrary strings, most often the first initial and last name of the user. To send to user *jlevine* (that's me, by the way), type

```
jlevine@delphi.com
```

Easylink

Easylink is a mostly mail service formerly run by Western Union and now run by AT&T. Users have seven-digit numbers. To mail to user *3141592,* type

```
3141592@eln.attmail.com
```

FIDONET

FIDONET is a very large, worldwide BBS network. On FIDONET, people are identified by their names, and each individual BBS (called a *node*) has a three- or four-part number in the form *1:2/3* or *1:2/3.4.* To send a message to Grover Cleveland at node *1:2/3.4,* type

```
grover.cleveland@p4.f3.n2.z1.fidonet.org
```

If a node has a three-part name, like *1:2/3,* type

```
grover.cleveland@f3.n2.z1.fidonet.org
```

GEnie

GEnie is an on-line service run by General Electric. It's the consumer end of GE's commercial on-line service, which dates back into the 1960s. Each user has a username, which is an arbitrary and totally unmemorable string, and a mail name, which is usually related to the user's name. You need to know a user's mail name, something like *J.SMITH7:*

```
J.SMITH7@genie.geis.com
```

MCI Mail

MCI Mail is a large, commercial e-mail system. Each user has a seven-digit user number guaranteed to be unique and a username that may or may not be unique. You can send to the number, username, or the person's actual name, using underscores instead of spaces:

```
1234567@mcimail.com
jsmith@mcimail.com
john_smith@mcimail.com
```

If you send to a username or an actual name, and the name turns out not to be unique, MCI Mail thoughtfully sends you a response listing the possible matches so that you can send your message again to the unique user number. MCI user numbers are sometimes written with a hyphen, like a phone number, but you needn't use the hyphen in your address.

Prodigy

Prodigy is a very large on-line system run by IBM and Sears. (We hear that they can have upwards of 10,000 simultaneous users.) They say (and have been saying for at least a year) that they will have an Internet mail gateway. Users have arbitrary usernames like *KS8GN3*. If and when the gateway works, you should be able to send mail to

```
KS8GN3@prodigy.com
```

Sprintmail (Telemail)

Sprintmail is an e-mail system provided by Sprintnet. Sprintmail used to be called Telemail because Sprintnet used to be called Telenet. (It was a technological spin-off of the original ARPANET work that led to the Internet.) Sprintmail is the major X.400 mail system in the United States. As I mentioned before, to send a message to a user named Samuel Tilden who is with Tammany Hall in the United States, type

```
/G=Samuel/S=Tilden/O=TammanyHall/C=US/ADMD=TELEMAIL/@sprint.com
```

UUCP

UUCP is an old and cruddy mail system that is still used by a lot of UNIX systems because (how did you guess?) it's free. UUCP addresses consist of a system name and a username, which are both short, arbitrary strings. For example, the system here at *The Internet For Dummies* Central, for historical reasons, has a UUCP address — *iecc* — as well as its normal Internet address, so you could address mail to *iecc!dummies.* (The ! is pronounced "bang," and this is called a *bang path address.*) Multihop UUCP addresses also exist: *world!iecc!dummies* says to send the message first to the machine called *world,* which can send it to *iecc,* where the address is *dummies.* (Think of it as e-mail's *whisper down the lane.*) Most often, UUCP addresses are written relative to an Internet host that also talks UUCP, so you could address mail to

```
world!iecc!dummies@uunet.uu.net
```

(although it gets here faster if you send it to *dummies@iecc.com,* because that avoids the UUCP nonsense). This address means to send the message to *uunet.uu.net* using regular Internet mail, then by UUCP to *world,* and another UUCP hop to *iecc,* and there to the mailbox called *dummies.* If you think this is ugly and confusing, you're not alone.

UUNET Communications is a large, non-profit outfit that, among other things, brings e-mail to the UUCP-speaking masses, so it's the Internet system most often seen with UUCP addresses. Most of UUNET's customers also have regular Internet addresses that internally are turned into the ugly UUCP addreses. If you know the Internet address rather than the UUCP address, use it.

Chapter 10
Using Mailing Lists

Are You Sure This Isn't Junk Mail?

Now that you know all about how to send and receive mail, only one thing stands between you and a rich, fulfilling, mail-blessed life: you don't know very many people with whom you can exchange mail. Fortunately, you can get yourself on lots of mailing lists, which ensures that you arrive every morning to a mailbox with 400 new messages. (Well, maybe you should start out with one or two lists.)

The point of a mailing list is quite simple. The list itself has a mail address, and anything (more or less) that someone sends to that address is sent to all the people on the list, who often respond to the messages. The result is a running conversation. Different lists have different styles. Some are fairly formal, hewing closely to the official topic of the list. Others tend to go flying off into outer space, topic-wise. You have to read them for a while to be able to tell which list works which way.

USENET news is another way to have running e-mail-like conversations, and the distinction between the two is blurry. (Some topics are available both as mailing lists and on USENET, so people with and without access to news can participate.) Chapter 11 discusses USENET.

Getting on and off Mailing Lists

The way that you get on or off a mailing list is simple: you send a mail message. Two general schools of mailing list management exist: the *manual* and the *automatic*. Manual management is the more traditional way: Your message is read by a human being who updates the files to put people on or take them off the list. The advantage to manual management is that you get personal service; the disadvantage is that the list *maintainer* may not get around to servicing you for quite a while if more pressing business (such as his or her real job) intervenes.

These days it's more common to have lists maintained automatically, which saves human attention for times when things are fouled up. The most widely used automatic mailing managers are a family of programs known as *LISTSERV*, which get their own section later in this chapter.

For the manual lists, there is a widely observed convention regarding list and maintainer addresses. Let's say that you want to join a list for fans of James Buchanan (the 15th President of the United States, the only one who never married, in case you slept through that part of history class), and the list's name is *buchanan-lovers@blivet.com.* The manager's address is almost certainly *buchanan-lovers-request@blivet.com.* In other words, just add *-request* to the list's address to get the manager's address. Because the list is maintained by hand, your request to be added or dropped needn't take any particular form, so long as it's polite. *Please add me to the buchanan-lovers list* does quite well. When you decide that you've had all the Buchanan you can stand, another message saying *Please remove me from the buchanan-lovers list* does equally well.

How to avoid looking like an idiot

Here's a handy tip: after you subscribe to a list, don't send anything to it until you've been reading it for a week. Trust me, it's been getting along without your insights since it started and it can get along without them for one more week.

This gives you a chance to learn the sorts of topics that people really discuss, the tone of the list, and so forth. It also gives you a fair idea about which topics people are tired of. The classic newcomer gaffe is to subscribe to a list and immediately send a message asking a dumb question that isn't really germane to the topic and that was beaten to death three days earlier. Bide your time and don't let this happen to you.

The number two newcomer gaffe is to send a message directly to the list asking to subscribe or unsubscribe. Such a message should go to a request or LISTSERV address, where the list maintainer (human or robotic) can handle it, and *not* to the list itself, where all the other subscribers can see that you screwed up.

Messages to -request addresses are read and handled by human beings who sometimes eat, sleep, and work regular jobs as well as maintain mailing lists. This means that they don't necessarily read your request the moment it arrives. It can take a day or so to be added to or removed from a list, and after you ask to be removed, you usually get a few more messages before they actually remove you. If it takes longer than you'd like, be patient. And *don't* send cranky follow-ups — they just cheese off the list maintainer.

LISTSERV, the studly computer's mail manager

The *BITNET* network (see Chapter 9) was originally set up so that the only thing it could do was ship files and messages from one system to another. As a result, BITNET users quickly developed lots and lots of mailing lists because no other convenient way — like USENET news — was available to stay in touch.

Maintaining all those mailing lists was (and still is) a lot of work, so in order to manage the mailing lists the BITNET crowd came up with a program called LISTSERV, which runs on great big IBM mainframe computers. (The IBM mainframe types have an inordinate fondness for eight-letter uppercase names EVEN THOUGH TO MOST OF US IT SEEMS LIKE SHOUTING.) Originally, only users on machines that were directly connected to BITNET could use LISTSERV, but current versions have been improved so that anyone with an Internet address can use them. Indeed, LISTSERV has grown to the point where it is an all-singing, all-dancing mailing list program with about 15 zillion features and options, almost none of which you care about.

LISTSERV is a little klunky to use but it has the great advantage of being able to handle with ease enormous mailing lists containing thousands of members, something that makes the regular Internet mail programs choke. (For example, LISTSERV can send mail to 1000 addresses in about five minutes, whereas that would take the regular Internet sendmail program over an hour.)

Urrp! Computer's Digest messages!

Some mailing lists are *digested*. No, they're not dripping with digital gastric juices — they're digested more in the sense of *Reader's Digest*. All the messages over a particular period of time (usually a day or two) are gathered into one big message with a table of contents added at the front. Many people find this more convenient than getting messages separately because you can easily look at all the messages on the topic at once.

Some mail and news-reading programs give you the option of dividing digests back into the individual messages so that you can see them one at a time yet still grouped together. This is sometimes known as *undigestification* or *exploding* a digest. (First it's digested and then it explodes, sort of like a burrito.) Ask a nearby guru if and how you can turn on digest exploding in your local mail program.

You put yourself on and off a LISTSERV mailing list by sending mail to *LISTSERV@some.machine.or.other,* where *some.machine.or.other* is the name of the particular machine where the mailing list *lives.* Some lists live on several machines (see the section "Stupid LISTSERV tricks" later in this chapter). Being computer programs, LISTSERV list managers are pretty simpleminded, so you have to speak to them clearly and distinctly.

Let's say, for example, that you want to join a list called *SNUFLE-L* (LISTSERV mailing lists usually end with *-L*) which lives at *ntw.org.* To join, send a message to *LISTSERV@ntw.org* that contains this line:

```
SUB SNUFLE-L Roger Sherman
```

You needn't add a subject line or anything else to this message. *SUB* is short for subscribe, *SNUFLE-L* is the name of the list, and anything after that is supposed to be your real name. (You can put whatever you want there, but keep in mind that it will show up in the return address of anything you send to the list.) Shortly afterward, you should get two messages back:

- ✔ A chatty, machine-generated welcoming message, telling you that you've joined the list, along with a description of some commands you can use to fiddle with your mailing list membership.

- ✔ An incredibly boring message, telling you that the IBM mainframe ran a program to handle your request and reporting the exact number of milliseconds of computer time and number of disk operations that the request took. *Whoopee.* (It is sobering to think that somewhere people find these messages interesting.)

To send a message to this list, mail to the list name at the same machine — in this case, *SNUFLE-L@ntw.org.* Be sure to provide a descriptive `Subject:` for the multitudes who will benefit from your pearls of wisdom. Within a matter of minutes, people all over the world will be reading your message.

To get off a list, you again write to LISTSERV@some.machine.or.other, this time sending

```
SIGNOFF SNUFLE-L
```

or whatever the list's name is. You don't have to give your name again, because after you're off the list, LISTSERV has no further interest in you and completely forgets you ever existed.

Some lists are harder to get on and off than others. Usually, you ask to get on a list and you're on the list. However, in some cases the list isn't open to all comers, and the human list owner screens requests to join the list. In other cases, after you ask to subscribe, LISTSERV sends you a message to make sure it got your address right, and you have to respond with OK or something. (These messages tend to say pretty clearly what you're expected to do.)

To contact the actual human being who runs a particular list, the mail address is *OWNER-* followed by the list name, for example *OWNER-SNUFLE-L.* The owner can do all sorts of things to lists that mere mortals can't. In particular, the owner can fix screwed-up names on the list or add a name that for some reason the automatic method doesn't handle. You have to appeal for manual intervention if your mail system doesn't put your correct network mail address on the From: line of your messages, as sometimes happens when your local mail system isn't set up quite right.

Stupid LISTSERV tricks

The people who maintain the LISTSERV program have added so many bells and whistles to it that it would take an entire book to describe them all, and, frankly, they're not that interesting. But here are some stupid LISTSERV tricks. For each of them, you send a message to LISTSERV@some.machine.or.other to talk to the LISTSERV program itself. You can send several commands in the same message if you want to do two or three tricks at once.

- ✔ **Temporarily stopping mail:** Sometimes you're going to be away for a week or two and you don't want to get a lot of mailing-list mail in the meantime. But because you're planning to come back you don't want to take yourself off all the lists, either. To temporarily stop mail from the SNUFLE-L mailing list, send

```
SET SNUFLE-L NOMAIL
```

  and it'll stop sending you messages. To turn the mail back on, send

```
SET SNUFLE-L MAIL
```

- ✔ **Getting messages as a digest:** If you're getting a lot of messages from a list and would rather get them all at once as a daily digest, send

```
SET SNUFLE-L DIGEST
```

  Remember, not all lists can be digested (again, think of burritos), and the indigestible ones will let you know.

✔ **Finding out who's on a list:** To find out who subscribes to a list, send

```
REVIEW SNUFLE-L
```

Some lists can only be reviewed by people on the list, and others not at all. Some lists are enormous, so be prepared to get back an enormous message listing 1000s of subscribers.

✔ **Getting or not getting your own mail:** When you send mail to a LISTSERV list of which you're a member, it usually sends you a copy of your own message to confirm that it got there OK. Some people find this needlessly redundant. (*Your message has been sent. You'll be receiving it shortly.* Huh?) To avoid getting copies of your own messages, send

```
SET SNUFLE-L NOACK
```

To resume getting copies of your own messages, send

```
SET SNUFLE-L ACK
```

✔ **Finding out what lists are available:** To find out what LISTSERV mailing lists are available on a particular host, send

```
LIST
```

Note: Keep in mind that just because a list exists doesn't necessarily mean you can subscribe to it. But it doesn't hurt to try.

✔ **Getting LISTSERV to do other things:** Lots of other commands lurk in LISTSERV, most of which apply only to people on IBM mainframes. If you are such a person, or if you're just nosy, send a message containing

```
HELP
```

and you'll receive a helpful response listing other commands.

Sending Messages to Mailing Lists

OK, you're signed up on a mailing list. Now what? First, as I said a few pages ago, wait a week or so and see what sort of messages arrive from the list — that way you can get an idea of what you should or should not send to it. When you think you've seen enough to avoid embarrassing yourself, try sending something in. That's easy — you mail a message to the mailing list. The list's address is the same as the name of the list: *buchanan-lovers@blivet.com* or *snufle-l@ntw.org* or whatever. Keep in mind that hundreds or thousands of people will be reading your pearls of wisdom, so try at least to spell things correctly (you may have thought that this was obvious but you'd be sadly misteaken.) On popular lists, you may start to get back responses within a few minutes of sending a message.

Some lists encourage new subscribers to send in a message introducing themselves and saying briefly what their interests are. Others don't. So don't send anything until you have something to say.

After you watch the flow of messages on a list for a while, all this will become pretty obvious.

Some mailing lists have funny rules about who is allowed to send messages, meaning that just because you're on the list doesn't automatically mean that any messages you send will appear on the list. Some lists are *moderated*, meaning that any message you send in gets sent to a human *moderator*, who decides what goes to the list and what doesn't. This may sound kind of fascist, but in practice the arrangement makes a list about 50 times more interesting than it would be otherwise, because a good moderator can filter out the boring and irrelevant messages, keeping the list on track. Indeed, the people who complain the loudest about moderator censorship are usually the ones whose messages most deserve to be censored.

Another rule that sometimes causes trouble is that many lists for some reason only allow messages to be sent from people whose addresses appear on the list. This becomes a pain if your mailing address changes. Say, for example, that you get a well-organized new mail administrator and your official e-mail address changes from *jj@shamu.pol.ntw.org* to *John.Jay@ntw.org,* although your old address still works. You may find that some lists start *bouncing* your messages (sending them back to you rather than to the list) because they don't understand that John.Jay@ntw.org, the name under which you now send messages, is the same as jj@shamu.pol.ntw.org, the name under which you originally subscribed to the list. What's worse, LISTSERV doesn't let you take yourself off the list for the same reason. To resolve this mess, you have to write to the human list owners of any lists in which this problem arises and ask them to fix the problem by hand.

Boing!

Computer accounts are created and deleted often enough and mail addresses change often enough that, at any given moment, a large list always contains some addresses that are no longer valid. So if you send a message to the list, your message is forwarded to these invalid addresses, and a return message reporting the bad addresses is generated for each of them. Normally, mailing list managers (both human and computer) try to deflect the error messages so that they go to the list owner, who can do something about them, rather than going to you. But as often as not a persistently dumb mail system sends one of these failure messages directly to you. Just ignore it because there isn't anything you can do about it.

Fine Points of Replying to Mailing List Messages

Lots of times you receive an interesting message from a list and want to respond to it. But when you send your answer, does it go *just* to the person who sent the original message, or does it go to the *whole list?* It depends, mostly on how the list owner set up the software than handles the list. About half the list owners set it up so that replies automatically go just to the person who sent the original message, on the theory that your response is likely to be of interest only to the original author. The other half set it up so that replies go to the whole list, on the theory that the list is like a running public discussion. In messages coming from the list, the mailing list software automatically sets the Reply-To: header to the address where replies should be sent.

Fortunately, you're in charge. When you start to create a reply, your mail program should show you the address it's replying to. If you don't like the address it's using, change it. If you're using UNIX's hoary mail program, type ~h to change the headers, including the To: address. If you're using some other mail program, a menu option should allow you to fix the headers.

While you're fixing the recipient's address, you may also want to fix the Subject: line. After a few rounds of replies to replies to replies, the topic of discussion often wanders away from the original topic, and it is nice to change to subject to better describe what is actually under discussion.

TIP

Mailing lists vs. USENET news

A lot of mailing lists are gatewayed to USENET newsgroups (see Chapter 11), which means that all the messages that you would receive if you subscribed to the mailing list appear as items in the newsgroup, and vice versa. Most gateways are two-way, meaning that anything you mail to the list also shows up in the newsgroup, and anything you post as a news item also goes to the list. A few are one-way, usually due to sloppy gateway code, and a lot of them are moderated — which means that you have to mail any items to the moderator, who filters out inappropriate messages.

Whether you get a particular list as mail or news is largely a matter of personal taste. The advantages of receiving lists as mail are: mail items tend to arrive faster than news items (usually by only a few hours), mail items stick around until you explicitly delete them whereas news is deleted automatically, usually after a few days, and some mail programs are more flexible than the news-reading programs. The advantages of news are: items are collected into a newsgroup instead of being mixed in with your mail, items are automatically deleted unless you save them, and news programs usually do a better job than mail programs of collecting threads of related messages so that you can read them in order.

If you don't care which way you get your stuff, then get it as news, because the load on both your local computer and the network in general is considerably lower that way.

Some Interesting Lists

A great many lists reside on the Internet — so many, in fact, that entire *books* have been written that just enumerate all the *lists*. So, to get you started, here are a bunch of lists that I find interesting, along with short descriptions of what they are. Each is accompanied by at least one of the following code letters, describing what kind of list it is:

- ✔ **I:** Internet-type list. To get on or off, or to contact the human who maintains the list, write to *whatever-request@sitename*.

- ✔ **B:** BITNET LISTSERV-type list. To get on or off, send a stylized message to *LISTSERV@sitename*. To contact the relevant human, send mail to *owner-whatever@sitename*.

- ✔ **M:** Moderated list. messages are filtered by the human list owner (moderator).

- ✔ **N:** List is also available as USENET News, which is usually the best way to receive it (see previous sidebar "Mailing lists vs. USENET news." Nearly all BITNET lists are also available as a special kind of newsgroup, so this only marks lists available as regular news. (See Chapter 11 for more about what this means.)

- ✔ **D:** Messages normally arrive as a digest rather than one at a time.

Telecom Digest
telecom@eecs.nwu.edu
IMND

Discussions of telephones ranging from the technical to the totally silly, like what the official telephone song should be. This is a very heavily moderated, high-volume list (with the only full-time moderator on the Net).

Risks Digest
risks@csl.sri.com
IMND

Forum on risks to the public in computers and related systems. Discusses the risks of modern technology, particularly of computer technology. Lots of great war stories.

Weather Talk
WX-TALK@vmd.cso.uiuc.edu
B

Weather discussions. Fairly technical. If you join WX-NATNL@vmd.cso.uiuc.edu, you get the National Weather Service's nationwide forecasts twice daily, which is probably more weather than you want in your mailbox unless you have some way to sort it out and discard it automatically after a day or two. Other Weather Service bulletins are:

- **WX-SWO:** for severe weather warnings in nearly incomprehensible weather shorthand
- **X-WATCH:** for tornado and thunderstorm watches also in shorthand
- **WX-WSTAT:** for other weather watches in shorthand
- **WX-TROPL:** for daily tropical storm and hurricane outlooks
- **WX-PCPN:** for heavy rain and snow reports
- **WX-SUM:** for the national weather summary
- **WX-STLT:** for satellite observations
- **WX-LSR:** for local storm reports
- **WX-MISC:** for other weather bureau reports.

Subscribe to them all and your mailbox will fill so fast your head will swim. If you just want to check the weather now and then, see Chapter 15.

Privacy Forum Digest
privacy@vortex.com
IM

A running discussion of privacy in the computer age. Lots of creepy reports about people and organizations you'd never expect were snooping on you (ambulance drivers, for example).

Tourism Discussions
travel-l@trearn.bitnet
B

Travel and tourism, airlines, guidebooks, places to stay, you name it. Participants come from all over the world (the system host is in France), so you get lots of tips you'd never get locally.

Frequent Flyers
frequent-flyer@ames.arc.nasa.gov
I

For and about frequent air travellers. Lots of tips and war stories.

Transit Issues
transit@gitvm1.bitnet
B

Mass transit, notably subways and streetcars. It's mostly about transit today, not nostalgia. (Yes, the United States still has lots of subways and streetcars.)

Info-IBMPC Digest
info-ibmpc@brl.mil
<u>IMD</u>

Moderately technical discussions of using, programming, and maintaining IBM PCs and clones. If you have access to USENET, the USENET equivalents are better.

Computer Professionals for Social Responsibility
cpsr@gwuvm.bitnet
<u>B</u>

CPSR is an organization of computer people interested in the social effects of computing. This list mostly contains reports about CPSR activities.

Desktop Publishing
user@powerhouse.com
<u>I</u>

Desktop publishing and document creation. Mostly about DTP tools and tips, not terribly technical.

Offroad Enthusiasts
offroad@ai.gtri.gatech.edu
<u>I</u>

Partly about off-road driving, mostly about 4-wheel-drive vehicles. Full of fun-lovers.

White House Press Releases
clinton-info@campaign92.org
<u>M</u>

Press releases and transcripts of press conferences direct from the White House. (A lot goes on in a press conference that they don't bother to report in the paper.) Subscribing is a little different from other lists: send a message to *Clinton-Info@campaign92.org* containing the word *help,* and it sends back a subscription form for you to edit and return. This service was set up during the 1992 presidential campaign, hence the mailing address, but proved so popular that it continued after the inauguration.

Compilers and Language Processors
compil-l@american.edu
<u>BMN</u>

A totally technoid list about programs that translate one computer language into another. I moderate it, so of course I think it's totally fascinating. (Your mileage may vary.)

Finding Other Mailing Lists

SRI in Los Angeles keeps the *list of lists,* a fairly complete listing of Internet mailing lists. To get a copy by e-mail (*warning: it's really big,* about 30,000 lines of text), send a message to *mail-server@nisc.sri.com* containing the line

```
send netinfo/interest-groups
```

If you have access to FTP (see Chapter 16), you can more easily FTP it from *ftp.nisc.sri.com* where it is called *netinfo/interest-groups* and a compressed version is called *netinfo/interest-groups.Z.* (You can also buy it neatly printed and indexed as a book called *Internet: Mailing Lists,* eds. Edward T.L. Hardie, Vivian Neou, PTR Prentice Hall, 1993 — though the book seems kind of pricey when compared to getting the material on-line.)

The USENET group *news.lists* also has an extensive monthly list of mailing lists. If you get USENET news, you can probably find this list there (see Chapter 11). Or you can get it by mail by sending this cryptic message to *mail-server@rtfm.mit.edu:*

```
send USENET/news.lists/P_A_M_L,_P_1_5
send USENET/news.lists/P_A_M_L,_P_2_5
send USENET/news.lists/P_A_M_L,_P_3_5
send USENET/news.lists/P_A_M_L,_P_4_5
send USENET/news.lists/P_A_M_L,_P_5_5
```

(That last weird part stands for Publicly Accessible Mailing Lists, Part 1 of 5, and so forth.) FTP users can FTP the list from *rtfm.mit.edu* where it's in the directory *pub/USENET/news.lists* under the same names.

Chapter 11
Using Network News

In This Chapter

▶ What and why is Net news?

▶ How to navigate around Net news

All the News That Fits and Considerably More as Well

Mailing lists are an OK way to send messages to a small number of people but they're a lousy way to send messages to a lot of people. For one thing, just maintaining a big list with thousands of people is a lot of work, even if you automate most of it with something like *LISTSERV,* which I discussed in Chapter 10. (On a large list, every day a few of the addresses go bad as people move around and system managers reconfigure addresses.) For another thing, just shipping the contents of messages to thousands and thousands of addresses puts a huge load on the system that sends them out.

USENET news (also known as *Net news*) solves that problem and creates a whole host of others. USENET is a very large, distributed *BBS (bulletin board system).* The principle is quite simple: every USENET site ships a copy of all *articles* (news-speak for messages) that it has received to all its neighbors several times a day. (To avoid wasted effort, each article contains a list of sites that it's already been sent to.) It's sort of a global game of *whisper down the lane,* although computers don't scramble the messages at each stage like people do. Different host-to-host connections run at different speeds, but for the most part news articles slosh around to nearly every directly connected USENET site within a day or two of being sent. (If your machine is directly on the Internet rather than connected over the phone, most news arrives within a few hours.)

I assume that your local news system has already been set up and is running (if not, you'll have to persuade your system administrator to set it up), so a pile of news presumably is waiting for you to read. You should learn three *Important News Skills:*

  ✔ How to read the news that interests you

  ✔ How not to read the news that doesn't interest you, because far more news is sent every day than any single human could ever read

  ✔ How to post articles of your own (definitely optional)

Being a Newsgroupie

Every day over 20,000 articles appear at a typical, well-connected news machine. To make it possible to sort through this mass of stuff, all items are assigned to *newsgroups,* which are topic headings. In all, several thousand newsgroups exist ranging from the staid and technical (computer data communications, for example) to the totally goofy (such as urban legends, like the one about the poodle in the microwave). Most news users pick a small number of groups to read and ignore the rest.

Where did USENET come from?

USENET came from North Carolina originally. In 1980 two students came up with the first version to run on a couple of UNIX machines. Their original version, now known as *A* news, seemed pretty cool because it could transfer as many as a dozen articles a day from one machine to another using a networking scheme called *UUCP (UNIX-to-UNIX Copy),* which is a klunky but reliable dial-up communication program that comes with all UNIX systems. Within a few years, USENET had spread to several other universities and several software companies in a completely rewritten version called *B* news. USENET was established enough to be featured in an article in the October 1983 issue of *Byte* magazine, which boasted that over 500 news sites were in existence. (My site was called *ima* — you can find it near the upper righthand corner of the network map on page 224 of the issue.)

Throughout the ensuing decade, USENET has spread like a disease. Now, over 30,000 sites send out news, and probably at least that many more sites just read it. Many of the original dial-up links have been replaced by permanently connected Internet *network* links using a communication scheme called *NNTP (Net News Transfer Proto-*

col). (And you thought all acronyms were obscure.) A lot of news is still sent over the telephone via UUCP, but an increasing amount of it is sent via exotic means, including satellite (using a spare channel that belongs to a national beeper company), CD-ROM, and even magnetic tapes (the tapes are sent to countries like Malaysia, where long modem phone calls are impractical, and also to places like the FBI, where internal computer users are prohibited from connecting to outside networks).

The volume of news has increased from a few hundred articles per day in 1983 to 30,000 articles (over 50MB of text) per day now. And USENET is still growing.

A lot of sites still use B news, even though its own authors officially pronounced it obsolete more than five years ago. Current news systems include C news, which is a faster, more maintainable, complete rewrite of B news, and INN, which is a new version designed to work well in Internet networked environments. Fortunately, they all function pretty much the same way, so for the most part you don't have to worry about which version you're using.

You can very easily *subscribe* and *unsubscribe* to any group received by your machine — unlike getting on and off mailing lists, newsgroups just require an update to a local file. Many people start reading a group by looking at a few articles and then stop reading it if it looks boring. Depending on how much time you plan to spend reading news, you may add a lot of groups when you're less busy and then drop all but the ones directly related to work when the crunch hits. (I suppose theoretically you could stop reading news altogether, just like you could stop drinking coffee altogether — way too painful to contemplate.)

The newsgroup thicket

If you're eager to start using news, you can skip this section and come back to it later when you want to refine your news-reading skills.

Newsgroups have multipart names separated by dots, as in *comp.dcom.fax* (a group devoted to fax machines and fax modems). The plan is that newsgroups are arranged into *hierarchies*. The first part of the name describes the general kind of newsgroup. When a bunch of newsgroups are related, their names are related, too. So, for example, all the newsgroups having to do with data communication are filed as *comp.dcom.something*. Here are the top-level names of the *official* hierarchies that are distributed to nearly every news site:

- ✔ **comp:** Topics having something to do with computers (lots of fairly meaty discussions)

- ✔ **sci:** Topics having something to do with one of the sciences (also fairly meaty)

- ✔ **rec:** Recreational newsgroups (sports, hobbies, the arts, and other fun endeavors)

- ✔ **soc:** Social newsgroups (both social interests and plain socializing)

- ✔ **news:** Topics having to do with Net news itself (a few groups with introductory material and the occasional important announcement should be read by everyone — otherwise not very interesting unless you're a news *weenie*)

- ✔ **misc:** Miscellaneous topics that don't fit anywhere else (the ultimate miscellaneous newsgroup is called *misc.misc*)

- ✔ **talk:** Long arguments, frequently political (widely considered to be totally uninteresting except to the participants)

Note: lots of less widely distributed sets of newsgroups are mentioned in the next chapter.

Regional groups

All the mainstream groups, in theory at least, are of interest to people regardless of where they live. But a lot of topics are quite specific to a particular place. For example, let's say that you live near Boston and you want recommendations of restaurants where you can take small children and not be snarled at (this topic actually came up recently). Although some newsgroups in the rec hierarchy discuss food, because most readers are likely to be nowhere near Boston, you're likely to get more snappy comments than useful restaurant tips (for example, someone in Texas may note that if you don't mind driving to Dallas for dinner, you can find one there).

Fortunately, local and regional groups exist for local and regional discussions. An *ne* hierarchy for topics of interest to New England includes groups like *ne.food*, which is just the place to ask about kiddie restaurants. (The answers, by the way, turned out to be practically any ethnic restaurant and one yuppie place in the suburbs that makes a big deal about having an annex featuring hot dogs and baby-sitters so that Mom and Dad can eat their fancy meal in elegant silence.) State and regional hierarchies exist for most places that have enough USENET sites to make it worthwhile: *ny* for New York, *ba* for the San Francisco bay area, and so forth.

Universities and other organizations that are big enough to have a lot of Net news users often have hierarchies of their own, like *mit* for MIT. Many companies have their own local sets of newsgroups for announcements and discussions about company matters. For example, at a software company where I used to work, every time someone logged in a change to one of our programs, the description of the change was sent out as a local news item so that everyone else could keep up with what was changing. Naturally, local company groups are only sent around within the company. Ask around to find out what organization or regional newsgroups your system gets, because it's basically up to your system manager to decide what to get.

Hand-to-Hand Combat with News

OK, you're probably dying to try out news for yourself. (If you're not, you may as well skip ahead to Chapter 13.) USENET is designed so that anyone who wants to can write a new news-reading program, so a lot of people have done so. Here, I look mostly at UNIX news programs called *trn* and its predecessor *rn,* which are the most widely used.

All news-reading programs do pretty much the same thing (they let you read news, what did you expect?), so most of them work in more or less the same way, give or take differences in the appearance of the screen and a few command letters. All news programs are written to be more or less full screen, although (as you'll see) some of them take advantage of the screen better than others. They're all designed to enable you to flip though news as quickly as possible (because there's so much of it), so they all use single-letter commands, which are a pain to remember, of course, until you get used to them.

In nearly all news-reading programs, you don't need to press Enter after single-letter commands. Some commands, however, require that you type a line of text after the letter, such as a filename or a newsgroup name. In that case, you *do* press Enter to tell the program that you're done with the line of text.

You start the news-reading program by typing **trn** (or if that doesn't work, **rn**). You should shortly see something like this:

```
% trn
Trying to set up a .newsrc file
running newsetup...
Creating .newsrc in /usr/johnl to be used by news programs.
Done. If you have never used the news system before, you may
find the articles in news.announce.newusers to be helpful.
There is also a manual entry for rn. To get rid of newsgroups
you aren't interested in, use the 'u' command.
Type h for help at any time while running rn.
Unread news in general                          14 articles
(Revising soft pointers—be patient.)
Unread news in ne.food                          47 articles
Unread news in ne.forsale                     1177 articles
Unread news in ne.general                      268 articles
Unread news in ne.housing                      248 articles
etc.
********  14 unread articles in general—read now? [+ynq]
```

If the program complains that it can't find either trn or rn, you have to ask for help to find out what the local news reader of choice is. Microsoft Windows users may have a program called Trumpet, which uses a typical Windows screen interface to handle news. Even if you aren't using trn or rn, it's probably worth your while to look through the rest of this chapter because what you do with news is the same even if the exact keys you type are different.

Assuming that you manage to start trn or rn, it tells you that it sees that you've never used news before, so it's creating a file called *.newsrc* (yes, it starts with a dot, and you don't really want to know why), which it uses to keep track of which articles you've already seen. Then, in a fit of wild optimism, it guesses that you want to subscribe to every single newsgroup available on your system. Naturally, the list of newsgroups that it shows depends on what's available on your system.

First things first: when you're tired of reading news, you leave it by pressing q (for quit). Depending on where you are, you may need to press it two or three times, but you can always q your way out.

Assuming that you're not ready to give up yet, trn or rn now goes through all the newsgroups. For each group, you basically have three choices: you can look at its articles now, you can choose to not look now but maybe come back later, or you can unsubscribe so that you never see that newsgroup again unless you specifically resubscribe. Press y to say yes (you want to read the newsgroup), n to skip it for now, or u to unsubscribe and never see the group again. (Of course, there's also q to quit trn or rn.)

If you press y, trn displays the first screen of the first unread article in the newsgroup *general,* which is the group for articles that are theoretically of interest to users of your machine only. (In practice, the newsgroup general tends to fill up with junk.) The screen looks something like this:

```
general #6281
(1)
From: 0000-Admin(0000)
(1)
[1] backup
(1)
Organization: I.E.C.C.
(1)
Date: Sat Aug  7 06:48:03 1993
(1)
+
[1] src/xgopher.1.3/subst.h
src/xgopher.1.3/text.h
src/xgopher.1.3/typeres.h
src/xgopher.1.3/util.h
src/xgopher.1.3/version.h
src/xgopher.1.3/xglobals.h
1898999 blocks
61684+132852 records in
7417+1,0 records out
End of article 6281 (of 6281)—what next? [npq]
```

While you're looking at an article, you once again have a bunch of choices. If the article is more than one screenful, pressing the spacebar advances to the next screen, much like the familiar *more* and *pg* commands. If you're done looking at the article, press n to go on to the next article or q to leave the newsgroup and go on to the next newsgroup. If you find an article to be totally uninteresting, you can skip both the rest of that article and any other articles in the newsgroup that have the same boring title by pressing k (for kill). You can arrange to have articles with known boring titles killed every time you enter a newsgroup (see the sidebar "Arrgh! It's a kill file" further on in this chapter). The article you're looking at here (see preceding screen shot) shows the result of last night's tape backup, so unless you're the one in charge of changing tapes, you probably want to press k to skip any other backup reports.

You'll find that after you get the hang of it, you mostly press the spacebar to go to the next article or newsgroup, n to skip to the next article or newsgroup, and k to skip a group of articles. Until you prune down to something reasonable in the set of newsgroups you're subscribed to, you'll probably also be pressing u frequently to get rid of the large majority of groups that you don't want to read.

Where do newsgroups come from?
Where do newsgroups go?

Here are two things you need to know that are related to getting rid of newsgroups. The first is that new newsgroups appear several times a week because USENET is still growing like crazy. Every time you run rn or trn, you have the opportunity to subscribe to any new newsgroups that have appeared. The trn or rn program asks a question like this:

```
Checking active list for new newsgroups...
Newsgroup alt.comp.hardware.homebuilt not in .newsrc—subscribe?
[ynYN]
```

You can answer y if you do or n if you do not want to subscribe. If you press y, it asks you where in the list of newsgroups you'd like to see this one appear.

```
Put newsgroup where? [$^L]
```

The most likely answers to this question are $ (to put it at the end), or + followed by the name of an existing group (to put it after that group).

Eventually, you may also regret having unsubscribed to a newsgroup, in which case you want to turn it back on. If so, press g followed by the name of the group you want to see. If you've never subscribed to the group at all, rn or trn may ask you where in the list you would like to put it and offer you the same choices ($ or +). You can also use g to go directly to a particular newsgroup to read its new articles.

TECHNICAL STUFF

Arrgh! it's a kill file

In most newsgroups, a bunch of running discussions go on, and some of those discussions are a lot more interesting than others. You can arrange to permanently ignore the uninteresting ones by using a *kill file.* When you're reading along and you encounter a hopelessly uninteresting article, press K (capital K, for *KILL!*) to kill all current articles with the same title and also to put the title into the kill file for the current newsgroup. In the future, whenever you enter that newsgroup, rn or trn checks for any new articles with titles in the kill file and automatically kills them so you never see any of them. Using kill files can save a great deal of time and lets you concentrate on discussions that are actually interesting.

You can edit kill files to remove entries for discussions that have died down or to add other kinds of article-killing commands. If you press Ctrl-K while reading a newsgroup, it starts the text editor (usually *vi* or *emacs* on UNIX machines) on the group's kill file. Kill files look like this:

```
THRU 4765
/boring topic/j
/was George Harrison in another
band before Wings?/j
```

The first line notes how many articles have been scanned for killable topics (to save time by not rescanning the whole group each time). Subsequent lines are topics that you don't want to read. You remove a topic by deleting its line in the kill file. After you're done, save the file, leave the editor, and you're back where you were reading news.

Sometimes you may also find that *certain people* write articles that you never want to read. You can arrange to kill all the articles that they write! Type Ctrl-K to edit the newsgroup's kill file and at the end add a line like this:

```
/Aaron Burr/h:j
```

Between the slashes, type the author's name as it appears in the `From:` line at the beginning of his (obnoxious authors are nearly all male) articles. You don't need to type the entire contents of the `From:` line, just enough of it to uniquely identify the guy. At the end of the line, after the second slash, place the magic incantation **h:j**. Then save the kill file, exit the editor, and you're set. *Sayonara,* pal.

Ignoring articles faster with trn

If you're using trn rather than rn, you have a better way to select which articles you want to see and which ones you don't. The important difference between trn and rn is that trn supports *threads* (that's what the *t* stands for), which are groups of related articles. You can select or ignore a thread at a time rather than an article at a time.

If you press spacebar or + to enter a newsgroup, you see a table of contents screen like the following, which shows the titles of the unread messages in the group:

```
general                            14 articles
a 0000-uucp(0000)    3   New mail paths
b 0000-Admin(0000)  10   backup
c Chet Arthur        1   System down to clean hamster cages

Select threads — All [Z>] —
```

Again, this newsgroup is called *general,* the group that exists on every machine for local messages that don't belong anywhere else. There are 14 unread articles. To make it easier to choose what to read, trn groups together related articles based mostly on the titles. In this case, three articles are called *New mail paths,* ten are called *backup,* and one is about hamsters. The letters in the left column are key letters you type to select articles to read. For example, you'd press c to see the article about the hamsters.

After you're done picking interesting-looking articles, you have a few choices. You can press the spacebar to go on to the next page of the table of contents, if any, and start reading selected articles if you've seen all the titles. Or you can press D (uppercase) to read the selected articles and kill any unselected articles on the screen (d is for delete). Or you can press Z (uppercase) to read any selected articles and *not* kill the unselected ones.

Honest, It's a Work of Art

USENET allows exactly one kind of message: plain old text. (Well, special versions of news handle Japanese and Russian characters, but this chapter is confusing enough without worrying about them.) But a few widely used conventions exist for sneaking through other kinds of files.

Binary files

Some newsgroups consist partly or entirely of encoded binary files, most often executable programs for IBM PCs, Macs, or other personal computers, or *GIF* or *JPEG bitmap* files (see Chapter 17 for details on file formats) of, um, artistic images. (Well, if you must know, the newsgroup with the largest amount of traffic, measured in megabytes per day, is called *alt.binaries.pictures.erotica,* and it contains exactly what it sounds like. It's an equal-opportunity group — that is, it has about the same number of pictures of unclad men as of unclad women.)

The usual way to pass around binary files of whatever type is called *uuencode*. You can recognize uuencoded messages because they start with a `begin` line followed by lines of what looks like garbage, as in the following:

```
begin plugh.gif 644
M390GNM4L-REP3PT45G00I-05[I5-6M30ME,MRMK760PI5LPTMETLMKPY
ME0T39I4905B05Y0PV30IXKRTL5KWLJR0JT0U,
6P5;3;MRU05OI4J5OI4
```

You unscramble this with a program called *uudecode*. Fortunately, rn and trn have a built-in decoder which you can invoke by pressing e (for extract). For *really* big files, it's customary to split the uuencoded file among several articles. The extract feature is smart enough to handle this if you press e for each article in sequence.

Groups of files

Sometimes an article contains a group of files. These are packed up as *shell archive* or *shar* files which are *UNIX shell (command language) scripts* that, when executed, re-create the desired files. Shar files usually start something like this:

```
—cut here—
# This is a shar file created on 4 Jul 1826 ...
```

You can also extract shar files with the trn or rn e command, just like you do with uuencoded messages. (It's smart enough to figure out which kind of message it is.)

Be aware that shar files are a horrendous *trojan horse* loophole (a way for a bad guy to run his program, but make it act as though you had done it) because a shar file can contain any command that you could type from the terminal. In the worst case, it can delete all your files, send obscene e-mail with your signature, and so forth. In the past, prank shar files haven't been much of a problem, but it's worth it to be a little skeptical. For the acutely apprehensive, shar-sanitizing programs are available (your system administrator should have one handy that comes with C news) that can scan a shar article, looking for suspicious commands.

Just a few notes for our files

Now and then an article is so interesting that you want to save it for posterity. You save it with the s (for save) command. To save an article, press s followed by the name of the file into which you want to save it. If the file doesn't already exist, rn or trn asks you whether it should format the file as a plain file or a

Don't say I didn't warn you

You may occasionally find an article that is just plain gibberish, neither uuencoded nor a shar file. (See preceding section, "Honest, It's a Work of Art.") Such articles use the notorious *rot13 cipher*. Rot13 is a simple-minded scheme that replaces each letter of the alphabet with the letter that is 13 places ahead of or behind it. For example, A turns into N and vice versa, B turns into O, and so forth. This isn't a very secure code (I believe it was cracked about 2,000 years ago by the Carthaginians), but it's not supposed to be.

The point of rot13 is to warn you that a message contains rude words or something else gross and offensive, so you shouldn't read it if you think you may be offended. If you want to read it anyway, press X (uppercase) to get rn or trn to unscramble it.

Don't expect much sympathy if you complain about an offensive rot13 message. After all, you didn't have to read it.

mailbox (a special kind of file that usually contains mail messages). Usually, you should make the save file a mailbox. If you save several articles into the same file and make it a mailbox, you can later use mail programs (see Chapter 7) to review and change the contents of the mailbox. Saved files (or mailboxes) are put in your *News* directory, unless you give a different directory to the s command.

You can also save an article and pass it to a program. To do so, press | (vertical bar) rather than s and follow it with the command you want to execute. This choice is most often useful for printing a message by making the command *lpr* or *lp* or whatever your local print command is. UNIX pipelines are also permitted, as in

```
|pr -h "An important message" | lpr
```

A trn and rn cheat sheet

By this point, you've probably lost track of all the keys that control trn and rn. Here's a summary of the keys described in this chapter, along with a few others that you might want to try. The rn program can be in two different *states:* newsgroup state (see Table 11-1), in which you pick which group to read, and *article state* (see Table 11-2), in which you're in a particular group and are looking at articles. The Trn program adds a third state, the *table of contents state* (see Table 11-3), in which you're looking at a list of titles of unread articles in a group.

Table 11-1	Newsgroup State
Key	*Meaning*
Spacebar	Enter the next group that has unread news.
y	Same as spacebar.
n	Skip this group.
u	Unsubscribe from this group, so you won't see it any more.
g	Go to a group. Type the group name after the g. If you're unsubscribed to the group, it resubscribes you.
q	Quit, leave news.
p	Go to the previous group with unread news.
h	Show extremely concise help.
^L	Redraw screen.

Table 11-2	Article State
Key	*Meaning*
Spacebar	Read the next page of the current article, or the next unread article.
n	Skip to the next article.
k	Kill this article and any others with the same title.
K	Same as k, also enter the title in the kill file so that the title is re-killed each time you enter the group.
q	Leave this group.
c	Catch up, pretend you've read all articles in this group.
u	Unsubscribe.
spdq	Save article to file pdq.
l lpr	Feed article to command lpr (easiest way to print an article).
/xyz	Find the next article whose title contains xyz.
=	Show titles of unread articles.
^L	Redraw screen.
^R	Restart current article (redraws first page).
X	Unscramble rot13 message (not for the squeamish).
e	Extract uudecoded or shar file.
edir	Extract into directory dir.
h	Show extremely concise help.
q	Leave this group.

Table 11-3	Table of Contents State
Key	**Meaning**
Spacebar	Read the next page of the table of contents, or start reading selected articles if there's no more TOC.
d	Start reading selected articles, mark unselected articles as read.
z	Read selected articles.
/xyz	Select articles whose titles contain xyz.
c-g	Select articles c through g in the current TOC.
h	Show extremely concise help.
q	Leave this group.

Most letters and digits are used to mark articles to select.

The quick reference manual entry for trn is 25 pages long, so it has a lot more commands. But you should be able to get along with just these.

What's in a Number?

Every USENET message has a *message ID,* which is supposed to be different from the message ID of any other message ever, *from the beginning to the end of time.* (These people thought big.) A typical message ID looks like this:

```
<1993Jul9.055259.15278@chico.iecc.com>
```

The part after the @ is the name of the site where the article originated, and the part before the @ is some garbage made up to be unique and usually includes the date, time, phase of moon, and so forth.

Messages also have numbers, which are assigned in order at each newsgroup as articles arrive. So the first message in *comp.fooble* is number 1, the second is number 2, and so forth. *Note:* An important difference distinguishes the IDs and the numbers: the IDs are the same everywhere, but the numbers only apply to *your local system.* So don't refer to article's message numbers when you write a response because people at other sites won't be able to tell which articles you mean.

If you use the rn or trn f or F commands to write a follow-up article, they automatically stick in a line starting with References: which has the message ID of the original article, along with any articles that it in turn referenced. Trn uses the references to gather articles into related threads.

So You Want to Be Famous?

Sooner or later, unless you are an extraordinarily reticent person, you'll want to send out some messages of your own so that people all over the world can at last find out just how clever you are. (This can be a mixed blessing, of course.) In this section, I look first at how you respond to an existing message and then take the plunge, writing an all-new message from scratch.

That's a Roger, Roger

The easiest and usually most appropriate way to respond to an article is to send e-mail to its author in case you want to ask a question or offer a comment. You can send e-mail by pressing r or R. In either case, rn or trn pops you into a text editor where you can compose your message. The file you're given to edit contains header lines for the e-mail message, notably `Subject:` and `To:`, which you can edit if you want. The difference between r and R is that the uppercase R command also puts a copy of the text of the article into the message so that you can quote parts of it. Edit out irrelevant parts of the quoted article, keeping in mind that the author already knows what he or she said.

When you leave the editor, rn or trn asks whether it should send the message (s), edit it again (e), or abandon it (a). Press s, e, or a as appropriate.

I'll follow you anywhere

If you have a comment on an article which is of general interest, you can post it as a USENET article by using the f or F (follow-up) keys. The program asks you whether you're sure you want to send a USENET follow-up. If you respond that you are sure, you are popped into the editor where you can compose your message. Uppercase F includes a copy of the original message, which you should again edit down to the minimum.

Many news systems reject messages that contain more quoted text than new material to discourage lazy typists who quote an entire 100-line message to add a two-line comment. Some people are under the peculiar impression that if an article is rejected with too much quoted text, they should add garbage lines at the end to pad out the unquoted part. *Don't ever do that.* Edit down the text — your readers will thank you.

After you leave the editor, it again asks whether you want to send the article, edit it again, or abort (abandon the follow-up). Press the appropriate key (s, e, or a).

Give me a sign

Whenever you post an article, if a file called *.signature* exists in your home directory, the news system appends the file's contents to your article. Your .signature file should contain your name, e-mail address, and anything else you feel is relevant— so long as it all fits in no more than three lines. Some people have huge, fancy, 20-line signatures that are never as clever as one may hope. Keep it to three lines. **Note:** many news systems enforce the three-line limit by only in-

cluding the first three lines of the file, no matter how long it is.

You don't have to copy your .signature file into messages that you send because the news-sending program adds it automatically. If you *do* include it yourself, your message will have two copies of your signature, which looks tacky and marks you as a rank amateur. You wouldn't want that to happen.

When you send your follow-up, in most cases the article is posted either immediately or in a few minutes (the next time a background posting program runs). Some groups are moderated, which means that you can't post to them directly. For moderated groups, your message is mailed to the group's modera- tor, who posts it if it meets the group's guidelines. Moderators are all volun- teers and all have work to do other than running their moderated groups, so it may take a while for your message to appear. Most moderators handle mes- sages every day or two, but the slowest ones can take as long as two weeks. Remember: patience is a virtue. As a newsgroup moderator (I run one called *comp.compilers,* a technoid group that discusses techniques of translating one computer language to another), I can assure you that writing cranky letters to a moderator — in which you complain that it's taking too long to process your pearls of wisdom — is utterly counterproductive.

First Past the Post

The final topic I discuss in this chapter is how to send an all-new news article. You send your article with the *Pnews* command. No rn or trn single-letter command does this. When you run Pnews, it asks you a few questions. The first is the name of the newsgroup or newsgroups. (You can post a single article to several groups at once if it's appropriate.) Type the name of the group or groups (separate them with commas). It asks for the subject of the message and then for the *distribution* (see the following section, "Distributions Are Your Friend") with a suggested default that you can use if you haven't figured out distributions yet. Then it asks once more whether you're absolutely, positively certain that you want to post an article, and if you say yes, it puts you into the text editor. From then on, it's just like when you're sending a follow-up article (as discussed earlier in this chapter).

Distributions Are Your Friends

Even though USENET is a worldwide network, a lot of times you're posting an article that doesn't really need to go to the whole world. For example, if you're posting something to *misc.forsale.computers* to advertise an old disk drive you want to sell and you're in the United States, there's no point in sending the article outside the country because it wouldn't be worth the shipping and customs hassles to sell it overseas. USENET distributions enable you to limit where an article is sent. A line like the following in your article header limits its distribution to the United States:

```
Distribution: usa
```

If you're sending a new article using Pnews, you're asked which distribution to use. If you're sending a follow-up, the news system guesses that you want to use the same distribution that the original article did. In either case, you can edit the Distribution: line in the message yourself as needed.

A long list of possible distributions exists. Some commonly used distributions are

- **world:** Everywhere (default)
- **na:** North America
- **usa:** United States
- **can:** Canada
- **uk:** United Kingdom
- **ne:** New England
- **ba:** Bay Area (California)

Dying boy makes mailing list about modem tax

Back in Chapter 8, a sidebar lists well-known topics about which you should never, *ever* write to any mailing list. The same warning applies to USENET news. For review, the top three topics to not write about are the following:

- Dying boy wants cards to set Guinness world record

- FCC will pass modem tax and impoverish us all

- Make big bucks with a chain letter

See Chapter 8 for details on why nobody wants to hear about any of these things.

All the regional hierarchy names, like ne, ny, uk, ba, and so forth, are also used as distributions. (People occasionally use worldwide hierarchy names like comp and rec as distributions by mistake — that doesn't do anything useful.)

Unless you're sure that people on the other side of the world will be as fascinated by what you say as people next door, you should use the smallest appropriate distribution for any articles you post, both originals and follow-ups.

In practice, distributions are pretty leaky, and articles often get sent places that the distribution says they shouldn't go, due to peculiarities in the way news is passed from one system to the next. But it's a courtesy to faraway readers to at least *try* to avoid sending articles to places where the articles are not interesting. Also, keep in mind that international phone links are expensive, so if you avoid sending an article to countries where people aren't interested, you can actually save people some money.

"I guess there's a little corner of the Internet for just about everyone these days."

Chapter 12
A Sampler of
Network News Resources

In This Chapter

▶ Favorite groups

▶ Standard and not-so-standard hierarchies

▶ Lots of news groups

So What Is There to Read Already?

Now that you learned all about how to read and write USENET news in Chapter 11, the only little detail remaining is to figure out what there is to read. This chapter lists some of the more interesting groups that exist as of mid-1993. Remember: New groups appear practically everyday, old groups occasionally go away, and system managers can reject any groups they want to for lack of interest or other reasons. First, I present some popular groups to get you acquainted with the mainstream hierarchies. Then you learn about hierarchies that are a tad more obscure. And finally, Tables 12-1 thru 12-6 list numerous groups in the various hierarchies that you may want to explore.

Some Favorite Groups

Here are a few groups that you may want to start with:

news.announce.newusers

Every new user should at least skim this group, which contains introductory material for new news users. One of the messages is pretty funny, but you have to read them to find out which one.

news.answers

This contains all the periodic (weekly and monthly, mostly) postings to all the groups on the Net. Many of these have evolved into pithy and well-written introductions to their subjects. When you need to learn something fast about something that might have been discussed on the Net, start here.

rec.humor.funny

This is a highly competitive, moderated group containing jokes, most of which are pretty funny. Compare to *rec.humor,* which contains articles that the authors think are funny but usually aren't.

comp.risks

The *Risks Digest* (same digest that was discussed in Chapter 10 as a mailing list) has lots of swell war stories of computer screwups.

comp.compilers

Well, I think it's interesting, but then I'm the moderator.

alt.sex

Everybody reads it, but nobody admits to doing so. I certainly don't.

Computers, on Computers, about Computers

Traditionally, the largest set of newsgroups have been the computer-related ones under the hierarchy *comp* (many of which are listed in Table 12-1). It's not surprising: if you listen in on ham radio conversations, you realize that they're mostly about ham radio. So you may expect that when people used computers to create USENET, they mostly talked about computers.

The comp groups can tend toward the esoteric and the technoid, but they're also a treasure trove when your computer acts up and you need advice from people who've seen it all before.

Many groups offer usable computer programs. The ones under *comp.binaries* are the places to look for free programs for PCs, Macs, and other personal systems.

Table 12-1	Groups in the Comp Hierarchy
Name	**Description**
comp.ai	Artificial intelligence discussions
comp.ai.nat-lang	Natural language processing by computers
comp.ai.neural-nets	All aspects of neural networks
comp.ai.philosophy	Philosophical aspects of Artificial Intelligence
comp.ai.shells	Artificial intelligence applied to shells
comp.answers	Repository for periodic USENET articles (moderated)
comp.apps.spreadsheets	Spreadsheets on various platforms
comp.arch	Computer architecture
comp.arch.storage	Storage system issues, both hardware and software
comp.archives	Descriptions of public access archives (moderated)
comp.archives.admin	Issues relating to computer archive administration
comp.bbs.misc	All aspects of computer bulletin board systems
comp.bbs.waffle	The Waffle BBS and USENET system on all platforms
comp.benchmarks	Discussion of benchmarking techniques and results
comp.binaries.apple2	Binary-only postings for the Apple II computer
comp.binaries.atari.st	Binary-only postings for the Atari ST (moderated)
comp.binaries.ibm.pc	Binary-only postings for IBM PC/MS-DOS (moderated)
comp.binaries.ibm.pc.d	Discussions about IBM/PC binary postings
comp.binaries.ibm.pc.wanted	Requests for IBM PC and compatible programs
comp.binaries.mac	Encoded Macintosh programs in binary (moderated)
comp.binaries.ms-windows	Binary programs for Microsoft Windows (moderated)
comp.binaries.os2	Binaries for use under the OS/2 ABI (moderated)
comp.cog-eng	Cognitive engineering
comp.compilers	Compiler construction, theory, and so on (moderated)
comp.compression	Data compression algorithms and theory
comp.databases	Database and data management issues and theory
comp.dcom.fax	Fax hardware, software, and protocols
comp.dcom.lans.ethernet	Discussions of the Ethernet/IEEE 802.3 protocols
comp.dcom.modems	Data communications hardware and software

(continued)

Table 12-1 *(continued)*

Name	Description
comp.dcom.servers	Selecting and operating data communications servers
comp.dcom.telecom	Telecommunications digest (moderated)
comp.doc	Archived public-domain documentation (moderated)
comp.doc.techreports	Lists of technical reports (moderated)
comp.dsp	Digital Signal Processing using computers
comp.edu	Computer science education
comp.emacs	EMACS editors of different flavors
comp.fonts	Type fonts — design, conversion, use, and so on
comp.graphics	Computer graphics, art, animation, image processing
comp.human-factors	Issues related to human-computer interaction (HCI)
comp.infosystems	Any discussion about information systems
comp.infosystems.gis	All aspects of Geographic Information Systems
comp.infosystems.gopher	Discussion of the Gopher information service
comp.infosystems.wais	The Z39.50-based WAIS full-text search system
comp.infosystems.www	The World Wide Web information system
comp.internet.library	Discussing electronic libraries (moderated)
comp.lang.c	Discussion about C
comp.lang.c++	The object-oriented C++ language
comp.lang.fortran	Discussion about FORTRAN
comp.lang.lisp	Discussion about LISP
comp.misc	General topics about computers not covered elsewhere
comp.multimedia	Interactive multimedia technologies of all kinds
comp.newprod	Announcements of new products of interest (moderated)
comp.object	Object-oriented programming and languages
comp.os.ms-windows.advocacy	Speculation and debate about Microsoft Windows
comp.os.ms-windows.announce	Announcements relating to Windows (moderated)
comp.os.ms-windows.apps	Applications in the Windows environment
comp.os.ms-windows.misc	General discussions about Windows issues

Name	Description
comp.os.ms-windows.programmer.misc	Programming Microsoft Windows
comp.os.ms-windows.programmer.tools	Development tools in Windows
comp.os.ms-windows.setup	Installing and configuring Microsoft Windows
comp.os.msdos.apps	Discussion of applications that run under MS-DOS
comp.parallel	Massively parallel hardware/software (moderated)
comp.patents	Discussing patents of computer technology (moderated)
comp.periphs	Peripheral devices
comp.programming	Programming issues that transcend languages and OSs
comp.risks	Risks to the public from computers and users (moderated)
comp.robotics	All aspects of robots and their applications
comp.security.misc	Security issues of computers and networks
comp.simulation	Simulation methods, problems, uses (moderated)
comp.society	The impact of technology on society (moderated)
comp.society.cu-digest	The Computer Underground Digest (moderated)
comp.society.development	Computer technology in developing countries
comp.society.folklore	Computer folklore and culture, past and present (moderated)
comp.society.futures	Events in technology affecting future computing
comp.society.privacy	Effects of technology on privacy (moderated)
comp.sources.misc	Posting of software (moderated)
comp.speech	Research and applications in speech science and technology
comp.text	Text processing issues and methods
comp.unix.questions	UNIX neophytes group
comp.unix.shell	Using and programming the UNIX shell
comp.unix.wizards	Questions for only true UNIX wizards
comp.virus	Computer viruses and security (moderated)

(continued)

None of the Above

Despite all the careful (well, sort of careful) arrangement of USENET into meaningful hierarchies, some topics just didn't fit anywhere else; these topics ended up in *misc,* the miscellaneous hierarchy. Topics range from the totally staid to the hopelessly argumentative. The ultimate miscellaneous group is *misc.misc,* for discussions that don't fit anywhere at all.

Table 12-2	Groups in the Misc Hierarchy
Name	*Description*
misc.answers	Repository for periodic USENET articles (moderated)
misc.books.technical	Discussion of books about technical topics
misc.consumers	Consumer interests, product reviews, and so on
misc.consumers.house	Discussion about owning and maintaining a house
misc.education	Discussion of the educational system
misc.entrepreneurs	Discussion on operating a business
misc.fitness	Physical fitness, exercise, and so on
misc.forsale	Short, tasteful postings about items for sale
misc.int-property	Discussion of intellectual property rights
misc.invest	Investments and the handling of money
misc.jobs.contract	Discussions about contract labor
misc.jobs.misc	Discussion about employment, workplaces, careers
misc.jobs.offered	Announcements of positions available
misc.jobs.offered.entry	Job listings only for entry-level positions
misc.jobs.resumes	Postings of resumes and *situation wanted* articles
misc.kids	Children, their behavior and activities
misc.kids.computer	The use of computers by children
misc.legal	Legalities and the ethics of law
misc.legal.computing	Discussing the legal climate of the computing world
misc.misc	Various discussions not fitting in any other group

Fun and Games

Even computer weenies like to have fun. (Stop laughing. It's true.) USENET has lots of recreational groups (in the *rec* hierarchy) for hobbies ranging from the strenuous, such as watching fish in an aquarium, to the totally relaxing — mountain climbing, for example. There are certainly a few here that you'll like.

Table 12-3	Groups in the Rec Hierarchy
Name	*Description*
rec.answers	Repository for periodic USENET articles (moderated)
rec.antiques	Discussing antiques and vintage items
rec.aquaria	Keeping fish and aquaria as a hobby
rec.arts.books	Books of all genres and the publishing industry
rec.arts.movies	Discussions of movies and movie making
rec.arts.movies.reviews	Reviews of movies (moderated)
rec.arts.poems	For the posting of poems
rec.arts.prose	Short works of prose fiction and followup discussion
rec.arts.sf.announce	Major announcements of the SF world (moderated)
rec.arts.startrek.current	New Star Trek shows, movies and books
rec.arts.startrek.info	Information about the universe of Star Trek (moderated)
rec.arts.startrek.misc	General discussions of Star Trek
rec.arts.startrek.reviews	Reviews of Star Trek books, episodes, films, and so on (moderated)
rec.arts.theatre	Discussion of all aspects of stage work and theatre
rec.arts.tv	The boob tube, its history, and past and current shows
rec.audio	High fidelity audio
rec.audio.car	Discussions of automobile audio systems
rec.autos	Automobiles, automotive products and laws
rec.autos.antique	Discussing all aspects of automobiles over 25 years old
rec.autos.driving	Driving automobiles
rec.autos.tech	Technical aspects of automobiles
rec.backcountry	Activities in the Great Outdoors
rec.birds	Hobbyists interested in bird watching

(continued)

Table 12-3 *(continued)*

Name	Description
rec.boats	Hobbyists interested in boating
rec.climbing	Climbing techniques, competition announcements, and so on
rec.crafts.brewing	The art of making beers and meads
rec.crafts.metalworking	All aspects of working with metal
rec.crafts.misc	Handiwork arts not covered elsewhere
rec.crafts.textiles	Sewing, weaving, knitting and other fiber arts
rec.equestrian	Discussion of things equestrian
rec.food.cooking	Food, cooking, cookbooks, and recipes
rec.food.recipes	Recipes for interesting food and drink (moderated)
rec.food.restaurants	Discussion of dining out
rec.games.chess	Chess and computer chess
rec.games.corewar	The Core War computer challenge
rec.games.design	Discussion of game design and related issues
rec.gardens	Gardening, methods and results
rec.humor	Jokes and the like — may be somewhat offensive
rec.humor.d	Discussions on the content of rec.humor articles
rec.humor.funny	Jokes that are funny (in the moderator's opinion)
rec.nude	Hobbyists interested in naturist/nudist activities
rec.railroad	For fans of real trains
rec.roller-coaster	Roller coasters and other amusement park rides
rec.running	Running for enjoyment, sport, exercise, and so on
rec.scouting	Scouting youth organizations worldwide
rec.scuba	Hobbyists interested in SCUBA diving
rec.skate	Ice skating and roller skating
rec.skiing	Hobbyists interested in snow skiing
rec.sport.football.college	U.S.-style college football
rec.sport.football.misc	Discussion about American-style football
rec.sport.football.pro	U.S.-style professional football
rec.travel	Traveling all over the world
rec.travel.air	Airline travel around the world

Ask Dr. Science

A lot of USENETters are in university or industrial research labs, so you encounter a lot of scientists in the *sci* hierarchy (both professional and amateur). You'll also find many computer science types, although (despite its name) this area isn't actually a science.

In this hierarchy you'll find pretty much any kind of pure or applied science you can think of, from Archaeology to Zoology and everything in between. Here's a choice few:

Table 12-4	Groups in the Sci Hierarchy
Name	**Description**
sci.aeronautics	The science of aeronautics and related technology (moderated)
sci.aeronautics.airliners	Airliner technology (moderated)
sci.answers	Repository for periodic USENET articles (moderated)
sci.archaeology	Studying antiquities of the world
sci.astro	Astronomy discussions and information
sci.classics	Studying classical history, languages, art, and more
sci.crypt	Different methods of data encryption/decryption
sci.math	Mathematical discussions and pursuits
sci.med	Medicine and its related products and regulations
sci.military	Discussion about science and the military (moderated)
sci.misc	Short-lived discussions on subjects in the sciences
sci.skeptic	Skeptics discussing pseudoscience
sci.space	Space, space programs, space-related research, and so on

C'mon By and Stay a While

USENET is a sociable place, so naturally there's a lot of socializing going on in the *soc* hierarchy. About half the soc groups are in *soc.culture,* where they discuss particular countries or ethnicities, and the other half are devoted to other sociable topics.

Table 12-5	Groups in the Soc Hierarchy
Name	*Description*
soc.answers	Repository for periodic USENET articles (moderated)
soc.college	College, college activities, campus life, and so on
soc.couples	Discussions for couples (compare with soc.singles)
soc.culture.british	Issues about Britain and those of British descent
soc.culture.canada	Discussions of Canada and its people
soc.culture.tamil	Tamil language, history, and culture
soc.history	Discussions of things historical
soc.men	Issues related to men, their problems and relationships
soc.misc	Socially-oriented topics not in other groups
soc.singles	Newsgroup for single people, their activities, and so on
soc.women	Issues related to women, their problems and relationships

Blah Blah Blah

A few topics provoke running arguments that never *ever* get resolved. USENET puts these in the *talk* hierarchy, mostly to warn you to stay away. Most find these groups to be argumentative and repetitious, and mostly populated by students. However, *you* may not mind this or you may feel differently — so take a look at any that seem interesting to you.

Table 12-6	Groups in the Talk Hierarchy
Name	*Description*
talk.abortion	All sorts of discussions and arguments on abortion
talk.answers	Repository for periodic USENET articles (moderated)
talk.bizarre	The unusual, bizarre, curious, and often stupid
talk.religion.newage	Esoteric and minority religions and philosophies
talk.rumors	For the posting of rumors

More Hierarchies

Along with the standard hierarchies, there are a bunch of less widely distributed ones.

alt

This designates so-called *alternative* groups. Setting up a group in a regular hierarchy is fairly difficult, requiring a formal charter and an on-line vote by its prospective readers and non-readers. On the other hand, any fool can (and often does) set up an *alt* group. Often, after an alt has been around for a while, its proponents go through the procedure to create a corresponding mainstream group, and the alt group goes away.

bionet

This is a bunch of groups of interest to *biologists,* with the latest news on fruit flies and the like. If you're not a biologist, don't bother.

bit

These are BITNET mailing lists (see Chapter 10) that are passed around as USENET news.

biz

Designates *business* groups that are more commercial than the generally noncommercial traffic in the mainstream groups.

clari

This refers to *ClariNet* (see sidebar "Listen to the ClariNet" later in this chapter).

gnu

This is the *GNU project,* which develops freely available software including, eventually, a complete reimplementation of the UNIX system. (GNU stands for Gnu's Not UNIX, by the way.)

hepnet

This is *HEPnet (High Energy Physics)'*. Like bionet, you know if you're interested.

IEEE

This is IEEE, the professional organization for electrical and electronics engineers.

k12

The K-12 net is for elementary and high school students and teachers. Students and teachers are welcome on all of the other groups, of course, but these groups contain topics of particular interest.

relcom

These are Russian-language groups. They are unintelligible unless you have a news-reading program that handles Cyrillic characters. You have to be able to read Russian, too.

vmsnet

Groups discuss the VMS system that runs on some Digital (DEC) computers. Primarily, they are for VMS fans.

Of all these hierarchies, only alt has many groups that are of general interest. A few of them can be found in Table 12-7. The character of alt groups varies wildly. Some, like *alt.dcom.telecom*, are just as staid as any comp group. Others, like *alt.buddha.short.fat.guy*, verge on the indescribable.

Table 12-7	Groups in the Alt Hierarchy
Name	*Description*
alt.activism	Activities for activists
alt.angst	Anxiety in the modern world
alt.answers	As if anyone on alt has the answers (moderated)
alt.appalachian	Appalachian region awareness, events, and culture
alt.backrubs	Lower...to the right...aaaah!
alt.bbs	Computer BBS systems and software
alt.binaries.pictures.erotica	Gigabytes of erotic copyright violations
alt.binaries.pictures.erotica.d	Discussing erotic copyright violations
alt.binaries.pictures.fine-art.d	Discussion of the fine-art binaries (moderated)
alt.binaries.pictures.utilities	Posting of pictures-related utilities
alt.books.isaac-asimov	Fans of the late SF/science author Isaac Asimov
alt.buddha.short.fat.guy	Religion, and not religion, both, neither
alt.cobol	Relationship between programming and stone axes
alt.dcom.telecom	Discussion of telecommunications technology
alt.dreams	What do they mean?
alt.drugs	Recreational pharmaceuticals and related flames
alt.evil	Tales from the dark side
alt.flame	Alternative, literate, pithy, succinct screaming
alt.folklore.college	Collegiate humor

Name	Description
alt.folklore.computers	Stories and anecdotes about computers (some true!)
alt.folklore.urban	Urban legends, *a la* Jan Harold Brunvand
alt.hackers	Descriptions of projects currently under development (moderated)
alt.manga	Discussion of non-Western comics
alt.online-service	Large, commercial online services and the Internet
alt.paranormal	Phenomena which are not scientifically explicable
alt.parents-teens	Parent-teenager relationships
alt.party	Parties, celebration, and general debauchery
alt.rhode_island	Discussion of the great little state
alt.save.the.earth	Environmentalist causes
alt.sex	Postings of a prurient nature
alt.sources	Alternative source code, unmoderated — caveat emptor
alt.sources.d	Discussion of posted sources
alt.sources.index	Pointers to source code in alt.sources. (moderated)
alt.supermodels	Discussing famous and beautiful models
alt.surfing	Riding the ocean waves
alt.tv.mash	Nothing like a good comedy about war and dying
alt.tv.mst3k	Hey, you robots! Down in front!
alt.tv.muppets	Miss Piggy on the tube
alt.tv.prisoner	The Prisoner television series from years ago

NAVIGATE

Listen to the ClariNet

It had to happen someday—USENET meets real life. A guy named Brad (same guy that created *rec.humor.funny,* USENET's most widely read group) had a simple goal for his computer: he wanted to get his weekly Dave Barry column in his electronic mail. How hard could that be, considering that newspaper features are all distributed by satellite, anyway? Pretty hard, it turned out, mostly because of the legal issues of who owns what on the satellite.

Brad kept at it, though, and ended up with the right to distribute by network not just Dave Barry, but the entire UPI newswire and a lot of other features, too. That was *far* too much data to send out as e-mail, so Brad did the obvious thing and decided to use USENET software instead. The result is a group of about 250 newsgroups known as ClariNet. Each group contains a particular category of news (actual newspaper-type news,

not just Net news), such as *clari.news.economy* for stories about the economy.

If your system has a direct (not just dial-up) Internet connection, you can get ClariNet news about as fast as the news comes off the ticker. It costs money, of course, but for a site with dozens or hundreds of users, the price per user is quite low — on the order of a few dollars per user per month. For information, send e-mail to *info@clarinet.com.*

Brad also did get his e-mail Dave Barry. You can, too, for under $10 per year (less than the cost of a Sunday paper each week). If your system gets ClariNet news, Dave may already be filed under *clari.feature.dave_barry.* If not, send e-mail to *info@clarinet.com* to get subscription details. You can get Mike Royko and Miss Manners, too.

Chapter 13
While-You-Wait Conversation: Talk and Chat

Talking the Talk

Sometimes e-mail just isn't fast enough. If you need to get in touch with some-one right now, what's the best way to establish contact? Pick up the phone and call, of course. But sometimes that's not practical (see the sidebar, "Why use talk if you have a telephone?" later in this chapter). When calling isn't practical, the next best thing is the Internet *talk* command. To talk to some other user somewhere, type

```
talk username@hostname
```

If the other person is on the same machine as you are, you can leave out the *@hostname* part (although leaving it in never hurts). If you're using a fancy, windowed system, such as Microsoft Windows or Motif, you probably double-click on the talk icon in a program menu and then type the victim's — er, recipient's — name into a box. The talk command clears your screen and draws a dotted line across the middle of it. (The top half of the screen is where you type, and the bottom half is where the other person's typing appears, so even if you both type at the same time, the messages don't get scrambled.) The program then says something like this:

```
[Checking for invitation on caller's machine]
```

That message means that talk is checking to see whether the other person has already asked to talk to *you*. Most likely that's not the case, and if not, talk displays something like the following on the other person's screen (you don't see this):

```
Message from Talk_Daemon@whitehouse.com at 10:08 ...
talk: connection requested by elvis@ntw.org.
talk: respond with:  talk elvis@ntw.org
```

The recipient (if someone else were trying to talk to you, you would be the recipient) should then type a corresponding talk command, and then the connection is established. It indicates the connection by displaying

```
[Connection established]
```

Now the two of you can talk back and forth:

```
How about some lunch?
-------------------------------------------------------------------
Sure, call me at 6-3765 and we'll figure out where to meet.
```

When you're done talking, either party can exit talk by typing the local system's *interrupt character,* which is usually Ctrl-C or Delete. On windowed systems, you usually disconnect by clicking on a menu item. If you are trying to talk to someone and there's no answer, talk keeps sending the notification message until you press Ctrl-C or Delete.

Finding your victim

If your intended recipient (or *talkee,* making you the *talker*) is using a workstation with a windowing system, talk picks, more or less at random, one of the windows on the screen and sends that window the invitation to talk. As likely as not, your friend isn't looking at that window at that moment. The window may not even be visible on the screen. Try *fingering* (see Chapter 9) the machine to see which window is active, as in the following example:

```
finger @tammany.org
[suit.tammany.org]
Login      Name              TTY Idle    When    Where
tweed    Boss Tweed         co 1:35 Wed 02:37
tweed    Boss Tweed         p0    4d Wed 02:37   :0.0
tweed    Boss Tweed         p1       Wed 02:37   :0.0
tweed    Boss Tweed         p2 1:35 Wed 02:38   :0.0
```

In this case, the user has several windows on the screen. (The glop in the Where column means that it's a window rather than some other kind of connection; the colon is the giveaway, so all but the first here are windows.) Only one of them is actually active at the moment. You can tell that p1, in the TTY column, the name of the *pseudoterminal* that the window uses, is the active window because all the other windows have entries in the Idle column showing that the window's been idle for over an hour or, in one case, four days. You can include a terminal name in the talk command, after the name of the talkee, as in the following:

```
talk tweed@suit.tammany.org ttyp1
```

Note: You have to type **ttyp1**, not just **p1**. (You don't really want to know why, just prefix **tty** to whatever finger shows as the terminal name.) Adding this argument tells talk to send its invitation to ttyp1, where your friend presumably will see it.

Why use talk if you have a telephone?

This is a darned good question, actually. Most of the time, if you can call someone on the phone, it's a lot more effective to call them than to use talk. (Using talk has been likened to communicating with someone on the moon.) Here are a few examples of times when it is sensible to use talk rather than the phone:

🡪 The other person isn't answering the phone or isn't logged in from her usual office, so you use talk to encourage her to call you from wherever she is.

🡪 The other person isn't near a phone. (Unlikely — how many networked computers don't have a phone nearby?)

🡪 The other person is on another continent, and phone calls are difficult or very expensive. (I hear that people at the Amundsen-Scott Base at the South Pole use the Internet as their primary means of communication.)

🡪 One or both of you don't speak English very well, so it's easier to type than to speak.

🡪 The other person can't hear at all. (Quite a few deaf people are on the Internet, and you never know who they are unless they decide to tell you.)

🡪 You don't know the other person's phone number, so use talk to find out the number to call.

Talk with care

Unlike e-mail, talk sends everything you type directly to the recipient as soon as you type it. You can backspace over your errors, but the recipient *sees you do it.* This means that if your fingers slip, causing you to type something really rude, even if you backspace over it, you're *in deep sneakers.* For example, don't do this:

```
Can you come by for a meeting?
------------------------------------------------------------------------
stick it←←←←←←←←←←Sure, Boss, no problem.
```

Serious Time Wasting

The talk command only enables you to talk to one person at a time. Chat programs let you talk to *dozens* of people at a time, who can be located all over the world. Most of the people you chat with are students who have nothing better to do (or who have lots better to do but don't feel like doing it at the moment).

The most widely used chat program is called *Internet Relay Chat,* or *IRC.* Some systems (particularly UNIX workstations) may have an IRC client program, in which case you merely type the command **irc** to get on it. (You can ask your system manager to install IRC, but don't expect much sympathy unless your manager is also a chat addict.)

In the absence of a local chat client, you can *telnet* (see Chapter 14) to a *public IRC server* and chat from there. IRC servers come and go all the time because they are widely (and not without justification) viewed as useless resource hogs. The best way to find current IRC telnet servers is to look at the USENET newsgroup *alt.irc.* (See Chapters 11 and 12.)

After you're connected to IRC, you have to pick a nickname to identify yourself for the duration of your chat (your username does nicely). Then you have to decide which *channel* (discussion topic) you want to join. Type

```
/list
```

to see the names of all the channels that are available on your IRC. For example, to join one called #penpals, type

```
/join #penpals
```

and wait a minute or so for IRC to find the other people on your channel and announce on your screen what their nicknames are. Then start typing. Each person's contributions are prefaced with the appropriate nickname on your screen. IRC conversation tends to be pretty vapid:

```
<Gier> Why do people start doing quickies today..
<DrScott> re Buster!
<Gier> Do a quick one and you're dead Buster!
<DrScott> Gier: well, just for fun :))
<Gier> I ain't gonna say anything...
<Gier> til I'm sure...
<DrScott> Gier.... ;)
> That could take a while.
```

When you lose interest, type:

```
/QUIT
```

to exit.

There are lots of other commands. Type

```
/HELP
```

to find out what they are.

In principle, IRC could be used for on-line help desks and things like that. In practice, though, it isn't. It's just gossip. Oh well.

Part III
Instant Gratification

The 5th Wave   By Rich Tennant

"I THINK WHAT WE LIKE MOST ABOUT IT IS ITS TRANSPARENCY IN THE SYSTEM."

In this part...

So far I've been looking at staid, slow-moving ways to communicate with other people and other computers. But face it, mail is *still* mail. How exciting is walking down to the mailbox? In this part, you start using the Internet for while-you-wait communication. If you're into instant gratification (and who isn't these days?), read on.

Chapter 14
The Next Best Thing to Being There

How You Can Be in Two Places at Once

By far, the most widely used interactive Internet services are the various forms of remote login. What these services do is simple: you log into a remote *host* (telnet-ese for a computer) as though your *terminal* (workstation, PC, whatever) were attached directly to that host. Because all hosts on the Internet are officially equal, you can log into a host on the other side of the world as easily as you can log into one down the hall, the only difference being that the connection to the distant host may be a little slower.

Although *telnet*, the most comonly used remote login program, is in principle simplicity itself, because computers are involved simplicity isn't what it used to be. To run telnet, you type the telnet command followed by the name of the host you want to use. If everything goes well, you are then connected to that host.

In the following example, I telnet to my home computer and log in as myself. (No, I'm not going to tell you what my password is. Sorry.)

```
% telnet iecc.com
Trying 140.186.81.1 ... Connected to iecc.com.
Escape character is '^]'.

System V UNIX (iecc)
login: john1
Password:

Terminal type (default VT100):
...
```

Notice a couple of points here:

- ✔ Some versions of telnet report the numeric addresses of the hosts they contact. If your version does this, note that number in case of later trouble with the network connection.

- ✔ The thing that's absolutely essential to note is the *escape character,* which is your secret key to unhooking yourself from the remote host should it become recalcitrant and stop doing anything useful.

- ✔ The escape character in my example, the most common one on UNIX systems, is ^], which means that you hold down the Ctrl key and press] (the right bracket character on your keyboard).

- ✔ If you use a program on the remote system that needs to use that escape character for its own purposes, you can pick another escape character. See the sidebar "Whipping telnet into line" later in this chapter.

After you're logged in, you can work pretty much as if you were indeed directly logged into the remote host. The main difference is that characters take a little longer to appear on-screen — as long as a full second or more. In most cases, you can keep typing even when what you typed hasn't yet appeared; the remote host eventually catches up.

Terminal Type Madness

If you use a full-screen program, such as the UNIX text editors emacs and vi or the mail programs elm and pine, you need to set your *terminal type.* This problem shouldn't exist in the first place. But it does, so you have to deal with it.

The problem is that about a dozen different conventions exist for screen controls like *clear screen, move to position (x,y),* and so forth. The program you're using on the remote host has to use the same convention that your terminal does (if you're using a terminal), or that your local terminal program does (if you're on a PC or a workstation).

If the conventions are not the same, you get *garbage* (funky-looking characters) on-screen when you try to use a full-screen program. In most cases, the remote system asks you what terminal type to use. The trick is knowing the right answer.

- ✔ If you're using a PC, the best answer is usually *ANSI* because most PC terminal programs use ANSI terminal conventions. (*ANSI* stands for the *American National Standards Institute.* One of their several thousand standards defines a set of terminal control conventions that MS-DOS PCs — which otherwise wouldn't know an ANSI standard if they tripped over one — invariably use.)

> ✔ If you're using a windowing system, such as Motif or Open Look, the answer is more likely to be *VT-100*, a popular terminal from the 1970s that became a defacto standard.

> ✔ In places where a great deal of IBM equipment is used, the terminal type may be *3101*, an early IBM terminal that was also quite popular.

The ANSI and VT-100 conventions are not very different from each other, so if you use one and your screen is only somewhat screwed up, try the other.

TECHNICAL STUFF

More than you want to know about terminal types

Back in the good old days — like about 1968 — only one kind of terminal was ever used: a genuine Teletype brand *Teletype*. Teletype machines, direct descendants of the news Teletypes (familiar from old movie footage of newspaper production), were simple beasts. That is, they were simple conceptually — physically, they had an incredible number of moving parts. The only things these machines did other than type text was return the carriage and ring the bell.

Then people realized that you could combine a keyboard with a slightly modified television screen and build a video terminal. Dozens of manufacturers appeared, most now long forgotten, and they all noticed that you could do a great deal more with a screen than you could with an old Teletype. For example, you could clear the screen, draw text in specific places, shift text up and down — all sorts of handy stuff. So each manufacturer assigned otherwise unused character codes as *control characters* to handle these special functions. Naturally, no two terminals used the same assignment.

Meanwhile, on a small planet far, far away . . . *oops, sorry, wrong book.* Meanwhile, in Berkeley, California in the late 1970s, what is now known as Berkeley UNIX was taking shape. People at Berkeley had amassed large and completely miscellaneous collections of incompatible terminals. Which terminals would Berkeley UNIX support? Here's a hint: terminals had to be bought from outside and cost real money, whereas software was written by students and was free. Naturally, they supported every single terminal type on the campus, using a large database of hundreds of terminal types with the particular control sequences needed for each terminal.

By the early 1980s, it was apparent that the dominant terminal in the non-IBM market was the DEC VT-100. Many clone terminals started to appear that understood exactly the same control sequences as VT-100s, so they'd work all the places that VT-100s did. ANSI, the organization in charge of technical standards in the United States, adopted control sequences almost identical to the VT-100 sequences as an official standard.

So now you can assume that every terminal is a VT-100, right? Well, no. For one thing, many of those old terminals refuse to die. For another, terminal manufacturers progressed far beyond the VT-100, adding features like color and graphics that the VT-100 didn't have. So most terminals made today are more or less ANSI-compatible, but with their own grotty warts. The world is stuck with multiple terminal types for the foreseeable future. But at this point, if you don't know what kind of terminal you have, either VT-100 or ANSI is your best guess.

For another failed attempt at terminal standardization, see the sidebar on Network Virtual Terminals (NVTs) later in this chapter.

Depending on how well-implemented your local version of telnet is, it may automatically advise the remote system of what kind of terminal you're using. So with luck, you won't actually have to set your terminal type, or perhaps you'll just have to reply **y** when it says something like `Terminal type VT100 OK?`

Help! I've Telnetted and I Can't Get Out!

The normal way to leave telnet is to log out from the remote host. When you log out, the remote host closes its end of the telnet connection, which tells your local telnet program that it's done. Easy enough — normally. Sometimes, though, the other end gets stuck and pays no attention to what you type. Or it doesn't get permanently stuck, but the host responds so slowly that you have no interest in waiting for it any more. (This sometimes happens when network congestion occurs between you and the other host.)

Some versions of host software, which I won't name for looking-gift-horses-in-the-mouth-type reasons, get hopelessly slowed down by congestion, much more than the congestion itself causes. So you need to know how to escape from telnet. Here's where the magic escape character comes in handy.

- ✔ First, you have to get telnet's attention by typing the escape character. (If nothing happens after a few seconds, try pressing Enter as well.) Telnet should come back with a prompt telling you that it's there.

- ✔ Then type **quit** to tell it that you're done. You should see something like the following:

```
^]
telnet> quit
Connection closed.
```

You can give telnet a dozen other commands (press **?** to see them), but none of them is anywhere near as useful as quit.

Terminals Served Here

One specialized host increasingly found on the Internet is a *terminal server*. The terminal server is basically a little computer with a number of modems or hard-wired terminal ports, and all it does with its life is telnet to other hosts. This makes sense if you have a lot of regular terminals around the office, or many people who dial in over the phone, because it enables many terminals to get onto the Net at low cost. (Terminal servers are so carefully tuned to their task that even though a typical one has the computing power of a 1985 PC, it can handle upwards of 30 modem connections at 14,000 bps *each*.)

Using a terminal server is like logging into a very single-minded computer (indeed, that's just what it is). You dial in and usually have to enter a site password that keeps 12 year-old hackers from calling in at random. (Or hackers of any age, for that matter.) Then you type the name of the host you want to connect to, and you're telnetted in. Here's a session on a typical Cisco terminal server:

```
User Access Verification Password: *****
TS>iecc.com
Translating "IECC.COM"...domain server (155.178.247.101) [OK]
Trying IECC.COM (140.186.81.1)... Open System V UNIX (iecc)
login:

. . . regular telnet session deleted here ...

[Connection to IECC.COM closed by foreign host]
TS>
```

Terminal servers have escape characters just like regular telnet programs, although they tend to be harder to guess. The usual escape for Cisco servers is actually two characters, Ctrl-^ (which you usually enter as Ctrl-Shift-6), followed by a lowercase x. Other brands of terminal servers have different escape sequences; inquire locally to find out which ones to use.

Most terminal servers also have a small set of commands that they understand to customize your terminal session. Press ? rather than a host name and see what it says.

PCs Can't Leave Well Enough Alone

If you use a Macintosh, a PC under Microsoft Windows, or some other windowing system, you start telnet somewhat differently that you do on a UNIX system. You start the telnet program from an icon, and a window pops up with menu choices at the top. One of the choices is usually Connect (or something like it). Click on that choice, type in the name of the host you want, or maybe select it from a list, and away you go.

Figure 14-1 shows the same session as shown previously in the chapter, but this time from a Windows machine. A windowing system has no escape character because you do all the escape-type stuff from the program's menu. To disconnect from a recalcitrant host, for example, click on a menu item called Disconnect (or something similar).

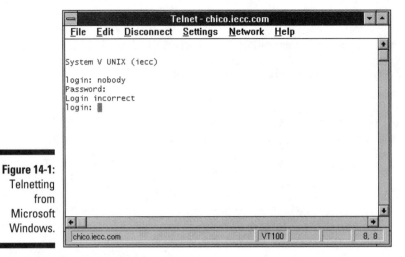

Figure 14-1:
Telnetting
from
Microsoft
Windows.

Whipping Telnet Into Line

You can tell telnet to change its behavior in a few ways. The two most notable are to turn on and off *local echo* and *line mode*. Local echo means that the characters you type are sent to your screen by the local host (the one running telnet) rather than the one you have telnetted to. If your remote host echoes slowly, or doesn't echo at all (some IBM hosts are like that), you can try to turn on local echo. Usually, pressing Ctrl-E turns local echo on and off.

Nearly all hosts on the Internet want to process the characters you type one at a time, as soon as you type them. A few ancient ones prefer a line at a time. You usually can recognize them because they don't handle any backspacing over errors. To work around that problem, type the telnet escape character, then

```
telnet> mode line
```

This line tells your local host to save up the characters and send them along a line at a time, handling the backspaces before passing them on. The number of hosts using line mode is small and shrinking. If you think you've found a host that needs it, ask around to see if you've overlooked something. If the host sends text a screen at a time and uses acronyms like VM or MVS (the two most common IBM operating systems), you've probably run into an IBM host and should use *tn3270* instead. See the section "We're from IBM . . ." coming up in this chapter.

Disregard this discussion about network virtual terminals

Back in 1983 when telnet was defined, the folks working on it were acutely aware of the various kinds of terminals in use. Their solution to the incompatible terminal explosion was to define a *Network Virtual Terminal (NVT)*. The plan was that the telnet *client* (the program that you run) would turn the local control glop into standard NVT codes; the telnet *server* (the program at the other end that makes your network connection act like a terminal on that host) would turn NVT codes into whatever the local convention was. So long as each system was configured correctly for the terminals physically attached to it, NVTs would take care of everything.

This didn't work. What happened? The problem was that telnet came along slightly too early, and the kinds of terminals they were worried about were line-at-a-time printing terminals, particularly some IBM terminals known by four-digit numbers such as 2741 and 1050. The 2741 was a slightly beefed up Selectric typewriter with a

computer interface, but it wasn't beefed up quite enough to handle the wear and tear of being run at full speed by a computer rather than at 30 WPM by a typist. I used a terminal room for several years that contained about a dozen 2741s, and I cannot remember all of them ever being in working order at the same time.

NVTs magnificently solve incompatibilities among 2741s, Teletypes, Flexowriters, and many other printing terminals. Unfortunately, video terminals were just coming into fashion, and NVTs didn't address them at all. So Internet users are stuck with multiple terminal types on all the hosts.

(Actually, that's not quite true. Major manufacturers such as Digital Equipment Corporation (DEC) tend to support only their own terminals, so if you telnet into a DEC VMS system with anything other than a DEC terminal or clone thereof, you lose. Fortunately, the ubiquitous VT-100 was made by DEC.)

Any Port In a Storm

When you telnet into a remote host, you have to select not just the host, but also a *port* on the host. The port is a small number that identifies what service you want. The usual port for telnet is (for obscure historical reasons) the number 23, which is taken to mean that you want to log into the host. You pick another port by putting the port name after the host name as follows:

```
telnet ntw.org 13
```

Port 13 is the *daytime* port. It tells you that host's idea of the time of day and then disconnects. This is not a terribly useful exercise, although occasionally you may need to see what time zone another host is in.

Some hosts are set up so that the regular telnet to port 23 gets a login prompt for regular users of the system, whereas telnet to some other port gets you into a special, publicly usable subsystem. Some of these systems are mentioned in Chapter 15.

We're from IBM and We Know What's Good for You

All the terminals discussed previously that are handled by telnet are basically souped-up Teletypes, with data passed character by character between the terminal and the host. This kind of terminal interaction can be called *Teletype-ish.*

IBM developed an entirely different model for its 3270-series display terminals. The principle is that the computer's in charge. The model works more like filling in paper forms. The computer draws what it wants on the screen, marks which parts of the screen the user can type into, and then unlocks the keyboard so that users can fill in whichever blanks they want. When the user presses Enter, the terminal locks the keyboard, transmits the changed parts of the screen to the computer, and awaits further instructions from headquarters.

To be fair, this is a perfectly reasonable way to build terminals intended for dedicated data-entry and retrieval applications. The terminal on the desks at your bank, electric company, and such are probably 3270s — or more likely these days, cheap PCs *emulating* 3270s. The 3270 terminal protocol squeezes a great deal more onto a phone line than Teletype-ish, so it's quite common to have all the 3270s in an office sharing the same single phone line, with reasonable performance.

The Internet is a big place, and plenty of IBM mainframes run applications on the Net. Some of them are quite useful. Most of the large library catalogs, for example, speak 3270-ish. Usually, if you telnet to a system that wants a 3270, it converts from the Teletype-ish that telnet speaks to 3270-ish so that you can use it anyway. But some 3270 systems only speak 3270-ish, and if you telnet to them, they connect and disconnect without saying anything in between.

A variant of telnet that speaks 3270-ish is called *tn3270.* If you find that a system keeps disconnecting, or if you see full-screen pictures like the one shown in Figure 14-2, try typing the command **tn3270** instead. (Large amounts of UPPER-CASE LETTERS and references to the IBM operating systems VM or MVS are also tip-offs that you're talking to a 3270.) Even if a 3270 system allows regular telnet, you'll get a snappier response if you use tn3270 instead.

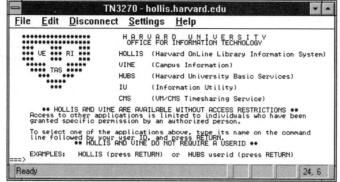

Figure 14-2:
Using tn3270
to log into
the Harvard
Library
Catalog.

Remote Login:
The Next Best Thing to Being There

Most UNIX systems also include a different, somewhat incompatible telnet-like program called *rlogin*. (Most PC network packages that support telnet have rlogin as well.) I use rlogin in the following example:

```
rlogin pumpkin.ntw.org
Last login: Fri Jan  8 14:30:28 from squash
SunOS Release 4.1.2 (PUMPKIN) #3: Fri Oct 16 00:20:44 EDT 1992
Please confirm (or change) your terminal type.
TERM = (vt100)
```

Hey! It didn't ask you to log in. What happened? That's the main advantage of rlogin over telnet. When you find yourself logging into the same machines over and over again, you easily can arrange it so that after you log into one of them, you can rlogin to any of them. The rlogin program automatically passes your username and terminal type to the remote system so that you don't have to retype them yourself. By and large, if the hosts you use support rlogin, it's more convenient to use than telnet. But not every host supports rlogin, so sometimes you have to use telnet. If you try to rlogin to a system that doesn't accept it, you see a message like the following, which means that you should try telnet instead:

```
% Connection refused by remote host
```

Parting Is Such Sweet Sorrow

The rlogin program has a completely different set of escape characters from telnet. (Honestly, are you surprised?) All rlogin escapes start with ~ (the tilde) at the beginning of a line. The most important escape sequence you can type is exit, which is ~. (a tilde followed by a period or dot). So to get out of a stuck rlogin, your key to escape is to press Enter (to make sure that you're at the beginning of a line) and then type ~. (that's tilde followed by a period followed by another Enter).

Be My Guest

In some cases, a group of hosts share the same complete set of users, so that anyone logged into one of them can log into any of the others. In this case, there is a system file listing all the hosts whose users are equivalent to this one. It's called */etc/hosts.equiv* on UNIX systems and something similar on other machines. If machine *Able* has a hosts.equiv file that contains the name of host *Baker*, anyone on Baker can rlogin to Able without giving a password.

Some groups of workstations, particularly Suns, use something called *NIS* (Network Information System), which provides a group-wide database of usernames and the like. If you're using NIS, the system consults an NIS hosts.equiv database in addition to its regular file. To see it, type **ypcat hosts.equiv**. (Don't ask me why the command is called *ypcat*; you don't want to know.)

Be My Host

In another situation, you have accounts on several hosts, but they're not all under the same management. You can arrange your own rlogin setup. On each of your accounts, create a file called *.rhosts* (that's a dot in front of the *r*) that lists all the other hosts on which you have accounts. For systems in which you have a different username, put your username on that system *after* the host name, separated by a space. Then, when you use rlogin, the system you're logging into checks your .rhosts, sees that it's you, and you're all set. If you're using rlogin to log into a host where you have a different name, specify it like this (assuming that your username at *ntw.org* is *king*):

```
rlogin ntw.org -l king
```

If you're bewildered by now, here's an example that may help. Let's say that you have accounts on three machines called *Able, Baker,* and *Clarissa.* On Able and Baker, your username is *sam,* and on Clarissa it's *tilden.* You want to be able to rlogin from any of them to any of the others. Your .rhosts file on Able could contain the following:

```
Baker
Clarissa tilden
```

Your .rhosts on Baker could contain this:

```
Able
Clarissa tilden
```

Your .rhosts on Clarissa could contain

```
Able sam
Baker sam
```

But here's an easier way. It doesn't hurt to include the username, even if it's the same, and it also doesn't hurt to include a line for the local system. So all three .rhosts files can be the same:

```
Able sam
Baker sam
Clarissa tilden
```

If rlogin doesn't recognize you, it asks for your name and password just like telnet. Who would ever have expected something that sensible?

How to Hardly Be There at All

The rlogin program has a junior version called *rsh* (for *remote shell*). It executes a single command on a remote system:

```
rsh Able ls -R
```

If you have a different username on that system, you give it the same way as for rlogin:

```
rsh Clarissa -l tilden ls -R
```

You can't run full-screen programs using rsh, although you can run programs that read their input a line at a time. (I won't bore you with the obscure technical reasons for this.) This means that you can use line-at-a-time mail programs like mail or mailx, but not nice ones like elm or pine. A simple workaround is available, however: use rlogin instead.

Finally, rsh never asks for a username or password. If it can't recognize you using hosts.equiv or .rhosts, it just fails.

Chapter 15
Some Interesting Computers to Log Into

In This Chapter

▶ Telnetting around the world

▶ More useful information than any sane person would want

Come On By, Anytime

The Internet is a remarkably friendly place. Many systems let you telnet in with little or no prearrangement. Most just let you telnet in without restriction. Others require that you register the first time you log in, but still don't ask you to pay anything. They just want to have some idea who their users are.

This list doesn't include any of the many places where you can telnet to Gopher, Archie, WAIS, or WWW servers — these servers are covered in Chapters 19 through 22.

Some Important Libraries

Nearly every large library in the country (indeed, in the developed world) now has a computerized catalog, and most of those catalogs are on the Internet. Most of the on-line catalogs also have other research info that is certainly more interesting than the catalogs themselves. This section lists some of the more prominent library systems and how to access them.

Library: Library of Congress
Address: locis.loc.gov
Access code: T3

The Library of Congress is the largest library in the world, and it certainly has the biggest catalog system, called LOCIS. (It's your tax dollars at work, or maybe at play.) Along with the regular card catalog, in which you can look up pretty much any book ever published in the United States, the Library of

Your secret decoder ring

In the list of services in this chapter, the code letters have the following meanings:

Code Letter	Meaning
T	Connect via regular telnet.
Port Number	Specify a port number after the host name in your telnet command (see Chapter 14 for details).
3	Connect via tn3270. Most tn3270 systems listed in this chapter also allow regular telnet for people without tn3270.
R	Registration required. The first time you log in, you have to say who you are.
A	Account required. You have to sign up and arrange to pay money. (Not many of these are listed.)

Congress has an extensive and useful congressional legislation system that you can use to look up the bills that are in Congress. You can find out what bills have been introduced; what's happened to them (getting a bill through Congress is somewhat more complicated than getting someone canonized as a saint); who sponsored them; and what they say (in summary).

Figure 15-1 shows the summary of a bill that was, at the time of this writing, passed by the House of Representatives and waiting for committee action in the Senate. You also can check for bills by the name of the sponsor, if you're wondering what your local representative or senator has been up to.

Note: LOCIS is available only during the hours when the Library is open, generally 9 a.m. to 9 p.m. (Eastern Time) on weekdays, shorter hours on weekends. Other times it disconnects immediately.

Figure 15-1:
LOCIS
showing a
legislative bill
summary.

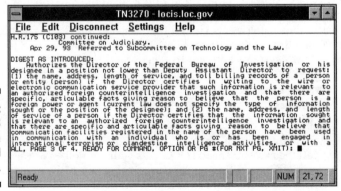

Library: Dartmouth College Library
Address: library.dartmouth.edu
Access code: T

Along with the card catalog, this service includes the full text of William Shakespeare's plays and sonnets and the works of other great authors. To search the plays, type **select file s plays**; for sonnets, type **select file s sonnets**. For example, Figure 15-2 shows a search string found in *Hamlet,* which was written by my literary colleague, Shakespeare.

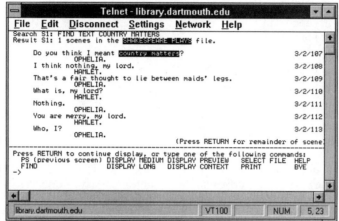

Figure 15-2: Searching for a phrase in *Hamlet.*

Library: Harvard Library
Address: hollis.harvard.edu
Access code: T3

Harvard has another huge library, and the service also provides campus info.

Library: Yale Library
Address: orbis.yale.edu
Access code: 3

This is yet another large library (and the only one where you can find a copy of my thesis, "A Data Base System for Small Interactive Computers," which may not matter to you, but I think it's interesting).

Library: Victoria University of Wellington
Address: library.vuw.ac.nz
Access code: T

This is a library catalog in New Zealand, if you're planning to head down that way. After you connect, press Enter a few times until it asks you to log in and then type **OPAC**.

Other libraries

A service called *hytelnet* is a database of and gateway to many other libraries. If you log into any one of them, it will help you find catalog information for dozens or hundreds of libraries. Current hytelnet servers include the following:

- ✔ access.usask.ca
  login: hytelnet

- ✔ info.ccit.arizona.edu
  login: hytelnet

- ✔ laguna.epcc.edu
  login: library

- ✔ info.anu.edu.au
  login: library
  Note: located in Australia

- ✔ nctuccca.edu.tw
  login: hytelnet
  Note: located in Taiwan

Large lists of on-line libraries also are available by FTP (see Chapter 18 for more information). For most purposes, I find that the Library of Congress is the most useful for finding names of books, unless I'm planning to physically visit one of the other libraries.

Miscellaneous Databases

On-line information on an astounding range of topics is only a few keystrokes away, as you can see in the following sections.

Agriculture and nutrition databases

Database: PENpages
Address: psupen.psu.edu
Access code: T

Log in as your two-letter state abbreviation. This database provides a wide range of agricultural info. It's handy if you are, or like to think of yourself as, a farmer.

Database: Clemson Forestry and Agriculture Network
Address: eureka.clemson.edu
Access code: T

Log in as *PUBLIC*. This database offers plenty of forestry facts.

Geography databases

Database: Geographic Server
Address: martini.eecs.umich.edu
Access code: TP
Port 3000

This database has the name, location, and other facts on every place in the United States. If you've ever wondered where Surf City, U.S.A. really is, then this database is for you. (It's in New Jersey, by the way — eat your heart out, California. However, it doesn't tell you not to miss the world famous Surf City Fire Breakfast, held on the second and fourth Sundays in August, but I guess I just did.)

Database: Earthquake info
Address: geophys.washington.edu
Access code: T

Log in as *quake,* and use the password *quake.* Did you know that the United States has earthquakes almost every day? And you thought you were paranoid!

Database: GLIS
Address: glis.cr.usgs.gov
Access code: TR

This is the government's *Global Land Use Info System (GLIS).* An enormous amount of map data is available in computer form, and GLIS enables you to locate and order it. Impress your friends by whipping out a computerized map of your town, state, and/or planet.

Ham radio databases

Several databases contain ham radio call signs. If you're a ham, you'll be interested in these:

- callsign.cs.buffalo.edu
  Port: 2000

- ham.njit.edu
  Port: 2000

- ns.risc.net
  login: hamradio

History databases

You history buffs can find lots of good stuff in a variety of history databases around the Net.

Database: University of Kansas
Address: ukanaix.cc.ukans.edu
Access code: T

Log in as *history* for databases on history, or as *ex-ussr* for databases on Russia and its neighbors. They list documents, bibliographies, and other info of interest to historians.

There are other history resources available by Gopher (see Chapter 20) and FTP (Chapter 16.) Also see the USENET group *soc.history* for announcements of any newly available resources.

Outer space databases

Care to roam the far reaches of the universe (or talk to people who do)? Then the outer space databases are for you.

Database: NASA
Address: nssdc.gsfc.nasa.gov
Access code: TR

This is NASA's *National Space Science Data Center.* This database contains many facts for the outer space crowd.

Database: Spacelink
Address: spacelink.msfc.nasa.gov
Access code: TR

This database contains NASA news, including the shuttle launch schedule.

Database: European Space Agency
Address: esrin.esa.it
Access code: T

This database tells you what's new in the European part of outer space.

Aviation database

Interested in the wild blue yonder? Here is someplace you can roam.

Database: DUATS
Address: duats.gtefsd.com
Access code: TR

This database provides pilot info, briefing, and flight plans. If you're a real certified pilot, log into *duat.gtefsd.com* instead. Log in using your last name as the login name.

Book databases

Looking for books, tapes, and CDs? Here are a few starting points.

Database: CARL
Address: pac.carl.org
Access code: TA

This is a database of book reviews, magazines, and articles, including fax article delivery. For many of the services, you need a library card (or at least the number of a library card) from a participating library in Colorado or Wyoming, such as the Denver Public Library.

Database: Consumer Access Services
Address: columbia.ilc.com
Access code: TR

Books, CDs, and videotapes are listed here. If you register, you can order these goodies by using a credit card.

Gateway Systems

The following systems act as gateways to other systems, like hytelnet does for libraries.

Gateway: Washington University Gateway
Address: wugate.wustl.edu
Access code: T

Log in as *services*. This is a gateway to hundreds of other services around the Net — the best place to start browsing. When you find an interesting service, make a note of its name (and port and login, if need be) so that you can telnet in directly next time.

Gateway: MERIT Network
Address: hermes.merit.edu
Access code: TA

MERIT is the regional network that serves Michigan, and it also runs some national network facilities. MERIT offers access to some commercial services, including CompuServe, at a modest hourly rate. If you're outside the United States and have access to telnet, MERIT is the least expensive way to get into CompuServe. The publicly available service is a gateway to *Sprintnet,* a commercial packet network from which you can reach CompuServe, and have the Sprintnet charges billed to your CompuServe account automatically. If you use CompuServe through this gateway very much, you can sign up for a paid (but very inexpensive) service that lets you dial out to local Detroit numbers including CompuServe's, which ends up being several dollars per hour less expensive than Sprintnet.

Commercial Services

Several commercial on-line services are available, too. Here are a few.

Service: DELPHI
Address: delphi.com
Access code: TA

Log in as *joindelphi,* and use the password *info* to find out about Delphi terms and services.

Service: The World
Address: world.std.com
Access code: TA

Log in as *new* both for information and to sign up.

Service: Anomaly
Address: ns.risc.net
Access code: TA

This is a regional system in Rhode Island. Log in as *newuser* for info.

Fun and Sheer Goofiness

Here are a few services you can access if you're in a frolicsome mood — or if you're just plain bored.

Service: Thought for the day
Address: astro.temple.edu
Access code: TP
Port: 12345

Each time you telnet to this service, you get a pithy saying. Here's one:

```
telnet astro.temple.edu 12345
Trying ASTRO.OCIS.TEMPLE.EDU (129.32.1.100, 12345)... Open
Nihilism should commence with oneself.
```

Service: Internet Relay Chat
Address: various
Access code: T

You can telnet to various systems to join the running on-line *IRC (Internet Relay Chat)* discussion (see Chapter 13 for more details). In each case, log in as *irc*. Here are a few servers that currently work, but be warned that they come and go frequently:

- ✔ wbrt.wb.psu.edu (Pennsylvania)

- ✔ irc.demon.co.uk (England)

- ✔ hastur.cc.edu (United States)

- ✔ prof.jpl.nasa.gov (California)

Consult the USENET group *alt.irc* for more recent information.

Service: Scrabble
Address: next2.cas.muohio.edu
Access code: TP
Port: 7777

Play the game *Scrabble* against the computer or other people.

Service: Network Go
Address: various
Access code: TPR
Port: 6969

Play the Oriental strategy game of *Go* against other people. The following are a few servers around the world:

- ✔ bsdserver.ucsf.edu (California)
- ✔ hellspark.wharton.upenn.edu (Pennsylvania)
- ✔ ftp.pasteur.fr (France)

Service: Sports Info
Address: culine.colorado.edu
Access code: TP

You should telnet to port 859 for NBA schedules, 860 for the NHL, 862 for Major League Baseball, or 862 for the NFL.

## Chapter 16

May We Have a Copy for Our Files?

In This Chapter

▶ Getting files from all over the Net

▶ Stashing files all over the Net

▶ Doing the same thing another way, for the easily bored

What's on File?

File transfer means to copy files from one system to another. You can copy files from other systems to your system and from your system to others. Two different (how did you know I was going to say this?) file-transfer programs are available: *FTP* and *RCP*. This chapter spends more time discussing FTP because it's more widely available and somewhat more flexible.

If your system doesn't have FTP or RCP, all is not necessarily lost. See Chapter 17 to find out how to FTP, slowly, by e-mail.

How hard can it be to copy a file from one place to another?

Basically, it's pretty simple to copy a file from one place to another (but don't forget — computers are involved). Here's how it works: Log into the other computer for FTP and tell it what you want to copy and where you want it copied to.

Here's an example in which I FTP to my computer and retrieve a file called *README*.

```
% ftp iecc.com
Connected to iecc.com.
220 iecc FTP server (Version 4.1 8/1/91) ready.
Name (iecc.com:johnl): johnl
331 Password required for johnl.
Password:
230 User johnl logged in.
ftp> get README
150 Opening ASCII mode data connection for README (12686 bytes).
226 Transfer complete.
local: README remote: README
12979 bytes received in 28 seconds (0.44 Kbytes/s)
ftp> quit
221 Goodbye.
```

Look at the preceding example step by step. First I run FTP, telling it the name of the *host* (computer) I want to talk to. After that host answers (the line starting with 220), it asks for a username because you have to log in the same way you do for a telnet login. Invariably, it also asks for the password, so type that in. (Usually, the password doesn't appear when you type it, just like when you log in via telnet.) Then I *get* the file README, which provokes a flurry of messages. Finally, I tell FTP to *quit*.

That's basically how FTP works, but of course you need to know about 400 other odds and ends to use FTP effectively.

When is a file not a file?

When it's a text file. The FTP definition specifies six different kinds of files, of which only two types are useful: *ASCII* and *binary*. An ASCII file is a text file. A binary file is anything else. FTP has two modes, ASCII and binary (also called *image* mode), to transfer the two kinds of files. When you transfer an ASCII file between different kinds of computers that store files differently, ASCII mode

Why is it called FTP?

I could say that FTP is short for *File Transfer Program,* and you'd probably believe me, but that would be wrong. It really stands for *File Transfer Protocol.* Way back in 1971, the Internet Powers That Be decided on a *protocol,* a set of conventions for copying files from one place to another on the Net. Then many people wrote programs that implemented the protocol and called them all FTP. Is this clear? Never mind.

By the way, RCP stands for *remote copy.* Nothing fancy there.

automatically adjusts the file during the transfer so that the file is a valid text file when it is stored on the receiving end. A binary file is left alone and transferred verbatim.

You tell FTP which mode to use with the *binary* and *ascii* commands:

```
ftp> binary
200 Type set to I.
ftp> ascii
200 Type set to A.
```

In the preceding example, the *I* is for binary or image mode (after 20 years, the Internet protocol czars still can't make up their minds what to call it), and the A is for ASCII mode. Like most FTP commands, binary and ascii can be abbreviated by lazy typists to the first three letters — so *bin* and *asc* will suffice.

How to foul up your files in FTP

The most common error made by inexperienced Internet users (and also by experienced users, for that matter) is transferring a file in the wrong mode. If you transfer a text file in binary mode from a UNIX system to an MS-DOS or Macintosh system, the file looks something like this (on a DOS machine):

```
This file
        should have been
                        copied in
                                ASCII mode.
```

On a Mac, the whole file looks like it's on one line. When you look at the file with a text editor on a UNIX system, you see strange ^M symbols at the end of each line. You don't necessarily have to retransfer the file. Many networking packages come with programs that do ex post facto conversion from one format to the other.

If, on the other hand, you copy something that isn't a text file in ASCII mode, it gets scrambled. Compressed files don't decompress; executable files don't execute (or they crash or hang the machine); images look unimaginably bad. When a file is corrupted, the first thing you should suspect is the wrong mode in FTP.

If you are FTP-ing (is that a verb? it is now) files between two computers of the same type, such as from one UNIX system to another, you can and should do all your transfers in binary mode. Whether you're transferring a text file or a non-text file, it doesn't require any conversion, so binary mode does the right thing.

Patience is a virtue

The Internet is pretty fast but not infinitely so. When you are copying stuff between two computers on the same local network, information can move at about 200,000 characters per second. When the two machines are separated by a great deal of intervening Internet, the speed drops — often to 1,000 characters per second or less. So if you're copying a file that's 500,000 charac-

ters long (the size of your typical inspirational GIF image, see Chapter 17), it only takes a few seconds over a local network, but it could take several minutes over a long haul connection.

It's often comforting to get a directory listing before issuing a get or put command, so that you can have an idea of how long the copy will take.

The Directory Thicket

Every machine that you can contact for FTP stores its files in many different directories, which means that to find what you want you have to learn the rudiments of directory navigation. Fortunately, you wander around directories in FTP pretty much the same way you do on your own system. The command you use to list the files in the current directory is *dir*, and to change to another directory you use the command *cd*, as in the following example:

```
ftp> dir
200 PORT command successful.
150 Opening ASCII mode data connection for /bin/ls.
total 23
drwxrwxr-x  19 root     archive        512 Jun 24 12:09 doc
drwxrwxr-x   5 root     archive        512 May 18 08:14 edu
drwxr-xr-x  31 root     wheel          512 Jul 12 10:37 systems
drwxr-xr-x   3 root     archive        512 Jun 25  1992 vendorware
    ... lots of other stuff ...
226 Transfer complete.
1341 bytes received in 0.77 seconds (1.7 Kbytes/s)
ftp> cd edu
250 CWD command successful.
ftp> dir
200 PORT command successful.
150 Opening ASCII mode data connection for /bin/ls.
total 3
-rw-rw-r—   1 root     archive      87019 Dec 13  1990 R
-rw-rw-r—   1 root     archive      41062 Dec 13  1990 RS
-rw-rw-r—   1 root     archive     554833 Dec 13  1990 Rings
drwxr-xr-x   2 root     archive        512 May 18 09:31 administrative
drwxr-xr-x   3 root     archive        512 May 11 06:44 ee
drwxrwxr-x   8 root     234            512 Jun 28 06:00 math
226 Transfer complete.
200 bytes received in 63 seconds (0.0031 Kbytes/s)
ftp> quit
221 Goodbye.
```

In a standard UNIX directory listing, the first letter on the line tells you whether something is a file or a directory. *d* means it's a directory — anything else is a file. In the directory *edu* in the preceding example, the first three entries are files, and the last three are other directories. Generally, you FTP to a host, get a directory listing, change to another directory, get a listing there, and so on until you find the files you want; then you use the get command to retrieve them.

You often find that the directory in which you start the FTP program is not the one in which you want to store the files you retrieve. In that case, use the *lcd* command to change the directory on the local machine.

To review: cd changes directories on the other host; lcd changes directories on your own machine. (You might expect cd to change directories correspondingly on both machines, but it doesn't.)

The File-Retrieval Roundup

Sometimes on your machine you need to give a file a name different from the name it has on a remote machine. (This is particularly true on DOS machines, where many UNIX names are just plain illegal.) Also, if you need to get a bunch of files, it can be pretty tedious to type all the get commands. Fortunately, FTP has workarounds for both of those problems. For example, let's say that you've found a directory with a bunch of files in it, as in the following:

```
ftp> cd r
250 CWD command successful.
ftp> dir
200 PORT command successful.
150 Opening ASCII mode data connection for /bin/ls.
-rw-rw-r—   1 root      archive      5248 Nov  1  1989 rose
-rw-rw-r—   1 root      archive     47935 Nov  1  1989 rose2
-rw-r—r—   1 jlc       archive    159749 Aug 16  1992 rtrinity
-rw-r—r—   1 jlc       archive     71552 Feb 10  1993 ruby
-rw-r—r—   1 jlc       archive    220160 Feb 10  1993 ruby2
-rw-r—r—   1 jlc       archive      6400 Jul 14  1992
ruger_pistol
-rw-rw-r—   1 ftp       archive    133959 Nov 30  1992
rugfur01
-rw-r—r—   1 jlc       archive     18257 Jul 14  1992 rush
-rw-r—r—   1 jlc       archive    205738 Sep  3  1992 rush01
-rw-r—r—   1 jlc       archive    202871 Sep  3  1992 rush02
-rw-r—r—   1 jlc       archive     51184 Jul 14  1992 ruth
226 Transfer complete.
9656 bytes received in 3.9 seconds (2.4 Kbytes/s)
```

In this example, you want to get the file *rose* but you want to name it *rose.gif* because it contains a GIF format image (see Chapter 17). First, make sure that you're in binary mode, and then retrieve the file with the get command. This time, however, you give two names to get — the name of the file on the remote host and the local name — so that it renames the file as the file arrives:

```
ftp> bin
200 Type set to I.
ftp> get rose2 rose2.gif
200 PORT command successful.
150 Opening BINARY mode data connection for rose2 (47935
bytes).
226 Transfer complete.
local: rose2.gif remote: rose2
47935 bytes received in 39 seconds (1.2 Kbytes/s)
```

Next, let's say that you want to get a bunch of the files that start with *ru*. In that case, you use the *mget* (which stands for *Multiple GET*) command to retrieve them. The names you type after mget can either be plain filenames or else wildcard patterns that match a bunch of filenames. For each matching name, FTP asks whether you want to retrieve that file, as in the following:

```
ftp> mget ru*
mget ruby? n
mget ruby2? n
mget ruger_pistol? n
mget rugfur01? n
mget rush? y
200 PORT command successful.
150 Opening BINARY mode data connection for rush (18257 bytes).
226 Transfer complete.
local: rush remote: rush
18257 bytes received in 16 seconds (1.1 Kbytes/s)
mget rush01? y
200 PORT command successful.
150 Opening BINARY mode data connection for rush01 (205738
bytes).
local: rush01 remote: rush01
205738 bytes received in 200.7 seconds (1.2 Kbytes/s)
mget rush02?
```

Note: If you find that mget matches more files than you expected, you can stop it with the usual interrupt character for your system — typically Ctrl-C or Delete:

```
^C
Continue with mget? n
ftp> quit
221 Goodbye.
```

You can even interrupt in the middle of a transfer if a file takes longer to transfer than you want to wait.

You also can do an *express* mget, which doesn't ask any questions and enables you to find exactly the files you want, as in the following:

```
ftp> dir 92-1*
200 PORT command successful.
150 Opening ASCII mode data connection for 92-1*.
-rw-rw-r—   1 john1     staff        123728 Jul  1 20:30 92-10.gz
-rw-rw-r—   1 john1     staff        113523 Jul  1 20:30 92-11.gz
-rw-rw-r—   1 john1     staff        106290 Jul  1 20:30 92-12.gz
226 Transfer complete.
remote: 92-1*
192 bytes received in 0.12 seconds (1.5 Kbytes/s)
```

Use the *prompt* command, which tells FTP to not ask any questions in mget but to just do it:

```
ftp> prompt
Interactive mode off.
ftp> mget 92-1*
200 PORT command successful.
150 Opening BINARY mode data connection for 92-10.gz (123728
bytes).
226 Transfer complete.
local: 92-10.gz remote: 92-10.gz 123728 bytes received in 2.8
seconds (43 Kbytes/s)
200 PORT command successful.
150 Opening BINARY mode data connection for 92-11.gz (113523
bytes).
226 Transfer complete.
local: 92-11.gz remote: 92-11.gz 113523 bytes received in 3.3
seconds (34 Kbytes/s)
200 PORT command successful.
150 Opening BINARY mode data connection for 92-12.gz (106290
bytes).
226 Transfer complete.
local: 92-12.gz remote: 92-12.gz 106290 bytes received in 2.2
seconds (47 Kbytes/s)
ftp> quit
221 Goodbye.
```

About, Face!

OK, now you know how to retrieve files from other computers. How about copying the other way? It's just about the same procedure, except that you use *put* instead of get. The following example shows how to copy a local file called *rnr* to a remote file called *rnr.new:*

```
ftp> put rnr rnr.new
200 PORT command successful.
150 Opening ASCII mode data connection for rnr.new.
226 Transfer complete.
local: rnr remote: rnr.new
168 bytes sent in 0.014 seconds (12 Kbytes/s)
```

(As with get, if you want to use the same name when you make the copy, leave out the second name.)

The *mput* command works just like the mget command, only in the other direction. If you have a bunch of files whose names start with *uu* and you want to copy most of them, issue the mput command, as in the following:

```
ftp> mput uu*
mput uupick? y
200 PORT command successful.
150 Opening ASCII mode data connection for uupick.
226 Transfer complete.
local: uupick remote: uupick
156 bytes sent in 0.023 seconds (6.6 Kbytes/s)
mput uupoll? y
200 PORT command successful.
150 Opening ASCII mode data connection for uupoll.
226 Transfer complete.
local: uupoll remote: uupoll
200 bytes sent in 0.013 seconds (15 Kbytes/s)
mput uurn? n
```

(As with mget, you can use prompt to tell it to go ahead and not to ask any questions.)

Most systems have protections on their files and directories that limit where you can copy files. Generally, you can use FTP to put a file anywhere that you could create a file if you were logged in directly.

A bunch of other file manipulation commands are sometimes useful, as in the following example of the *delete* command:

```
delete somefile
```

This command deletes the file on the remote computer, assuming that the file permissions enable you to do so. The *mdelete* command deletes multiple files and works like mget and mput. The *mkdir* command makes a new directory on the remote system (again assuming that you have permissions to do so), as in the following:

```
mkdir newdir
```

After you create a directory, you still need to use cd to change to that directory before you use put or mput to store files into it.

If you plan to do much file deleting, directory creation, and the like, it's usually a lot quicker to login to the other system using telnet to do your work using the usual local commands.

What's with All These Three-Digit Numbers?

You may notice that whenever you give a command to FTP, the response from the remote host starts with a three-digit number. (Or you may not notice, in which case never mind.)

The three-digit number is there so that the FTP program, which doesn't know any English, can figure out what's going on. Each digit means something to the program.

Here's what the first digit means:

- **1** means that it has started to process your request but hasn't finished it.
- **2** means that it finished.
- **3** means that it needs more input from you, like when it needs a password after you enter your username.
- **4** means it didn't work but may if you try again.
- **5** means *you lose.*

Here's what the second digit means: The second digit is a *message subtype.*

Here's what the third digit means: The third digit distinguishes messages that would otherwise have the same number (something that in the computer world would be unspeakably awful).

If a message goes on for multiple lines, all the lines but the last one have a dash rather than a space after the number.

Note: Most FTP users have no idea what the numbers mean, by the way, so now that you're one of the few who does know, you're an expert.

No Names, Please

So far, you have seen how to FTP to systems where you already have an account. What about the other 99.9 percent of the hosts on the Net, where nobody's ever heard of you? You're in luck. On thousands of systems, you can log in with the username *anonymous*. For the password, enter your e-mail address. (This is strictly on the honor system — if you lie, they still let you log in.) When you log in for *anonymous FTP*, most hosts restrict your access to only certain directories that are allowed to anonymous users. But you can hardly complain because anonymous FTP is provided free out of sheer generosity. Here's a typical example of what you see when you log into a large, anonymous FTP host:

```
ftp wuarchive.wustl.edu
Connected to wuarchive.wustl.edu.
220 wuarchive.wustl.edu FTP server (Version wu-2.1b(1) Fri Jun
25 14:40:33 CDT 1993) ready.
Name (wuarchive.wustl.edu:johnl): anonymous
331 Guest login ok, send your complete e-mail address as pass-
word.
Password: (typed my e-mail address here)
230-  If your FTP client crashes or hangs shortly after login
please try
230-  using a dash (-) as the first character of your password.
This will
230-  turn off the informational messages that may be confusing
your FTP
230-  client.
230-
230-  This system may be used 24 hours a day, 7 days a week.
The local
230-  time is Thu Aug 12 12:15:10 1993.
230-
230-  You are user number 204 out of a possible total of 250.
230-
230-  All transfers to and from wuarchive are logged.  If you
don't like
230-  this then disconnect now!
230-
230-  Wuarchive is currently a DEC Alpha AXP 3000, Model 400.
```

```
Thanks to
230-  Digital Equipment Corporation for their generous support
of wuarchive.
230-
230-Please read the file README
230-  it was last modified on Mon May 17 15:02:13 1993 - 87 days
ago
230-Please read the file README.NFS
230-  it was last modified on Tue Jun 29 12:12:27 1993 - 44 days
ago
230 Guest login ok, access restrictions apply.
ftp> dir
200 PORT command successful.
150 Opening ASCII mode data connection for /bin/ls.
total 23
-rw-r--r--  1 root     wheel          782 Aug  9 10:45 .Links
-rw-r--r--  1 root     archive          0 Nov 28  1990 .notar
-rw-r--r--  1 root     archive       2928 May 17 14:02 README
  ... tons of other stuff, this is a very large archive ...
```

When you're logged in, you use the same commands to move around and retrieve files as you always do.

A few anonymous FTP tips

✔ Some hosts limit the number of anonymous users or the times of day that anonymous FTP is allowed. Please respect these limits, because no law says that the owner of the system can't turn off anonymous access.

✔ Don't store files in the other computer unless the owner invites you to do so. Usually a directory called *INCOMING* or something similar is available where you can put stuff.

✔ Some hosts only allow anonymous FTP from hosts that have names. That is, if you try to FTP anonymously from a host that has a number but no name, these hosts won't let you in. This is most often a problem with personal computers which, because they generally offer no services useful to other people, don't always have names assigned.

Once again, PCs don't leave well enough alone

If you are running under Microsoft Windows or some other windowing environment, you may find that the version of FTP that you're using has been *user-friendlyized*. Figure 16-1 shows a list of remote files and directories that you can click on with a mouse. In fact, under the covers these FTP programs are doing the same things you would do with a regular FTP program. You tell it to change directories, copy files, and perform other operations by clicking with the mouse, but what you can do is just the same as it always was.

The full-screen FTP programs can take a while to start up because before you can start pointing and clicking, they have to ask the remote host for a list of file and directory names to fill in the selection lists on the screen.

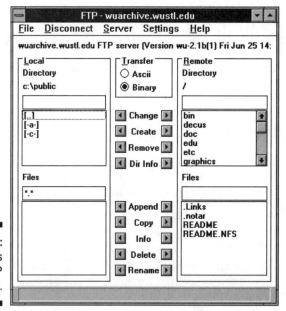

Figure 16-1:
A Windows
FTP
program.

An FTP Cheat Sheet

Table 16-1 gives a short list of useful FTP commands, including a few not otherwise mentioned:

Table 16-1	Useful FTP Commands
Command	*Description*
get old new	Copies remote file *old* to local file *new,* can omit *new* if same name as *old*
put old new	Copies local file *old* to remote file *new,* can omit new if same name as *old*
del xxx	Deletes file *xxx* on remote system
cd newdir	Changes to directory *newdir* on the remote machine
cdup	Changes to next higher directory
lcd newdir	Changes to directory *newdir* on the local machine
asc	Transfers files in ASCII mode (use for text files)
bin	Transfers files in binary or image mode (all other files)
quit	Leaves FTP
dir pat	Lists files whose names match pattern *pat;* If no *pat,* lists all files
mget pat	Gets files whose names match pattern *pat*
mput pat	Puts files whose names match pattern *pat*
mdel pat	Deletes remote files whose names match pattern *pat*
prompt	Turn name prompting in mget and mput on or off

A Few Words from Berkeley

Berkeley UNIX systems and systems written by programmers who (for some reason) *like* Berkeley UNIX, have another file-copying command called *RCP*. The idea of RCP is that it works just like the standard file-copying command *cp* except that RCP works on remote files that you own or have access to. The RCP command uses the same username rules as do *rlogin* and *rsh,* so before you can use RCP, the remote computer must be set up so that you can use rlogin and rsh as well (see Chapter 14 for details).

To refer to files on another host, put the host name followed by : (a colon) before the filenames. For example, to copy a file named *mydata* from the host named *pumpkin* to the local machine and call it *pumpkindata,* enter the following command:

```
rcp pumpkin:mydata pumpkindata
```

To copy it the other way, use this command:

```
rcp pumpkindata pumpkin:mydata
```

If your username on the other system is different from your username on your *own* system, put the username and @ (at sign) before the host name, as follows:

```
rcp steph@pumpkin:mydata pumpkindata
```

If you want to copy files beloging to another user on the other system, the username goes after ~ (a tilde) and is separated by a slash from the filename. For example, to copy a file called *trfile* belonging to user *tracy:*

```
rcp pumpkin:~tracy/trfile tracyfile
```

When you want to copy a whole directory at a time, you can use the *-r* flag (-r is short for *recursive,* computerese for *go into the directory and do the same thing it's already doing*) to tell it to copy the entire contents of a directory, as in the following:

```
rcp -r pumpkin:projectdir .
```

The preceding line says to copy the directory *projectdir* on host *pumpkin* into the current directory (that's what the period or dot is, the nickname for the current directory) on the local machine.

You can combine all this notation into an illegible festival of punctuation, as follows:

```
rcp -r steph@pumpkin:~tracy/projectdir tracy-project
```

The preceding line means to go to host *pumpkin,* where your username is *steph,* and get from user *tracy* a directory called *projectdir.* Copy *projectdir* and its contents to a directory on this machine called *tracy-project.* Whew!

In the finest UNIX tradition, RCP is extremely taciturn and says nothing at all unless something goes wrong. Copying many files over a network can take a while, like a couple of minutes, so you may have to be more patient than usual while waiting for RCP to do its work.

If you copy stuff to another host and want to see if it worked, try using *rsh* to run an *ls* command afterwards to list the directory and see what files are actually there:

```
rcp -r projectdir pumpkin:squashproject
rsh pumpkin ls -l squashproject
```

RCP is pretty reliable. If it doesn't complain, the copy almost certainly worked — but it never hurts to make sure.

Chapter 17
Now That I've Got It, What Do I Do With It?

*N*ow that you know how to use FTP and RCP, you've probably already retrieved zillions of files (well, maybe three or four). But when you look at them with your text editor, you may notice that they're garbage. In this chapter, we consider the various kinds of files on the Net, how to tell what they are, and what to do with them.

How Many Kinds of Files Are There?

Hundreds, at least. Fortunately, they fall into some general categories.

Text files

Text files contain readable text (what did you expect?). Sometimes the text is actually human-readable text (like the manuscript for this book, which I typed into text files). Sometimes the text is source code to computer programs in languages like *C* or *Pascal*. And occasionally the text is data for programs. PostScript printer data is a particular kind of text file discussed later in this chapter.

Executable files

Executable files are actual programs that you can run on a computer. Executable programs are particularly common in archives of stuff for PCs and Macs. Some executable programs are also available on the net for other kinds of computers, such as various workstations.

Archives and compressed files

Often, a particular package requires a bunch of related files. To make it easier to send the package around, the files can be glommed together into a single file known as an *archive.* (Yes, the term *archive* also refers to a host from which you can FTP stuff. Sorry. So sue me. In this chapter, at least, *archive* means *a multifile file.*) After you retrieve an archive, you use an *unarchiving program* to extract the original files.

Some files are also *compressed,* which means that they're encoded in a special way that takes up less space but that can be decoded only by the corresponding *uncompressor.* Most files that you retrieve by anonymous FTP are compressed because compressed files use less disk space and take less time to transfer over the Net. In the PC world, archiving and compression usually happen together using utilities like PKZIP. In the workstation world, however, the two procedures are usually done separately — the programs *tar* or *cpio* do the archiving, and the programs *compress, pack,* or *gzip* do the compressing.

Data files

Some files are not text, executable, archived, or compressed. For lack of a better term, I refer to these as *data files.* Programs often arrive with some data files for use by the program. Microsoft Windows programs usually come with a data file that contains the help text.

The most common kinds of data files you find on the Net are pictures, most often digitized photographs in *GIF* or *JPEG* format. An increasing number of digitized movies in *GL* and *MPEG* format also can be found on the Net.

You also occasionally find formatted word-processor files to be used with programs like WordPerfect and Microsoft Word. If you encounter one of these files and don't have access to the matching word processor program, you can usually load them into a text editor where you will see the text in the file intermingled with non-printing junk representing formatting information. In a pinch, you can edit out the junk to recover the text.

The most commonly used text processing programs on the Net remain the elderly but servicable TeX and troff. Both of them take as their inputs plain text files with formatting commands in text form, something like this:

```
\begin{quote}
Your mother wears army boots.
\end{quote}
```

If you want to know more about TeX, see the USENET newsgroup *comp.text.tex*. Free versions are available for most computers, described in a monthly posting on the newsgroup. Troff is commonly distributed with UNIX systems; see *comp.text.troff*.

Just Plain Text

There isn't much to say about text files — you know them when you see them. As mentioned in Chapter 16, the way text is stored varies from one system to another, so you should FTP text files in ASCII mode to convert them to your local format automatically.

If you encounter a text file that starts out something like the following, you have a PostScript document:

```
%!PS-Adobe-2.0
%%Title: Some Random Document
%%CreationDate: Thu Jul 5 1990
/p1 transform 0.1 sub round 0.1 add exch
 0.1 sub round 0.1 add exch itransform bind def
```

A PostScript document is actually a program in the PostScript computer language that describes a document. Unless you are a world-class PostScript weenie, the only sensible thing to do with such a document is to run the program and see the document. And the normal way to do that is to send it to a PostScript printer. PostScript interpreters, such as *GNU Ghostscript* (see Chapter 18), are also available that can turn PostScript into other screen and printer formats.

A few text documents are really archives or nontext files in drag. See the discussions of *shar* and *uuencoded* files later in this chapter.

Any Last Requests before We Execute You?

The most commonly found executable programs are for DOS and Windows. These files have filenames like FOOG.EXE, FOOG.COM, or (sometimes for Windows) FOOG.DLL. You run them the same way you run any other DOS or Windows program.

Some chance always exists that any new PC or Mac program may be infected with a computer virus. (Because of the different ways that the systems work, it's much less likely for workstation executables to carry viruses.) Stuff from well-run repositories like SIMTEL-20 and wuarchive (see Chapter 18 for details) are unlikely to be infected; but if you run a random program from a random place, you deserve whatever you get. I'm not going to belabor the issue of safe software practices here — for more details see *DOS For Dummies* and *Macs For Dummies.*

Executable programs for workstations don't have easily recognizable filenames, although any file whose filename contains a dot is unlikely to be an executable. Even though nearly every kind of workstation runs UNIX, the executables are not interchangeable. For example, code for a SPARC won't work on an IBM RS/6000, or vice versa. Several different versions of UNIX run on 386 PCs, with different executable formats. Generally, newer versions of PC UNIX run executables from older versions, but not vice versa.

Packing It In

If you retrieve many files from the Net, you'll have to learn how to uncompress stuff. The three main compression schemes are

- ✔ compress
- ✔ gzip
- ✔ ZIP

Compression classic

Back in 1975, a guy named Terry Welch published a paper on a swell new compression scheme that he had just invented. A couple of UNIX programmers implemented it as the program *compress,* and it quickly became the standard compression program. Better compressors are available now, but compress is still the standard.

You can easily recognize a compressed program because its name ends with *.Z*. You recover the original file with *uncompress* (which is actually the same program as compress running in a different mode), as in this example:

```
uncompress blurfle.Z
```

This gets rid of blurfle.Z and replaces it with the original blurfle. Sometimes uncompress is unavailable, in which case you can do the equivalent using compress:

```
compress -d blurfle.Z
```

On PCs, compressed files often have names ending with *Z*, like *BLURFLE.TAZ*. A UNIX-compatible version of compress is available in the SIMTEL archive in the directory */msdos/compress* as *COMP430D.ZIP*. (You need to unzip that, see the section "ZIP-ing it up" later in this chapter.) Frequently, UNIX files are archived and compressed and have names like *blurfle.tar.Z*. In that case, you first uncompress to get *blurfle.tar* and then unarchive.

If you want to see what's in a compressed file without uncompressing the whole thing, you can use *zcat*, which sends an uncompressed copy of its input to the screen. Any file big enough to be worth compressing is longer than one screenful, so you should run it through a paging program like *more:*

```
zcat blurfle.Z | more
```

It's patently obvious

Something that the people who wrote compress didn't realize is that Welch not only published the scheme that compress uses, he also patented it. (Two guys at IBM named Miller and Wegman independently invented the same scheme at the same time and also got a patent on it, something that's not supposed to happen since only the first person to invent something is allowed to patent it. But the patents are definitely there.) UNISYS, which employs Welch, has said from time to time that it might someday start to collect royalties on compress.

So the Free Software Foundation, which runs the GNU free software project, wrote *gzip*, which uses 100 percent nonpatented algorithms. Files that are gzipped end with *.gz* and are uncompressed with the command *gunzip:*

```
gunzip blurfle.gz
```

It turns out that although compress's compression is patented, nobody bothered to patent the *de*compression technique, so gunzip can also decompress .Z files from compress as well as from some other earlier and less widely used schemes. It can even uncompress a ZIP archive so long as only one file is in it. If you have a mystery compressed file, try feeding it to gunzip and see what happens. There is also *gcat,* which, like zcat, sends its output to the screen. So a good way to peek inside a mystery file is to enter this command:

```
gcat mysteryfile | more
```

UNIX versions of gzip and gunzip are available in the GNU files at *ftp.uu.net* and elsewhere, and a DOS version is in the SIMTEL repository (See Chapter 18) as *GZIP123.ZIP* in */msdos/compress*.

ZIP-ing it up

The most widely used compression and archiving program for DOS is the shareware program PKZIP. Zipped files all end with *.ZIP* and can be uncompressed and unarchived with PKUNZIP, available at SIMTEL as well as at virtually every BBS in the world.

Compatible UNIX zip and unzip programs called *zip* and *unzip* (the authors are creative programmers but not creative namers) are available at ftp.uu.net and elsewhere. For situations where the shareware nature of PKUNZIP is a problem, a DOS version of UNIX unzip is available, although it's only about half as fast as PKUNZIP.

Other archivers

Dozens of other compressing archivers are out there with names like *LHARC, ZOO,* and *ARC.* DOS and Mac users can find unarchivers for all of them in the SIMTEL repository. A free unzipper called Unzip is available for the Mac.

In the Archives

Two different UNIX archive programs are *tar* and *cpio.* They were written at about the same time by people at two different branches of Bell Laboratories in different parts of New Jersey. They both do about the same thing; they're just different.

An important difference between UNIX-type archives and ZIP files is that UNIX archives usually contain subdirectories; ZIP files almost never do. You should always look at a UNIX archive's *table of contents* (the list of files it contains) before extracting the files so you'll know where the files will end up.

The tar pit

The name *tar* stands for *Tape ARchive* (it was originally designed to put archives of files on old reel-to-reel tapes). Files archived by tar usually have filenames ending with *.tar*. To see what's inside a tar archive, enter the following command:

```
tar tvf blurfle.tar
```

(The *tvf* stands for *Table of contents Verbosely from File*.) To extract the individual files, use this command:

```
tar xvf blurfle.tar
```

Copy here, copy there

The name *cpio* stands for *CoPy In and Out*. The program was also intended to copy archives of files to and from old reel-to-reel tapes. (It was a pressing issue back then because at the time the disks on UNIX systems failed about once a week — tape was the only hope for restoring work.) Files archived by cpio usually have filenames ending with *.cp* or *.cpio*. To see what's in a cpio archive, type the following:

```
cpio -itcv <blurfle.cpio
```

Note the < (left bracket) before the name of the input file. (If you wonder why it's needed, see *UNIX For Dummies*. The answer is pretty technoid.) The *-itcv* means *Input, Table of contents, Character headers* (as opposed to obsolete *octal* headers), *Verbosely*.

To extract the files, enter this:

```
cpio -icdv <blurfle.cpio
```

The letters here stand for *Input, Character headers, Verbosely*, and *create Directories as needed*.

PAX vobiscum

Modern versions of UNIX (versions since around 1988) have a swell new program called *pax* (for *Portable Archive eXchange*). It speaks both tar and cpio, so it should be able to unpack *any* UNIX archive. (Pretty advanced, huh? Only took them 20 years to think of it.) If your system has pax, you'll find it easier to use than either tar or cpio. To see what's inside an archive, enter this command:

```
pax -v <tar-or-cpio-file
```

(the v is for *verbose* listing).

And to extract its contents, enter this:

```
pax -rv <tar-or-cpio-file
```

(that's Read, Verbose output).

For the Artistically Inclined

A large and growing fraction of all the bits flying around the Internet is made up of increasingly high-quality digitized pictures. About 99.44 percent of the pictures are purely for fun, games, and worse. But I'm sure you're in the 0.56 percent of users who need them for work, so here's a roundup of picture formats.

You almost never find GIF or JPEG image files compressed or archived. That's because these formats already do a pretty fair job of compression internally, so compress, zip, and the like don't help any.

I could GIF a . . .

The most widely used format on the Internet is CompuServe's *GIF* (*Graphics Interchange Format*). The GIF format is well-matched to the capabilities of the typical PC computer screen — no more than 256 different colors in a picture and usually 640x480, 1024x768, or some other familiar PC screen resolution. Two versions of GIF exist: *GIF87* and *GIF89.* The differences are small enough that nearly every program that can read GIF can read either version equally well. GIF is very well standardized, so you never have problems with files written by one program being unreadable by another.

Dozens of commercial and shareware programs on PCs and Macs can read and write GIF files. On UNIX, under the X Window system, are quite a few free and shareware programs, probably the most widely used of which are ImageMagick and XV. You can find them in the USENET *comp.sources.x* archives, such as the one at wuarchive in */usenet/comp.sources.x*. (These are all in source form, so one needs to be able to compile C programs to install them. Grab some choco-late chip cookies and sweet-talk a local nerd into doing it for you.)

The eyes have it

A few years back, a bunch of digital photography experts got together and decided that: A.) it was time to have an official standard format for digitized photographs, and B.) none of the existing formats were good enough. So they formed the *Joint Photographic Experts Group (JPEG),* and after extended negotia-tion, JPEG format was born. JPEG is specifically designed to store digitized, full-color or black-and-white photographs, not computer-generated cartoons or anything else. As a result, JPEG does a fantastic job of storing photos and a lousy job of storing anything else.

A JPEG version of a photo is about ¼ the size of the corresponding GIF file. (JPEG files can actually be *any* size because the format allows a trade-off between size versus quality when the file is created.) The main disadvantage of JPEG is that it's considerably slower to decode than GIF, but the files are so much smaller that it's worth it. Most programs that can display GIF files now also handle JPEG. JPEG files usually have filenames ending in *.jpeg* or *.jpg.*

The claim has occasionally been made that JPEG pictures don't look anywhere near as good as GIF pictures do. What is true is that if you take a full-color picture and make a 256-color GIF file and then translate that GIF file into a JPEG file, it won't look very good. For the finest in photographic quality, however, demand full-color JPEGs.

A trip to the movies

As networks get faster and disks get bigger, people are starting to store entire digitized movies (still rather *short* ones at this point). The standard movie format is called *Moving Photographic Experts Group (MPEG).* MPEG was de-signed by a committee down the hall from the JPEG committee and — practi-cally unprecedented in the history of standards efforts — was actually designed using the earlier JPEG work.

MPEG viewers are found in the same places as JPEG viewers. You need a reasonably fast workstation or a top-of-the-line power-user PC to display MPEG movies in anything like real time.

Let a hundred formats blossom

Many other graphics file formats are in use, although GIF and JPEG are by far the most popular ones found on the Internet. Other formats that you'll run into include the following:

- **PCX:** This is a DOS format used by many paint programs — also OK for low-resolution photos.

- **TIFF:** This is an enormously complicated format with hundreds of options — so many that a TIFF file written by one program often can't be read by another.

- **TARGA:** (Called TGA on PCs.) This is the most common format for scanned, full-color photos. In Internet archives, TARGA is now supplanted by the much more compact JPEG.

- **PICT:** This is a format common on Macintoshes because the Mac has built-in support for it.

A few words from the vice squad

I bet you're wondering whether any on-line archives contain, er, *exotic* photography but you're too embarrassed to ask. Well, I'll tell you — they don't. Nothing in any public FTP archive is any raunchier than fashion photos from *Redbook* or *Sports Illustrated*.

That's for two reasons. One is political. The companies and universities that fund most of the sites on the Internet are not interested in being accused of being pornographers, nor in filling up their expensive disks with pictures that have nothing to do with any legitimate work. (At one university archive, when the *Playboy* pictures went away, they were replaced by a note that said that if you could explain why you needed them for your academic research, they'd put them back.)

The other reason is practical. From time to time someone makes his (almost always *his,* by the way) private collection of R-rated pictures available for anonymous FTP. Within five minutes, a thousand sweaty-palmed undergraduates try to FTP in, and that corner of the Internet grinds to a halt. After another five minutes, out of sheer self-preservation, the pictures go away.

WAAHHH! I Can't FTP!

Oh, no! You only have an e-mail connection to the Internet, so you can't FTP any of this swell stuff! Life isn't worth living!

Wait. There's hope even yet. Several kind-hearted Internet hosts provide FTP-by-mail service. You e-mail a request to them, and a helpful robot retrieves the file and mails it to you. It's not as nice as direct FTP but it's better than nothing. Only a few FTP-by-mail servers exist, so treat them as a precious resource. In particular, observe the following:

- ✔ Be moderate in what you request. When it mails you a nontext file (remember, compressed or archived files are nontext for FTP purposes, even if what they contain is text), it has to use a text-like encoding that makes the mailed messages 35 percent bigger than the file itself. So if you retrieve a 100K file, you get 135K of mail, which is a great deal of mail. If you use a commercial system where you pay for incoming mail, you'll probably find FTP by mail to be prohibitively expensive. (In that case, try a service like AT&T Mail or MCI Mail that doesn't charge for incoming mail, or a public Internet provider that provides direct FTP access.)

- ✔ Be patient. Nearly all FTP-by-mail systems ration their service. This means that if many people are using them (which is always true), there may be a delay of several days until they can get to your request. If you send in a request and don't hear back right away, *don't send it again.*

- ✔ Before you use a general-purpose FTP-by-mail server, check to see if the system from which you want to retrieve stuff has a server of its own that can send you files just from that system. If it does, use it, because that is much quicker than one of the general servers.

The most widely available FTP-by-mail server is known as *BITFTP*. It was originally intended for users of *BITNET,* an older, mostly-IBM network, which has great mail facilities but no FTP at all. In the United States, a BITFTP server is at Princeton University at *bitftp@pucc.princeton.edu.* European users should try *bitftp@vm.gmd.de* in Germany.

Before you send any requests to an FTP-by-mail server, send a one-line message containing the word *help.* You should do this for two reasons: to see if the help message contains anything interesting and to verify that you and the server can send messages to each other. Don't try to retrieve any files until you get the help message.

The message you send to a BITFTP server is more or less the sequence of commands that you would issue in an interactive FTP session. For example, to retrieve a text file with the index of FYI notes from INTERNIC (INTERnet Network Information Center) at *ftp.internic.net*, send this message to BITFTP:

```
FTP ftp.internic.net
USER anonymous
cd fyi
get fyi-index.txt
quit
```

You can enter multiple cd and get commands if need be, but keep in mind that you don't want to overwhelm your mailbox with huge numbers of incoming messages full of files.

How am I supposed to know what files to ask for?

An excellent question. I'm glad you asked. If you're lucky, someone has sent you a note that tells you what to look for. Failing that, you can get a directory listing and then ask for a file in a later request, like this:

```
FTP ftp.internic.net
USER anonymous
cd fyi
dir
quit
```

Many systems have a complete directory listing available as a file in the top-level directory. The file is usually called something like *ls-lR* or *ls-lR.Z*. (The odd name comes from the name of the UNIX command used to create it.) If such a file exists, try getting it instead of doing a zillion dir commands. If no ls-lR is available, but the file *README* is, get that because it often tells you where the directory listing is hidden.

If u cn rd ths u mst b a cmptr

So far, we've considered retrieving text files by mail. But what about the 95 percent of available files that aren't text? For those files there's a subterfuge called *uuencode*. (I mentioned this in Chapter 11, because it's the same way that binary files are sent as USENET news.) The program uuencode disguises binary files as text, something like this:

```
begin plugh.exe 644
M39OGNM4L-REP3PT45GOOI-O5[I5-6M3OME,MRMK76OPI5LPTMETLMKPY
MEOT39I4905B05YOPV3OIXKRTL5KWLJROJTOU,6P5;3;MRUO5OI4J5OI4
...
end
```

You have to feed it through the program *uudecode* to get back the original file. If a file is really big, its uuencoded version is sent as multiple mail messages, in which case you have to save all the messages in the correct order to a file and then uudecode that file.

To retrieve a binary file, you give a uuencode *keyword* on the FTP line to tell it to uuencode what it retrieves and, as always, a binary command to tell it to FTP the file in binary mode. For example, to retrieve the compressed directory listing from */INFO* on *wuarchive.wustl.edu*, send this to BITFTP:

```
FTP wuarchhive.wustl.edu uuencode
USER anonymous
binary
cd info
get ls-1R.Z
quit
```

After you've uudecoded this file, you uncompress it (just like a file you FTP-ed directly) to get the file listing.

If you don't have a copy of uudecode lying around but *do* have access to a *C compiler* (or to someone who knows how to use a C compiler), the first file you retrieve should be a uudecoder. At *wuarchive.wustl.edu* in the directory */info/ftp-by-mail* is a file called *uuconvert.c,* which is a superior version of uudecode that can decode large uuencoded files that have been sent as multiple mail messages.

Macintosh files are often encoded with a different uuencode-like scheme called *BinHex*. See Chapter 5 for details.

Chapter 18
FTP's Greatest Hits

In This Chapter

▶ Lotsa swell stuff for FTP

▶ Navigating in anonymous land

▶ Looking in a mirror

There's Gigabytes out There

Hundreds of gigabytes of stuff are available for FTP, if you know where to find them. (Remember that FTP stands for *File Transfer Protocol*. It's the way you can get files from one place to another on the Net, discussed in Chapter 16.) This chapter suggests some places to look. But first, a few words on strategy.

Ms. Manners says . . .

Please recall that all *anonymous FTP* servers (hosts that allow you to log in for FTP without having to have an account there) exist purely because someone feels generous. Any or all can go away if the provider feels taken advantage of. So remember these rules:

✔ Pay attention to restrictions on access times noted in the welcome message. Remember that servers are in time zones all over the world. So if the server says `only use between 6 p.m. and 8 a.m.`, but it's in Germany and you're in Seattle, you can use it between 9 a.m. and 11 p.m. your time.

✔ Do not upload material unless invited to. (And don't upload material inappropriate to a particular archive — I should hope that this would be obvious, but experience suggests otherwise.)

Mirror, mirror, on the Net

Many archives are *mirrored,* which means that the contents of an archive are mechanically copied from the home server to other servers. Usually, the mirroring systems are larger and faster than the home server, so it's easier to get material from the mirror than from the home system. Mirrors are usually updated daily, so everything on the home system is also at the mirrors.

When you have a choice of mirrors, use the one that's closest to you. You actually want the one that's closest in terms of the number of network links between you and it. But because the number of hops is practically impossible to figure out, use the mirror that's physically closest. In particular, use one in your own country if at all possible, because international network links are relatively slow and congested.

A Few Words on Navigation

All the FTP servers discussed in this chapter require you to log in using the username *anonymous*. For the password, use your e-mail address.

Many servers have a small file called *README* that you should retrieve the first time you use the server. That file usually contains a description of the material available and the rules for using the server.

If you log into an FTP server and don't see any interesting files, look for a directory called *pub* (for public). For reasons lost in the mists of history, it's a tradition on UNIX systems to put all the good stuff there.

The FTP Hit Parade

The rest of this chapter lists some available FTP systems. Each section in the chapter includes the following information:

- ✔ Name and location of the system
- ✔ Particular rules for use
- ✔ Mail or other non-FTP access, if any
- ✔ What's there

If you don't have FTP

Many archives have methods for retrieving files other than FTP. In most cases, the other method is a mail server. To get started, send a message containing the word *help* to the mail server's address, and it will send you instructions on how to use it.

Mail servers are all slightly different and are subject to constant improvement by the people who maintain them, so it's hopeless to try and give detailed instructions here. Generally, you use a few commands to mail a message saying what you want, and the server mails the answer back.

Most mail servers have capacity limits, so if a server has more business per day than its limits allow, your request may have to wait a few days for a response. This is a pain, but because it's free, it's hard to complain.

UUNET

UUNET Communications, Virginia
Only accepts FTP from hosts with registered names.
All material also available for uucp (dial-up system available on UNIX and DOS systems) via 1-900-GOT-SRCS, fifty cents per minute

UUNET is probably the largest archive available on the Net. It has masses of software (mostly for UNIX in source form), archives of material posted on USENET, files and documents from many publishers and vendors, and mirrors of many other archives around the Net.

SIMTEL20

wsmr-simtel20.army.mil
White Sands Missile Range, New Mexico
Mirrored at wuarchive.wustl.edu, oak.oakland.edu, ftp.uu.net, nic.funet.fi, src.doc.ic.ac.uk, archie.au, and nic.switch.ch.
Mail servers: listserv@ndsuvm1.bitnet, listserv@rpiecs.bitnet

SIMTEL-20 is the premier archive for MS-DOS material. It also has a great deal of stuff for Macs, CP/M (remember that?), and UNIX. By the time you read this, SIMTEL itself probably will have gone away because it is an ancient DEC-20 computer that costs the Army a fortune to maintain, but the mirror systems will still be available.

WUARCHIVE

wuarchive.wustl.edu
Washington University, Missouri

This is a large program and file archive. It includes mirrors of many other programming archives, with megabytes of stuff for DOS, Windows, Macintosh, and other popular computer systems. WUARCHIVE also contains the largest collection of GIF and JPEG pictures (all suitable for family viewing, by the way) on the Net.

RTFM

rtfm.mit.edu
Massachusetts Institute of Technology, Massachusetts
Mail server: mail-server@rtfm.mit.edu

RTFM is the definitive archive of all the *FAQs (frequently asked questions)* messages on USENET. Hence, RTFM is a treasure trove of information for everything from the state-of-the-art in data compression, to how to apply for a mortgage, to sources of patterns for Civil War uniforms. Look in the directories *pub/usenet-by-group* and *pub/usenet-by-hierarchy*.

RTFM also has an experimental USENET address database, containing the e-mail address of every person who has posted a message to USENET in the past several years. That database is in *pub/usenet-addresses*.

INTERNIC

ftp.internic.net
Internet Network Information Center, California

This is the central repository for information about the Internet itself, including copies of all the standards and RFC documents that define the network. Also, INTERNIC has information about many other FTP archives available on the Net.

NSFNET

nic.nsf.net
National Science Foundation c/o MERIT, Michigan
Mail server: nis-info@nic.merit.edu

The NSFNET is (or at least used to be) the largest backbone network in the Internet. It has a great deal of boring administrative stuff and some interesting statistics on how big the Net is and how fast it's growing. Look in *statistics/ nsfnet.* For example, in July 1993, the NSFNET carried 38,490,966,200 packets of data, totalling 7,367,382,469,700 bytes, of which 42 percent was FTP data.

NSF publications not related to the NSFNET can be found at *stis.nsf.gov,* mail server *stisserv@nsf.gov.*

The list of lists

ftp.nisc.sri.com
SRI International, California
Mail server: mail-server@nisc.sri.com

Look in the directory *netinfo* for the file *interest-groups,* or the compressed version, *interest-groups.Z.* This is a fairly complete list of public mailing lists on various topics.

The contents of this list is published in book form and sold for about $25, but you can get it by FTP or e-mail for free!

Of Academic Interest

Many sites are full of information that is fascinating to sections of the academic community.

Coombs Papers

Coombs.anu.edu.au
Australian National University

This is a databank of social science papers, offprints, bibliographies, directories, abstracts of theses, and other materials. It's in Australia, so the slant is different from what you get in the United States.

Behavioral Brain Sciences

princeton.edu in directory pub/harnad/BBS
Behavioral Brain Sciences Archive
Princeton University, New Jersey

This is the main meeting point for brain and cognitive scientists. It's also tied into a conventional print journal for those seeking publications necessary for tenure.

EJVC

byrd.mu.wvnet.edu in directory /pub/ejvc
Arachnet Electronic Journal of Virtual Culture, West Virginia

I wouldn't dream of telling you what *Virtual Culture* is. You have to look for yourself. For more info on this journal, e-mail yourself to *m034050@marshall.wvnet.*

Also at the same site is an archive on fractals, chaos, and more of that kind of stuff in */pub/estepp/fracha.*

Kermit

watsun.cc.columbia.edu in directory kermit
Kermit Archive, Columbia University, New York

Kermit is a popular dial-up communications program that runs on practically every kind of computer known to humankind. You can find versions of it for your computer here. If you have some computers on the Internet and others not on the Internet with modems, you can Kermit them all together.

Numerical Software

netlib@research.att.com
Bell Labs, New Jersey
Mail servers: netlib@research.att.com (New Jersey), netlib@nac.no (Norway), and netlib@draci.cs.uow.edu.au (Australia)
(use the closest one to you)

For upwards of thirty years, scientists have been writing programs to do things like *solve sparse systems of linear equations*. If you know what that means and are interested in doing some of it yourself, don't even consider writing any software of your own until you check in *netlib*.

Compilers

iecc.com
I.E.C.C., Massachusetts
Mail server: compilers-server@iecc.com

Complete archives of the *comp.compilers* USENET group along with various documents, bibliographies, and programs of interest to compiler writers are available from this service. It also contains documents for the *Journal of C Language Translation.*

Incidentally, unlike most archives sponsored by large organizations, this one is maintained and funded by a single individual who thinks having an Internet node in his house is fun.

NIH

cu.nih.gov
National Institutes of Health, Maryland

This system contains many NIH documents, including sometimes interesting reports from the General Accounting Office in the directory GAO-REPORTS, such as this:

```
Although GAO notes much good news in the enforcement of federal
milk bid-rigging laws, more work needs to be done.  On the plus
side, the Justice Department continues to aggressively
investigate milk bid-rigging cases and has taken legal action
against a number of violators. . . .
```

The messages from the NIH's FTP system look pretty strange, but it really does work like any other.

Go ask Archie

This chapter gives you only a handful of the FTP sites available on the Net. *Far* too many exist to list them all here, and new sites appear daily.

Fortunately, you have an ally to help you find the FTP material you need: *archie*. See Chapter 19 to learn all about Archie, the on-line FTP locator.

Part IV
Finding Stuff on the Net

The 5th Wave

By Rich Tennant

"I think this answers our question – no, it's not a good idea to try to download the entire Internet at one time."

In this part...

As I've already said too many times, the Internet is *really* big. It's so big that finding all the swell stuff that's available for the taking is itself a daunting task. (Imagine a very large library that has no card catalog, in which each shelf is arranged independently by the person who brought in the books on that shelf.) In these chapters, you learn about four new tools to help you navigate around and find the goodies: Archie, Gopher, WAIS, and the World Wide Web.

Chapter 19
Ask Archie

In This Chapter

▶ Finding files by name

▶ Log into Archie

▶ Send Archie a letter

I Know I Saw a Note about It Here Somewhere . . .

Somewhere on the Internet is probably everything you really want and a whole lot more you might want if you knew it existed. "But how do I *find* it?" you ask. Good question.

If it's software you're looking for, ask Archie.

If you know the name of what you're looking for — or kind of know the name, enough so that you can come up with a reasonable guess — Archie goes running around the world, checking database after database, looking for files that match your description.

Archie servers exist all over the world, but you should pick one close to home to help minimize traffic on the Net. Different Archie servers get different amounts of use, so you may have to try a few before you find one with a reasonable response time. If everything you try seems painfully slow, try early in the morning, late at night, or try sending your Archie request by e-mail (see the section "E-mail Archie" later in this chapter).

Table 19-1 lists several Archie servers you can try. If you try one, and it doesn't let you on because it's too full, chances are it provides you with another list of Archie servers you can try. Eventually, you'll get on.

Table 19-1	Archie Servers
Server Name	*Location*
archie.rutgers.edu	New Jersey
archie.sura.net	Maryland
archie.unl.edu	Nebraska
archie.ans.net	New York
ds.internic.net	U.S.A. (run by AT&T)
archie.mcgill.ca	Canada
archie.au	Australia
archie.th-darmstadt.de	Europe (Germany)
archie.funet.fi	Europe (Finland)
archie.luth.	Europe (Sweden)
archie.univie.ac.at	Europe (Austria)
archie.doc.ic.ac.uk	UK and Europe
archie.cs.huji.ac.il	Israel
archie.ad.jp	Japan
archie.kuis.kyoto-u.ac.jp	Japan
archie.sogang.ac.kr	Korea
archie.nz	New Zealand
archie.ncu.edu.tw	Taiwan

You can access Archie servers in several ways:

- ✔ If you have *Archie client software (archie or xarchie),* you can run directly from your machine (see the sections "Straight Archie" and "Xarchie" later in this chapter).

- ✔ You can telnet to an Archie server (see the following section "Telnet Archie").

- ✔ You can e-mail your request to an Archie server (see the section "E-mail Archie").

Telnet Archie

Unless you have Archie client software available to you locally (try using the command *archie,* or, on a machine with X Windows or one of its variants such as Motif, *xarchie*), you probably want to telnet to an Archie server. However, before you do, if you can, you probably want to start a *log file* (a file in which all of the text displayed in your window is captured) because Archie's output may come fast and furiously, gushing filenames, host names, and Internet addresses that you really don't want to have to copy down by hand if you can avoid it. If you're running on a machine with X Windows or one of its variants such as Motif, hold down Ctrl, press the left mouse button, and select Log to File from the Main Options window. If you're not running X, it's worth asking around to see if there is some locally available program that can capture the text on the screen to a file.

Now, pick a server, use telnet, and log in as *archie,* as in the following:

```
% telnet archie.ans.net
Trying...
Connected to forum.ans.net.
Escape character is '^]'.Archie
AIX telnet (forum.ans.net) IBM AIX Version 3 for RISC System/
6000
(C) Copyrights by IBM and by others 1982, 1991.
login: archie
```

Archie returns with an Archie prompt:

```
archie>
```

Tell Archie how to behave: the set and show commands

Every Archie server is set up with features that you can tune to suit your needs. You may need to change them to make Archie do what you want. Not all Archie servers are alike, and you have to pay attention to how things are set up on the server you land on.

To see how the server you're on is set up, use the *show* command:

```
archie> show
#  'autologout' (type numeric) has the value '15'.
#  'mailto (type string) is not set.
#  'maxhits' (type numeric) has the value '100'.
#  'pager' (type boolean) is not set.
#  'search' (type string) has the value 'sub'.
#  'sortby' (type string) has the value 'none'.
#  'status' (type boolean) is set.
#  'term' (type string) has the value 'dumb 24 80'.
```

You can also use show to see specific values one at a time (try typing **show term**, **show search**, and so on). Though all these values are explained next, the variables you need to pay careful attention to are *search* and *maxhits*. I also advise setting the *pager,* which tells Archie to stop after every screen full of text and wait for you to press the spacebar, to help control Archie's output.

Searching is such sweet sorrow, or something

Normally, Archie searches for a name that contains the string you type, disregarding uppercase and lowercase. So if you search for *pine*, it matches *PINE*, *Pineapple,* and *spineless,* among other things. If you use Archie very much, you find that you want more control over the searching process, so you probably want to use one of the other search methods for matching what you type. How much you know about the name of the file you're looking for should determine the search method you use.

To set the search method, use the *set* command:

```
archie> set search sub
```

The search methods that Archie supports are called *sub, subcase, exact,* and *regex.* The next sections discuss how they work.

Sub method

This method searches to match the substring anywhere in the filename. This search is case insensitive, meaning case doesn't matter. If you have an idea of a character string that's likely contained in the filename, choose sub.

Subcase method

This method searches to match the substring exactly as given anywhere in the filename. This search is case sensitive. Use this method only if you are sure of the case of the characters in the filename.

Exact method

This method searches for the exact filename you enter. This is the fastest search, and you should use it if you know exactly what file you're looking for.

Regex method

Use UNIX *regular expressions* to define the pattern for Archie's search. This is a particular kind of substring search and Archie tries to match the expression to a string anywhere in the file's name. In regular expressions, certain characters take on special meaning, and regular expressions can get absurdly complicated, if you want them to be.

- ✔ If you know that the string begins the filename, start your string with the ^ (caret) to tie the string to the first position of the filename.

- ✔ If you know the file ends with a particular string, end your string with the $ (dollar sign) to tie the string to the end of the filename.

- ✔ The . (period) is used to specify any single character.

- ✔ The * (asterisk) means zero or more occurrences of the preceding regular expression.

- ✔ Use [and] (square brackets) to list a set of characters to match, or a range of characters to match. Combined with ^ (caret) in the first position, square brackets list a set of characters to exclude or a range to not include.

- ✔ You can specify more than one range in the same search. If you need to use a special character as part of your string, put a \ (backslash) in front of it.

For example, to find any files containing the string *birdie,* and ending with *txt,* type

```
prog ^birdie.*txt$
```

To find filenames containing numeric digits, type

```
prog [0-9]
```

To exclude filenames containing lowercase letters, type

```
prog [^a-z]
```

How long do you want to look?

TIP

The *maxhits* variable determines how many matches Archie tries to find. On many servers, the default for this number is 1000 — but for most searches that's ridiculous. If you know the name of the file you want, how many copies do you want to choose from? 10 or 20 should give you sufficient choice. But if you don't reset maxhits, Archie continues traveling around the Net looking for up to 1000 matches.

Remember, too, that Archie's output is going to your screen and maybe to your log file — so think about how much data you can handle. After you decide just how much you want to know, set maxhits equal to that number (say that it's 100):

```
archie> set maxhits 100
```

Table 19-2 lists more set settings.

Table 19-2	Other Nifty Features to Set from Set
Variable	*What It Does*
autologout	Sets how long Archie waits around for you to do something before kicking you off.
mailto	Sets the e-mail address used by the mail command.
pager	When set, sends Archie's output through the pager program *less*, which stops after each screen full of output and waits for you to press the space bar. Using the command *set pager* switches the pager from off to on or from on to off, so do a *show* before you change the pager setting so you don't do the opposite of what you intend.
sortby	Sorts Archie's output in one of the following orders: by *hostname* in alphabetical order or reversed (*rhostname*); by most recently modified (*time*) or oldest (*rtime*); by *size,* largest first, or smallest first (*rsize*); by *filename* in lexical order, or reverse (*rfilename*); *unsorted* (usually the default). You type something like **set sortby time.**
status	If set, Archie shows the progress of the search. Can be reassuring when Archie is very slow.
term	Sets the type of terminal you're using so that Archie can tailor your output (try *vt100* if you're not sure).

Find It!

Archie's basic command is the *prog* command, and it takes the form

> **prog searchstring**

And that's it. That command launches the whole search. The nature and scope of the search are determined by the variables you set or didn't set.

Here's an example. Suppose that I want to find out what kind of font software is around:

```
archie>  prog font

Host csuvax1.murdoch.edu.au   (134.115.4.1)
Last updated 00:23 31 Jul 1993

     Location: /pub/mups
        FILE      rw-r-r—      4107  Nov 16  1992   font.f
        FILE      rw-r-r—      9464  Nov 16  1992   fontmups.lib

Host sifon.cc.mcgill.ca   (132.206.27.10)
Last updated 04:22 11 Aug 1993

     Location: /pub/packages/gnu
        FILE      rw-r-r—    628949  Mar  9 19:16   fontutils-
0.6.tar.z

Host ftp.germany.eu.net   (192.76.144.75)
Last updated 05:24  7 May 1993

     Location: /pub/packages/gnu
        FILE      rw-r-r—    633005  Oct 28  1992   fontutils-
0.6.tar.z
     Location: /pub/gnu
        FILE      rw-r-r—   1527018  Nov 13 16:11   ghostscript-fonts-
2.5.1.tar.z

Host ftp.uu.net   (192.48.96.9)
Last updated 08:17 31 Jul 1993

     Location: /systems/att7300/csvax
        FILE      rw-r-r—   1763981  Mar  5 23:30   groff-font.tar.z

Host reseq.regent.e-technik.tu-muenchen.de   (129.187.230.225)
Last updated 06:26 10 Aug 1993
```

```
     Location: /informatik.public/comp/typesetting/tex/tex3.14/
DVIware/laser-sett ers/umd-dvi/dev
     FILE      rw-r—r—        51  Sep 24  1991    fontdesc

Host nic.switch.ch    (130.59.1.40)
Last updated 04:48  7 Aug 1993


Host nic.switch.ch    (130.59.1.40)
Last updated 04:48  7 Aug 1993

     Location: /software/unix/TeX/dviware/umddvi/misc
     FILE      rw-rw-r—       607  Oct  2  1990    fontdesc
```

As you quickly find out, a great deal of duplication is out there. If you're looking for variety, you can make a series of inquiries that eliminate the stuff you've already found and make subsequent queries more fruitful.

Once you have found it, or some of it . . . what is it?

There sure is a lot of *stuff* out there. But what the heck is it? Sometimes Archie can help you to figure that out. I say *sometimes* because Archie's information is only as good as that provided by the folks who hung the stuff out there in the first place. But for those packages that have been supplied with a description, the *whatis* command might provide you with useful information. The whatis command is actually another kind of search — it searches a database of software descriptions provided by the individual archive managers looking for the string that you provide, instead of searching directories for filenames. If you're looking for software of a specific nature, regardless of what it's called, you can use the whatis command to augment your search.

For example, if I use whatis instead of prog in my search for font software, I get the following:

```
archie>  whatis font
afm2tfm                  Translate from Adobe to TeX
                         fage support)
gftodvi                  Converts from metafont to DVI format
gftopk                   Converts from metafont to PK format
gftopxl                  Converts from metafont to PXL format
her2vfont                Hershey fonts to 'vfont' rasterizer
hershey                  Hershey Fonts
hershey.f77              Hershey Fonts in Fortran 77
```

hershtools	Hershey font manipulation tools and data
hp2pk	HP font conversion tool
jetroff/bfont	Jetroff Basic Fonts
jis.pk	The JTeX .300pk fonts (Japanese language support)
k2ps	Print text files with Kanji (uses JTeX fonts) (Japanese language support)
mkfont	Convert ASCII font descriptions <-> device-independent troff (ditroff) format
ocra-metafont	METAFONT sources for the OCR-A "Alphanumeric Character Sets for Optical Recognition"

Note: The string *font* appears in some of these filenames, but only in the description of others.

You can't get there from here

Archie's great for *finding* stuff but no help at all in actually *retrieving* stuff for you. (Actually, xarchie is a big help, so if you have it, you probably want to use it.) In order to actually get stuff off the Net, you have to do what Archie did to find it in the first place: use *FTP (File Transfer Protocol)* to copy it from the archive where it lives back to your computer. Since you're not likely to have an account on any of the systems that Archie finds, you can use *anonymous FTP* (logging in as the generic user *anonymous*). Once you've logged in for FTP, you use the *cd* command to move to the appropriate directory, and *get* or *mget* to retrieve the files. See Chapter 16 for details.

If you're on a quest for related software, after you have FTP'd to a host that has relevant stuff, you might want to look around in the directory containing the file you know about (use the *FTP dir* command to list the contents of a remote directory) and in any subdirectories near it.

Straight Archie

If you try to type the *archie* command directly, and it returns a comment telling you how to use it, you're in luck. You can use the Archie client software directly without telnetting to an Archie server. One big advantage of using Archie from a command line is that you can easily redirect its output to a file, as in the following:

```
$ archie -ld font > fontfiles
```

(This stores the result of the search in a file called fontfiles, which you can later peruse at your leisure using any text editor or file viewer.) Be aware, however, that the client software is limited and that you may want to telnet to an Archie server in order to take advantage of more of Archie's capabilities. For one, you can't set all the tuning variables described in the section "Telnet Archie" earlier in this chapter. Also, you cannot use the *whatis* command.

Using Archie directly means using a command line that may get complex. You can specify the kind of search, the Archie server that you want to use, and format the output to a limited extent. If you supply the search string and no modifiers, Archie defaults to an exact search with a maximum of 95 matches. For details on selecting a search method, and other available options, see the section "Telnet Archie" earlier in this chapter.

Table 19-3 lists the modifiers you can supply.

Table 19-3		Search String Modifiers
Archie Modifier	*Telnet Equivalent*	*Archie Meaning*
-c	subcase	Set search mode for a case-sensitive substring
-e	exact	Set search mode for an exact string match (default)
-r	regex	Set search mode for a regular expression search
-s	sub	Set search mode for a substring search
-l		List one match per line
-t	sortby	Sort Archie's output by date, newest first
-m#	maxhits	Set the maximum number of matches to return (default 95)
-h		Specify the Archie server to use
-L		List the known Archie servers and the current default

For example, to use the server *archie.ans.net* to do a regular expression search for no more than 50 files that contain digits in their names:

```
$ archie -r -m50 -h archie.ans.net "[0-9]"
```

(Note that the pattern [0-9] is enclosed in double quotes to avoid having it misinterpreted as the name of a file to match locally. In general, put your patterns in quotes if they contain anything other than letters and digits.)

Xarchie

If you're lucky enough to be running X Windows or a near relative of X Windows, and xarchie is available to you, use it. It enables you to set most Archie settings from the main menu and the settings menu. Furthermore, after completing the search, xarchie allows you to scroll through the hosts and filenames and click on the selections that interest you (see Figure 19-1).

After you find something you want, you can choose Ftp from the main menu, and xarchie turns itself into a junior version of the FTP program and retrieves the remote file for you and puts the file in your current directory or in the directory you specify from the settings menu (see Figure 19-2).

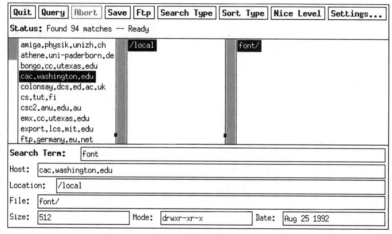

Figure 19-1: Using xarchie to search for files.

Figure 19-2: Xarchie's option menu.

E-Mail Archie

If you're unable to telnet to an Archie server either because of the limitations of your network connection or because you have been unsuccessful in logging into an Archie server, you can send your request to Archie using e-mail. If you're planning to launch a major search and don't want to wait for the response, using Archie from e-mail is a good way to go.

Not all of telnet Archie's capabilities are available to you through e-mail, but you can still carry out a substantial search. To send a request to Archie, send mail to: *archie@servername*, where *servername* is any of the Archie servers mentioned at the beginning of this chapter.

The body of the e-mail message that you send contains the commands you want to issue to Archie. Enter as many commands as you like, each beginning in the first column of a line. Choose from the following available commands:

Command	*What It Does*
prog	Searches for matching names; assumes a regular expression search (regex).
whatis	Supplies the keyword for the software description database search.
compress	Sends the reply in a compressed and encoded format.
servers	Returns a list of Archie servers.
path	Gives the e-mail address you want Archie to use to respond to your mail request, if the automatically generated return address on your e-mail isn't correct.
help	Returns the help text for e-mail Archie.
quit	Ends the request to Archie.

The most common commands are *prog* and *whatis*, which take exactly the same form you use in telnet Archie. For example:

```
prog font.*txt
whatis font
```

Archie has become extremely popular, so popular that it's common for each server to be handling several dozen requests at a time, all the time, all day. That means that telnet or command-line Archie can be *sssllllooowwww*. If it's going to be *that* slow, you may as well send in your request by e-mail and go do something else. As soon as Archie finishes your request, it drops its answer in your mailbox, where you can peruse it at your leisure. An added advantage of e-mail is that if the response turns out to be 400 lines long, it's easier to deal with a 400-line e-mail message than with 400 lines of stuff flying off your screen.

Chapter 20
Gopher Baroque

· ·

In This Chapter

▶ Looking for documents and files with Gopher

▶ Having considerably more fun with fancy Gopher programs

· ·

Welcome to Gopherspace

As the Internet has grown, users have run into two related problems. One is that so much information is available that nobody can find it all. (This is the same problem that Archie addresses.) The other is that umpteen different ways exist to get to different resources (telnet, FTP, finger, Archie, and so forth), and it's getting hard to remember what you say to what program in order to make it do its tricks.

Gopher solves this problem quite well by reducing nearly everything to menus. You start up Gopher, it shows you a menu. You pick an item, it shows you another menu. After a certain amount of wandering from menu to menu, you get to menus with actual, useful stuff. Some of the menu items are files that Gopher can display, mail to you, or (usually) copy to your computer. Some are telnet items that start a telnet session for you to a host that provides a particular kind of service. And some are search items that ask you to enter a *search string,* the name or partial name of what you're looking for, and then use the search string to decide what to get next — more menus, files, or whatever.

Another way to look at Gopher is like directories on your disk, in which some of the entries are files of various sorts, and other entries are other directories. Whether you think of it as menus or directories, Gopher gets much of its power from the fact that any item in any menu can reside on any host in Gopherspace. It's quite common to have a menu where every item refers to a different host. Gopher automatically takes care of finding whatever data you want, no matter where it is. You may use a dozen or more different Gopher servers in a single session, but you hardly know it.

This extremely simple model turns out to be very powerful, and Gopher is usually the fastest, easiest, and most fun way to wander around the Net looking for and frequently finding the information you need.

Why did they name it Gopher?

They named it Gopher for two reasons: one is that the gopher is an industrious little animal, always busy scurrying about on behalf of its family. The other is an obvious pun on *go fer*, because Gopher *goes fer* your files.

The fact that the mascot of the University of Minnesota, where Gopher was written, is a gopher is, of course, *completely* irrelevant.

Gopher has been so successful that an improved version has appeared, called *Gopher+*. Fortunately, the main difference between the two is that Gopher+ can handle more and different kinds of information than plain Gopher can. Other than that, they're so similar that you can think of them as interchangeable, and plain Gopher and Gopher+ items can intermix in the same menu.

The Good, the Bad, and the Ugly

All the services we've discussed up to this point have had a bunch of different client programs that run on different systems (the client is the program you run on your computer, the server is the one on the other end). But by and large, although the clients look different, anything that you can do with one client you can do with another.

Gopher is different. You can do a lot more with a good client than with a bad one. In particular, Gopher is moving into the multimedia era with a vengeance, but the classic UNIX client (the original Gopher program you get at all the telnet sites) only handles text. For anything else, it goes into what one may call *cruel joke mode,* in which it tells you that it has a swell picture that you'd just love to look at, but you can't. A good client, on the other hand, wastes no time in finding the picture, copying it to your computer, and popping it up in a window on your screen.

So in the interest of fairness, I look at two Gopher clients: the original, ugly, UNIX terminal Gopher and HGOPHER, a snazzy Microsoft Windows client written in England by Martyn Hampson. (Both are available for free, so I know which one *I'd* choose.)

Where Do I Find a Gopher?

In your vegetable garden of course, *yuk yuk* — oh, sorry, you mean the other kind of Gopher. The number of systems that have Gopher servers grows almost daily. Most of the servers only talk to Gopher clients, not to mere mortals using telnet. If you have a Gopher client available, use it, because it's faster and more flexible than the telnet version. The exact name of the program varies from system to system. The most common Mac version is called Turbogopher, there's an experimental Microsoft Windows version called Gopherbook that makes Gopher menus look like pages in a book, and so forth. Ask around locally if you don't see any obvious Gophers available.

If you don't have your own client, telnet to Gopher is much better than no Gopher at all. Fortunately, quite a few Gopher systems offer telnet access. Table 20-1 lists hosts offering telnet to Gopher. Because nearly all Gopher servers have references to each other (or at least to the master _every gopher in the world_ list in Minnesota), you can get to any Gopher information from any Gopher system. So pick one close to you. **_Note:_** Unless otherwise instructed, if it asks you to log in, log in as _gopher_.

Table 20-1	**Gopher Servers**	
Country	_Server Address_	_Special Instructions_
Australia	info.anu.edu.au	Log in as _info_
Austria	finfo.tu-graz.ac.at	Log in as _info_
Britain	info.brad.ac.uk	Log in as _info_
Britain	uts.mcc.ac.uk	
Canada	nstn.ns.ca	Log in as _fred_
	camsrv.camosun.bc.ca	
Chile	tolten.puc.cl	
Denmark	gopher.denet.dk	
Ecuador	ecnet.ec	
Germany	gopher.th-darmstadt.de	
Iceland	gopher.isnet.is	
Italy	siam.mi.cnr.it	
Poland	gopher.torun.edu.pl	
Spain	gopher.uv.es	
Sweden	sunic.sunet.se	
Sweden	gopher.chalmers.se	
U.S.A.	consultant.micro.umn.edu	
	seymour.md.gov	
	gopher.msu.edu	
	twosocks.ces.ncsu.edu	
	cat.ohiolink.edu	

(continued)

Table 20-1 *(continued)*

Country	Server Address	Special Instructions
U.S.A. *(continued)*	wsuaix.csc.wsu.edu	Log in as *wsuinfo*
	arx.adp.wisc.edu	Log in as *wiscinfo*
	scilibx.ucsc.edu	Log in as *infoslug*
	infopath.ucsd.edu	Log in as *infopath*
	sunsite.unc.edu	
	ux1.cso.uiuc.edu	
	panda.uiowa.edu	
	grits.valdosta.peachnet.edu	
	gopher.virginia.edu	Log in as *gwis* pronounced "gee whiz"
	ecosys.drdr.virginia.edu	
	gopher.ora.com	
	gopher.netsys.com	Log in as *enews*

Taking Gopher for a Spin

Enough of this Theory of Pure Gopherology — let's take Gopher for a test drive. If you have a Gopher client on your system, type **gopher** (if you're not sure, try it). With any luck, you get a copyright screen and when you press Enter you get a screen like the following:

```
               Internet Gopher Information Client v1.1
                   Root gopher server: gopher.micro.umn.edu   —
  > 1.  Information About Gopher/
    2.  Computer Information/
    3.  Discussion Groups/
    4.  Fun & Games/
    5.  Internet file server (ftp) sites/
    6.  Libraries/
    7.  News/
    8.  Other Gopher and Information Servers/
    9.  Phone Books/
   10.  Search Gopher Titles at the University of Minnesota <?>
   11.  Search lots of places at the University of Minnesota  <?>
   12.  University of Minnesota Campus Information/
  Press ? for Help, q to Quit, u to go up a menu
  Page: 1/1
```

If you don't have a local Gopher client, telnet to one of the systems listed in the section, "Where Do I Find a Gopher?" The items in the menu differ, but the general appearance of the screen is the same for local client Gopher and telnet Gopher. (If you're using Windows and HGOPHER, you see a screen like the one in Figure 20-1, which displays the same items, only more attractively.)

This particular menu contains two kinds of items. The ones that end with / (slash) are other menus, and the ones with <?> are search items, which I consider later. In HGOPHER, the icon to the left of the line tells you what kind of item it is. A large arrow means another menu, and a little arrow pointing into a book is a search item. (If you're wondering what the square icons to the left of some of the items are, they mean that extra Gopher+ info exists for that item. Ignore that for now.)

Although Minnesota is a swell place, gophers and all, let's look farther afield in our Gopher tour. So choose number eight, Other Gopher and Information Servers/. That is, either move the cursor down to line 8 (or go there directly by typing 8) and press Enter. When you press Enter, the next menu appears (*Note:* I'm leaving out the top and bottom headers to save space):

```
 ->    1.  All the Gopher Servers in the World/
        2.  Search titles in Gopherspace using veronica/
        3.  Africa/
        4.  Asia/
        5.  Europe/
        6.  International Organizations/
        7.  Middle East/
```

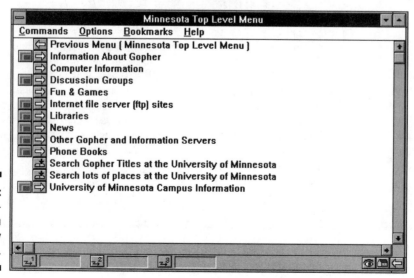

Figure 20-1:
Typical top-
level menu
displayed by
HGOPHER.

```
 8.  North America/
 9.  Pacific/
10.  South America/
11.  Terminal Based Information/
12.  WAIS Based Information/
```

Picking North America and then USA gives you a menu that lists all the states. The menu is too big to fit on a single screen, which it tells you by putting `Page: 1/3` at the bottom (meaning that this is page one of three). You move from page to page in the listing with + and – or to a particular item by typing its number. If you know the name of the item you want, you can search for it by typing / (slash), then part of the name, and pressing Enter, at which point Gopher finds the next menu item that matches what you typed.

Eventually (in this example), I end up at the National Bureau of Economic Research because I'm looking for a position paper they published. The menu looks like the following:

```
 ->   1.  NBER Information.
      2.  About this Gopher.
      3.  Search for any NBER publication <?>
      4.  Penn-World Tables v. 5.5/
      5.  Phone books at other institutions/
      6.  NetEc (Universal) Economics Working Paper Server/
```

These indexes are a mess

If you use Gopher much, you quickly notice that there isn't a great deal of consistency from one menu to another. That's because Gopher is a totally decentralized system. That is, anyone who wants to can put up a Gopher server. It's pretty easy to do, requiring only that the system manager install a few programs and create some index files containing the text of the local menus. If one site wants to include in its Gopher menu a link to an item or menu somewhere else, it can just do so without requiring any cooperation from the *linkee*.

So the *good* news is that hundreds of Gopher servers are on the Net, put up by volunteers who want to make it easier to get to their data. The *bad* news is that almost none of these people have any experience in indexing and information retrieval (for that, you'd need a degree in library science), so the same item may appear on five different menus under five different names, and no two Gopher menus are quite the same.

This means it can take some experimenting and poking around to figure out where people have hidden stuff. But it's invariably worth the effort.

Yoo Hoo, Gopher

Now let's take advantage of a search item, indicated by <?>. When I select it, Gopher pops up a box into which I type words to search for. In this case, I type the name of the author of the paper, and it shortly returns a menu of papers the author has written:

```
Search for any NBER publication: Krugman  —
>     1.  |TI| Pricing to Market when the Exchange Rate Changes
      2.  |TI| Industrial Organization and International Trade
      3.  |TI| Is the Japan Problem Over?
   . . .
```

Gopher search items are a very general feature. In this case, we searched through a local database, but the interpretation of any particular search key is entirely up to the Gopher server that does the search. People can and do write extremely clever servers that do all sorts of searching (see the section "Veronica, My Darling" later in this chapter).

Finally, Some Files

Now we have a menu of file items, which in this case contains citations of the papers we want. Selecting any of the items starts displaying its file on the screen, a page at a time. When the whole file has been displayed (or after you press Q to shut it up), Gopher says

```
Press <RETURN> to continue, <m> to mail, <s> to save, or <p> to
print:
```

If you decide that you liked that file, you can arrange to get a copy of it for your very own. If you press m, Gopher asks for your e-mail address and mails you a copy. If you press s, it asks for a filename and copies the file (invisibly, using FTP) to your computer. If you press p, it sends a copy to the printer. If you're telnetted in, the only option is m, because the disk and the printer may be thousands of miles away from where you are.

If you've dialed in from a PC running a terminal program like Crosstalk or Procomm, you can usually download files using a scheme like *Kermit* or *Zmodem*. At the end of a document, press Enter to get back to the menu, then *D* to download. Gopher pops up a box asking which download method to use. If your access to the Internet is via PC, this is by far the easiest way to get copies of files because it combines FTP retrieval and downloading into one step. (For more info on the mysteries of terminal programs, downloading, and the like, consult *Modems For Dummies* by Tina Rathbone (IDG Books, 1993). Gopher can download any file in its menus, even if it's not text, on the theory that you probably have a program that handles it.

UNIX Gopher Cheat Sheet

Table 20-2 contains all the keys for the basic UNIX Gopher. Except as noted, each key takes effect immediately as you type it.

Cursor up and down to move up and down in the current menu. Cursor left goes back to the previous menu. Cursor right selects the current item.

Table 20-2	Basic UNIX Gopher Commands
Command	**What It Does**
Enter	Select current item, same as cursor right
u	Up, go back to previous menu, same as cursor left
+	Move to next menu page
−	Move to previous menu page
m	Go to main menu
digits	Go to particular menu item, terminate with Enter
/	Search menu for string
n	Search for next match
q	Quit, leave Gopher
=	Describe current item
Bookmark commands	
a	Add current item to list
A	Add current menu to list
v	View bookmarks as a menu
d	Delete current bookmark
File commands	
m	Mail current file to user
s	Save current file (not for telnet)
p	Print current file (not for telnet)
D	Download current file

Leaping Tall Systems in a Single Bound

Some menu items are flagged with _<TEL>_. These are telnet items. When you select one of these, Gopher automatically runs telnet to connect you with a system that provides a service. More often than not, you have to log into the remote system — if so, just before it starts the connection, it tells you the login to use.

If your short-term memory isn't great, you may want to write down the login name that the telnetted-to system requires, because it can take a while before it gets around to asking you for the login name.

To get back to Gopher, log out of the new system. If you can't figure out how to do that, press Ctrl/] and then at the `telnet>` prompt type **quit**. (_Note:_ If you've telnetted to Gopher rather than running it directly, read the sidebar "How many telnets would a telnet telnet if a telnet . . ." before trying this maneuver.)

Some telnet items actually invoke _tn3270,_ a mutant version of telnet that works with IBM mainframes. The principle is the same, but figuring out the escape keys to use can be difficult (see Chapters 14 and 15).

When Gopher telnets to a system, it's not doing anything magical — if Gopher can telnet somewhere, so can you. If you find one of Gopher's on-line systems to be interesting, make a note of its hostname, which is displayed just before connection. Next time, you can telnet there yourself without Gopher's help.

How many telnets would a telnet telnet if a telnet . . .

Here's one of those problems that nobody had to worry about before computers existed. Let's say that you're working on your UNIX system and you telnet to a Gopher system. You use that Gopher to telnet to a _third_ system, and your session on the third system is messed up, so you want to stop it. As Gopher never tires of pointing out, you can interrupt its telnet session by pressing Ctrl/].

But wait a minute. Ctrl-] also interrupts the telnet session from your computer to the Gopher system. If you press Ctrl-], which one does it interrupt? The first session (you to Gopher) or the second session (Gopher to third system)? Both? Neither?

The answer is that it interrupts the first session. But in that case, how do you interrupt the second session? For that, a trick is available: change your interrupt character. Do this:

```
Ctrl/]
telnet> set escape ^X
```

Note: that last line ends with the two keys ^ (caret) and X. This tells the first telnet that henceforth you'll be typing Ctrl-X to interrupt it. Now, if you type Ctrl-], you interrupt the second telnet session, which is what you wanted to do in the first place. If Gopher itself messes up, you can use Ctrl/X to get the local telnet's attention.

Incidentally, once you've gotten telnet's attention, the command to tell it to quit is **quit**.

Veronica, My Darling

Gopher quickly became a victim of its own success. So many Gopher servers are out there that finding the Gopher menu that you want has itself become hard. *Veronica* comes to the rescue. Like Archie, Veronica has a big database of available services. Veronica tracks all the Gopher menus that can be accessed directly or (often very) indirectly from the mother Gopher in Minnesota.

Using Veronica is easy — it's just another search item. You can find Veronica under "Other Gophers" or a similar name in most public Gophers.

For example, one time I wanted to find the on-line computerized *Jargon Dictionary* (which has been around in various forms since the late 1960s). I picked a Veronica Gopher item — there are usually several, one for each of the available Veronica servers — and for the search string I entered *jargon dictionary.* Veronica constructed a custom menu for me, containing only entries that matched my search string:

```
  ->    1.  The Jargon Dictionary File/
        2.  The Jargon Dictionary File/
        3.  The Jargon Dictionary File/
        4.  The Jargon Dictionary File/
        5.  The New Hacker's Dictionary (computer jargon) <?>
        6.  jargon: The New Hacker's Dictionary <?>
        7.  jargon: The New Hacker's Dictionary <?>
        8.  Fuzzy search in "The New Hackers Dictionary"
   (jargon.txt) <?>
        9.  The Jargon Dictionary <?>
        10. Computer Jargon Dictionary <?>
```

Redundant items mean that a resource is available at more than one place. It usually doesn't matter which one you use.

Why did they name it Veronica?

According to its authors, the name Veronica is just a coincidence, unrelated to Archie, because it's an acronym for the true name, which is *Very Easy Rodent-Oriented Net-wide Index to Computerized Archives.*

But I hear that the next index searcher is called *Jughead,* which is supposed to stand for *Jonzy's Universal Gopher Hierarchy Excavation And Display.* This could make even the Easter Bunny a little suspicious.

Making Book

The final Gopher feature is *bookmarks*. As you move through Gopherspace, you often come to a menu that you'd like to revisit later. One way to do that is to carefully note the sequence of menus that led up to the one that you like — but that's exactly the sort of thing that computers do better than people. Gopher bookmarks, then, note your favorite places in Gopherspace.

To remember the current item, press *a* (lowercase), for *add* a bookmark. To remember the entire current menu, press *A* (uppercase).

To use your bookmarks, press *v* (for *view*), and Gopher constructs a menu that contains all your bookmarks. You can use that menu like any other menu and move ahead from there. You can prune that menu if you want by using *D* to *delete* the current item.

I find that I come up with a set of bookmarks that are close to most of the items I regularly use. That lets me get to my regular Gopher haunts in only one or two keystrokes, starting from my bookmark menu.

If you're running the Gopher client directly, your bookmarks are saved in a file so that they're available each time you go Gophering. If you telnet in, the bookmarks are discarded (unfortunately) at the end of each session.

High-Class Gopher

Well, enough of that grotty old user interface. Let's try HGOPHER (see Figure 20-2).

Figure 20-2 shows a fairly typical HGOPHER screen. The column of icons describes the file types. The eyeglasses mean a text file, arrows are menus, and the little arrow pointing at the book is a search item. The 1101 is a binary file, and telnet items (none is shown here) appear as little terminals.

Because Microsoft Windows lets you have lots of windows active at once, nonmenu items show up in windows of their own. Text items appear in the standard Notepad editor, telnet items start a telnet window, and so forth. To save a file, switch from *view* mode (click on the little eye in the lower right corner of the screen) to *copy to file* mode; for any incoming file, HGOPHER asks you for the name under which you would like to store the incoming info.

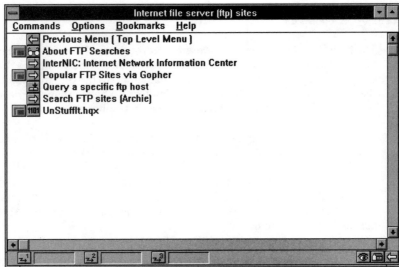

	Internet file server (ftp) sites	▼ ▲

Commands   Options   Bookmarks   Help

⇦ Previous Menu [Top Level Menu]
About FTP Searches
⇨ InterNIC: Internet Network Information Center
⇨ Popular FTP Sites via Gopher
⬆ Query a specific ftp host
⇨ Search FTP sites [Archie]
UnStuffIt.hqx

Figure 20-2:
Typical
HGOPHER
menu.

If you've retrieved a file in view mode, you can keep a copy by telling the application that's viewing it to save the file under a *different* name than the one that HGOPHER assigned. When the viewer exits, HGOPHER deletes the file it made, but if you made another copy, that copy stays on the disk.

HGOPHER understands Gopher+, so it knows considerably more about the formats of files than plain Gopher clients do. For example, Gopher+ can tag a file as being a *bitmapped picture* stored in *GIF* format (see Chapter 17) and can even say that a file is available in multiple formats, perhaps as a PostScript file and also as plain text. The optional icon to the left of the file type icon is the Gopher+ file type, which you can click on to see the types of the file.

HGOPHER keeps a list of viewer programs, so if you have a shareware program that can display GIF files and you enter it in the viewer list, then when you click on a Gopher+ file item which is a GIF file, the file is automatically copied to your machine and displayed with your GIF viewer. It's really cool.

But by far the coolest thing is that HGOPHER can do three things at once. You can click on three file items, and it copies all three at the same time into separate windows. You can continue to browse the Gopher menus while the transfers are happening — subject to a limit of three simultaneous transfers (moving from one menu to the next also requires a transfer) at any time.

This means that you can ask for a large item, such as a high-resolution picture, and keep Gophering along while the picture is being copied. This feature alone would make HGOPHER worth it, even if it *weren't* free.

There's considerably more to HGOPHER, but like most Windows applications, it's much easier to learn by using it than by reading about it.

TIP

It's a breath mint! No, it's a floor wax! No, it's both!

The astute reader (you, of course) may be wondering why Archie and Gopher both exist. They both let you look for files and retrieve them. Don't they really do the same thing?

Yes and no. Their original goals were quite different: Archie is an index to FTP files, and Gopher is a menuing system.

But they turn out to be quite complementary. In Chapter 19, you saw that at least five different ways are available to send a request to Archie (telnet, mail, and so on). The Gopherologists figured that a Gopher search item is as good a way as any to send a request to Archie. They then went beyond that and arranged to intercept the response from Archie so that the directory names that Archie returns turn into Gopher menus, and the files turn into items. This arrangement enables you to use Gopher to retrieve the files that Archie found. A marriage made in heaven, no?

The 5th Wave
By Rich Tennant

"OOPS - HERE'S THE PROBLEM. SOMETHING'S CAUSING SHORTS IN THE GOPHER SERVER."

Chapter 21
We Have WAIS of Finding Your Information

• •

In This Chapter

▶ "There are more things in heaven and earth, Horatio, than are dreamt of in your philosophy . . ."

▶ Finding documents by keyword

▶ Some great recipes

• •

*I*f you're keen on finding all there is to find about a given topic, it behooves you to learn to use *WAIS,* the software that knows its way around the databases of the world. WAIS stands for *Wide Area Information Servers* (pronounced *ways,* incidentally) and it is a system designed for retrieving information from networks.

WAIS's original developers were information-retrieval and database gurus at Thinking Machines, Apple Computer, and Dow Jones (yes, the Dow Jones that publishes the *Wall Street Journal*). Although it was developed to provide access to proprietary databases, like the ones that Dow Jones sells, most of the information accessible via WAIS at this point is available free. Thinking Machines even maintains a CM-5 Connection Machine supercomputer on the Internet for free WAIS access.

With WAIS, you enter a set of words that describe what you're looking for, and WAIS digs through whatever libraries you specify, looking for documents that match your request. Unlike Archie and Veronica, WAIS looks at the *contents* of documents rather than just at the titles. This requires much more work by the server (that's one reason why Thinking Machines is involved — its supercomputer does this kind of searching well), but makes it much easier to find what you want because you're not dependent on someone's coming up with properly descriptive titles.

WAIS also uses *relevance feedback,* which means that after WAIS performs a search it returns a list of documents that seem to match your request. You can then look at some of those documents, and if WAIS didn't find quite what you want, you can identify a few of the documents that matched best (the most *relevant* ones) and tell WAIS to find stuff more like that.

Why Z39.50 is good for you

In an anonymous building in Times Square in New York City, a little known organization called the *American National Standards Institute (ANSI)* labors away to make our lives easier. For example, an ANSI standard for light bulbs ensures that no matter which brand of light bulb you buy, it fits into your socket at home.

The scheme that WAIS uses to communicate between its clients and servers is based, amazingly enough, on an official ANSI standard called Z39.50. (The standards all have strange names like that. It means simply that it's the 50th standard

approved by the 39th subgroup of the library science division.)

Z39.50 defines rules for one computer to use when passing an information-retrieval query to another computer and the rules for passing back the result. Systems all over the world use Z39.50 because most libraries insist on it.

Splicing WAIS onto most existing information-retrieval systems that already speak Z39.50-ese should be relatively simple, so you can expect a lot more WAIS sources in the future as existing library databases get WAIS-ized.

The Bad News about Using WAIS

Unless you're thrilled at the thought of parallel parking an 18-wheeler in the city, you're probably not going to be really excited by the standard UNIX command-line interface for WAIS. The people who *like* WAIS say that the standard UNIX WAIS interface is clumsy, ugly, and nearly unusable. I can't tell you what the people who *dislike* WAIS think about that interface (at least not in a PG-rated book like this one).

Fortunately, there are window-based interface programs available for most window systems (including X Windows and its variants, Microsoft Windows, and Macs) that make WAIS quite usable.

If you do have access to a window-based interface, by all means use it. Not only will you be happier, you can do more than is available through the command-line interface.

I should tell you that all the information accessible by WAIS is also available to Gopher and through WWW (World Wide Web). I tell you this now so that if you lose patience with the WAIS interface program — or if it loses you (not unheard of) — you know that you have other alternatives. Anyway, the following is how you get started.

Go fer WAIS

Using WAIS through Gopher is simplicity itself. Find a WAIS menu in Gopherspace. (From the mother Gopher's main menu, select *Other Gopher and Information Sites* and then *WAIS Based Information*.) From there, select a WAIS source (which appears as a search item) and type the words to search for. Gopher conducts a WAIS search and gives you a menu of the matching documents. You don't get to select multiple sources and you can't use the relevance feedback features (described later in this chapter), but it's *much* easier than fighting with the standard horrible interface.

You also can get to WAIS from the World Wide Web. See Chapter 22 for details.

WAIS and Means

Unless you're fortunate enough to have a WAIS client program available to you locally (try the commands *wais*, *swais*, and *xwais*), you have to telnet to a machine that does. Telnet to *quake.think.com*, the home of WAIS, and log in as *wais*. Prepare to wait for a while because it starts up quite slowly.

New WAIS of thinking

Although WAIS provides access to tons of stuff, it's not exactly user-friendly. You kinda have to learn how to talk to it. For example, if you've just heard about a new cure for baldness and want to find out everything there is to know about this treatment, other treatments, and baldness in general, you can't just start by saying *tell me about baldness*.

Where to look

WAIS begins by displaying a lengthy list of databases that it's ready to search:

```
SWAIS                      Source Selection              Sources: 460
   #            Server              Source                   Cost
 001:  [           archie.au] aarnet-resource-guide          Free
 002:  [      munin.ub2.lu.se] academic_email_conf           Free
 003:  [wraith.cs.uow.edu.au] acronyms                       Free
 004:  [      archive.orst.edu] aeronautics                  Free
 005:  [ ftp.cs.colorado.edu] aftp-cs-colorado-edu           Free
 006:  [nostromo.oes.orst.ed] agricultural-market-news       Free
 007:  [      archive.orst.edu] alt.drugs                    Free
```

(continued)

```
008:  [      wais.oit.unc.edu]  alt.gopher              Free
009:  [sun-wais.oit.unc.edu]  alt.sys.sun             Free
010:  [      wais.oit.unc.edu]  alt.wais                Free
011:  [alfred.ccs.carleton.]  amiga-slip              Free
012:  [      munin.ub2.lu.se]  amiga_fish_contents     Free
013:  [   coombs.anu.edu.au]  ANU-Aboriginal-Studies  $0.00/minute
014:  [   coombs.anu.edu.au]  ANU-Asian-Computing     $0.00/minute
015:  [   coombs.anu.edu.au]  ANU-Asian-Religions     $0.00/minute
016:  [         150.203.76.2]  ANU-Australian-Economics $0.00/minute
017:  [         150.203.76.2]  ANU-CAUT-Academics      $0.00/minute
018:  [   coombs.anu.edu.au]  ANU-CAUT-Projects       $0.00/minute
```

It's up to you to tell it which of the nearly 500 servers to look at. That means that you review the lists and try to determine whether the information you seek is likely to be included in one of the databases whose title you see. No subject is too obscure. WAIS includes such databases as

- ✔ Astropersons

- ✔ Supreme Court

- ✔ Tantric News

- ✔ Livestock

- ✔ Quran (better known as the Koran, the Islamic holy book)

Slogging through WAIS lists

As you look through the list of databases, select those that you think likely contain the information you're looking for. Use ↓ or j (lowercase) to move down the list. Use ↑ or k (lowercase) to move up the list.

Sources are listed alphabetically, and you can page down using uppercase J or Ctrl-V or Ctrl-D. You can page back up using uppercase K or Ctrl-U. The list of sources wraps around so that if you go past the bottom, you find yourself at the top of the list again (and if you go above the top, you find yourself at the bottom).

If you know the name of a source, you can search for it by name using / (slash) followed by the name. You don't have to know the entire name; WAIS searches for whatever string you give it, starting with the first character of the entry. If you give it "USE" it finds "USENET" but if you give it "NET" it doesn't. WAIS always begins at the top of the list, so you should try to use a string that's likely to be unique.

After you see the source in the list, you can position the cursor on it by pressing the number of the source. **_Note:_** Positioning the cursor on the source and actually selecting that source as one that WAIS is to use are _not_ the same thing. That would be too simple.

To select a database, position your cursor on the line containing the database that interests you and press the spacebar or . (period). You probably want to select several databases for WAIS to search if you find many that look promising. If, after looking at the names of all the databases listed, you _still_ don't see anything that looks relevant to your search, you should select the database called _Directory of Servers_ and search it for more possible databases.

What to look for

In order for WAIS to find something in a database — even a database of databases — it needs to know what to look for. You have to supply it with keywords that indicate that the information it finds is likely relevant. For example, when I was trying to find information about baldness, I gave WAIS the following keywords: _bald skin head medicine._

WAIS returned the following:

```
SWAIS                       Source Selection         Sources: 460
  #          Server               Source                     Cost
001:   [          archie.au]  aarnet-resource-guide          Free
002:   [      munin.ub2.lu.se]  academic_email_conf          Free
003:   [wraith.cs.uow.edu.au]  acronyms                      Free
004:   [      archive.orst.edu]  aeronautics                 Free
005:   [ ftp.cs.colorado.edu]  aftp-cs-colorado-edu          Free
006:   [nostromo.oes.orst.ed]  agricultural-market-news      Free
007:   [      archive.orst.edu]  alt.drugs                   Free
008:   [     wais.oit.unc.edu]  alt.gopher                   Free
009:   [sun-wais.oit.unc.edu]  alt.sys.sun                   Free
010:   [     wais.oit.unc.edu]  alt.wais                     Free
011:   [alfred.ccs.carleton.]  amiga-slip                   Free
012:   [      munin.ub2.lu.se]  amiga_fish_contents          Free
013:   [   coombs.anu.edu.au]  ANU-Aboriginal-Studies   $0.00/minute
014:   [   coombs.anu.edu.au]  ANU-Asian-Computing      $0.00/minute
015:   [   coombs.anu.edu.au]  ANU-Asian-Religion       $0.00/minute
016:   [        150.203.76.2]  ANU-Australian-Economics $0.00/minute
017:   [        150.203.76.2]  ANU-CAUT-Academics       $0.00/minute
018:   [   coombs.anu.edu.au]  ANU-CAUT-Projects        $0.00/minute
```

WAIS scores its search results on a scale of 0 to 1000, 1000 being assigned to the item that meets your criteria most closely. (The numbers are only relevant within your search; the best match is always 1000, even if it didn't match all that well.) The search results are ordered, with the highest score appearing first.

To look further at an entry, select it using the same positioning and selection characters that you use to select sources (see the section "Slogging through WAIS lists" earlier in this chapter).

After you select it, item number 001 is revealed as

```
Catalogs of Autosomal Dominant, Autosomal Recessive, and X-
Linked Phenotypes
```

(Baldness is inherited, and a phenotype is a genetically determined characteristic, so this is in fact a fairly promising place to look.) Remember that this was the Directory of Servers. In keeping with the horribleness of this interface, to actually get to the information you want you have to anonymous FTP (Chapter 16) to the site listed and copy the files it found to your computer. Or use Gopher or World Wide Web (see Chapter 22 for details on WWW). As you'll see later in this chapter, not all WAIS interfaces are this nasty. For example, xwais enables you to add a new source to your source list and search from there.

Strictly optional

The WAIS server display format is determined by options, some of which may prove helpful to you. To see and set the options settings, press o (lowercase).

```
SWAIS                    Option Settings        Options: 6
  #     Option          Value
001:    widetitles      on
002:    sortsources     on
003:    sourcedir       tmp/sources-user.13337/
004:    commondir       /sources/
005:    pagerpause      on
006:    maxitems        40
```

The widetitles option provides you with the Internet name or address of the server. If you aren't interested in these, you can turn off its display.

If sortsources is off, the sources are displayed in the order that WAIS finds them rather than by relevance.

The maxitems option determines how many matches WAIS finds before returning.

To actually change an option, select it as you select a source (by first positioning the cursor on the line of the correct option and pressing the spacebar, or by
referencing the option by number). To change a value from on to off or vice
versa, press the spacebar. To change other values, press the spacebar and then
enter the new value at the prompt.

Simpler Searches

WAIS does know about a lot of things, and if you pick the right thing, you may
be easily satisfied. For example, suppose that you want new recipes for cherry
pie. If you select the sources *recipes* and *usenet-cookbooks* and the keywords
cherry and *pie,* WAIS happily provides you with a great selection:

```
SWAIS                   Search Results              Items: 40
  #    Score                      Source              Title Lines
001:  [1000] (cmns-moon.think)  CHERRYCHEESE-1(D)      USENET Cookbook    60
002:  [1000] (        recipes)  shafer@rig Re: BAKERY COLLECTION VEG App  445
003:  [ 917] (cmns-moon.think)  BLKFOREST-PIE(D)       USENET Cookbook    61
004:  [ 760] (cmns-moon.think)  CHERRY-PILAF(M)        USENET Cookbook   110
005:  [ 732] (cmns-moon.think)  CHEESECAKE-4(D)        USENET Cookbook    65
006:  [ 693] (        recipes)  Sanjiv Sin Re: REQUEST Pumpkin Pie       302
007:  [ 654] (        recipes)  shafer@rig Re: COLLECTION BAKERY Pumpkin  291
008:  [ 519] (cmns-moon.think)  PUMPKIN-PIE-3(D)       USENET Cookbook    87
009:  [ 500] (cmns-moon.think)  GRAPE-PIE(D)           USENET Cookbook    57
010:  [ 491] (cmns-moon.think)  STRAW-RHU-PIE(D)       USENET Cookbook    73
011:  [ 482] (cmns-moon.think)  SWEEPTO-PIE(D)         USENET Cookbook    48
012:  [ 482] (cmns-moon.think)  LEMON-PIE(D)           USENET Cookbook    56
013:  [ 481] (        recipes)  arielle@ta Re: COLLECTION: Vinegar PIE    155
014:  [ 473] (cmns-moon.think)  FRANGO-PIE(D)          USENET Cookbook    64
015:  [ 462] (        recipes)  arielle@ta Re: Sweet Potato Pie           180
016:  [ 462] (        recipes)  arielle@ta Re: Cheesecakes               1105
017:  [ 454] (cmns-moon.think)  SPANAKOPITA-2(M)       USENET Cookbook   108
018:  [ 454] (cmns-moon.think)  PUMPKIN-PIE-2(D)       USENET Cookbook    51
```

BLKFOREST_PIE **looks enticing, so I select item 3 and press the spacebar. WAIS goes and gets it, presenting me with the following:**

```
BLKFOREST-PIE(D)          USENET Cookbook          BLKFOREST-
PIE(D)

BLACK FOREST PIE

     BLKFOREST-PIE - A rich chocolate/cherry pie

     I got this recipe from my mom, I don't know where she got
     it. It is very rich, so be careful!

INGREDIENTS (1 pie)
     1          pie crust, cooked
     3/4 cup    sugar
     1/3 cup    unsweetened cocoa
     2 Tbsp     flour
     1/4 cup    butter
     1/3 cup    milk
     2          eggs, beaten
     1 1/4 lb   cherry pie filling (one large can)
     8 oz       whipped cream
     1 oz       unsweetened chocolate, coarsely grated

PROCEDURE
   (1)  Prepare your favorite crust for a  filled  1-crust pie.

   (2)  Preheat oven to 350 deg. F.  In a medium saucepan, com-
        bine  sugar,  cocoa  and  flour; add butter and milk.
        Cook until mixture begins to boil, stirring constantly.
        Remove from heat.

   (3)  Add small amount of hot mixture to eggs, mix well, then
        fold egg mixture into the chocolate mixture.

   (4)  Fold 1/3 of the pie filling  into  chocolate  mixture;
        save  the  rest for the topping.  Pour chocolate mix-
        ture into pie crust.

   (5)  Bake at 350 deg. F for  35-45  minutes  or  until
        center is set but still shiny. Cool, and chill one hour.

   (6)  Whip the cream.  Combine 2 cups whipped cream  and
        grated  chocolate and spread over cooled pie.  Top with
        remaining  pie  filling,  and  the  remaining whipped
        cream.  Chill at least half an hour before serving.
```

```
NOTES
    I use a pre-mixed whipped topping rather than  real  whipped
    cream when I make this pie.

RATING
    Difficulty: easy.  Time: 30  minutes  preparation,  3  hours
    cooking and cooling.  Precision: measure the ingredients.
CONTRIBUTOR
    Darrell Walker
    Hewlett Packard, Cupertino, California, USA
    hplabs!hpesocl!walker
```

To display the next screen, press the spacebar.

If you want WAIS to send you the article, press m (lowercase). WAIS prompts you for your e-mail address.

After you're done with the current selection, press q (lowercase). WAIS prompts you with Press any key to continue. When you do that, you are returned to the Search Results screen. Look through any of the goodies WAIS has brought you.

After you're done, press s (lowercase) to return to the sources selection screen to start another search or q (lowercase) to quit.

For searches of more obscure topics, begin with broad, general keywords. As WAIS finds articles, you can refine the search by choosing more specific keywords.

Windows into WAIS

If you have serious research to do, or if you expect to do it on an ongoing basis, investigate getting access to a decent WAIS client, like xwais on UNIX or WinWais on Microsoft Windows. They provide extra functions that enable you to add sources or even set things up so that when new information becomes available, the client lets you know. Let's try a search with WinWais.

WinWais is a WAIS client that was written at the United States Geological Survey (your taxes at play — er, work). It has some special features that enable you to choose geographical coordinates by rotating and zooming in and out of a picture of the earth, but because most WAIS databases don't include any longitude or latitude to match, I'll stick to the basics.

When you start WinWais, you get a very busy screen bristling with fields and buttons, as befits a complex application like WAIS. WinWais doesn't know about all the possible data sources, so before you do any searching you have to start by searching the Directory of Servers to find sources of interest, then add the sources that it finds to the list that WinWais knows about.

First, you have to select the source to use by clicking the Sources button, the large one at the upper left corner under the File menu in Figure 21-1. At this point, there's only the Directory of Servers source, so click on that to include it in the list to search. Then click Done.

Searching for recipes worked fairly well last time, so let's try it again. Type **food cooking recipes** into the top window and click on Search to have WinWais look for sources on those topics. After a few seconds, it comes back with a list, shown in the bottom window in Figure 21-2.

Rather than scoring sources on a scale of 0 to 1000, WinWais scores them like movies, giving them one to four stars. The first two sources seem promising.

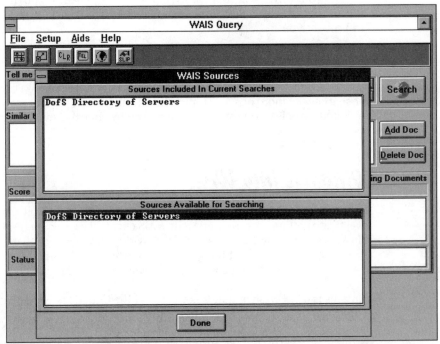

Figure 21-1:
Selecting
the source.

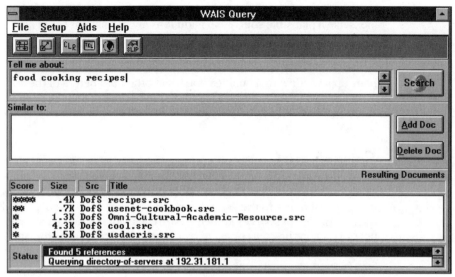

Figure 21-2:
Found some
sources.

To retrieve any found item, double-click on it. After double-clicking the first
found item, recipes.src, WinWais displays it in a window, as in Figure 21-3.

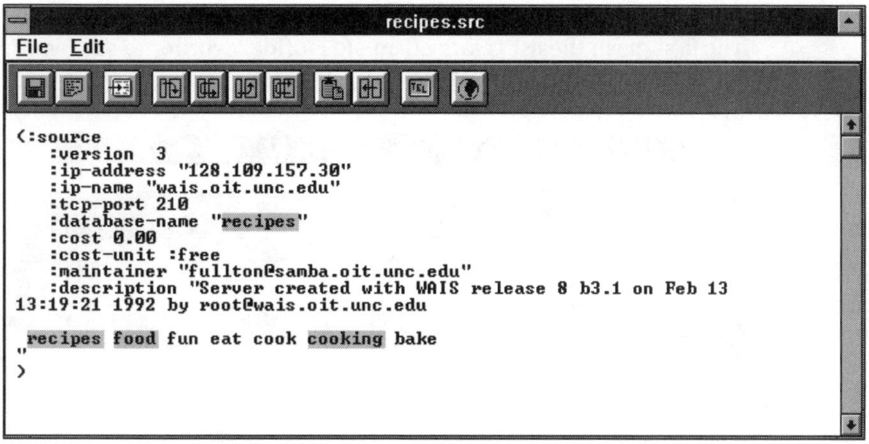

Figure 21-3:
A recipe
source.

The sources are in a special, rather ugly format that WAIS itself specifies. This looks like a plausible source, so I add it to my permanent list of sources by clicking the Save button (the one with the picture of the diskette on it in the upper lefthand corner of Figure 21-3). If this were a regular document, this action would save it to a file. But because it's a WAIS source, the Save button pops up a window that enables you to edit the parameters of the source — something which is rarely a good idea. Click Add and then Done to add the source to WinWais's list. Then add the second source in the same way.

Search ho!

Now you're ready to do some actual searching. First, you add the two sources that you just found to the list of sources to search. (What you just did added them to the list of sources known to WinWais, but *not* to the list to search right now.) You add the sources again by clicking the Sources button and then clicking the two new sources that now appear in the lower window in the Sources screen. Click Done to get back to the main screen.

Performing the actual search is practically anticlimactic. Just type the words to search for (**florida pie** in this case, to try and find a recipe for a pie I had on my last trip to Florida) into the top window and then click Search. WinWais queries each of the sources in turn and comes up with a ranked list of matches, as shown in Figure 21-4.

The first pie in the list is indeed an old Florida favorite, so double-click it to retrieve the recipe, as in Figure 21-5.

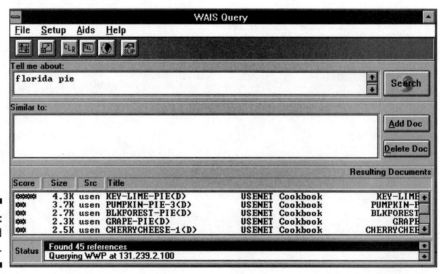

Figure 21-4:
WAIS found
some pies.

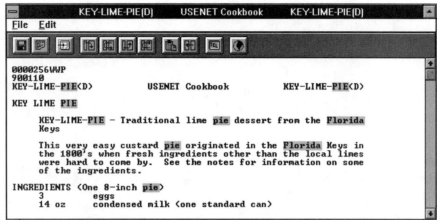

Figure 21-5:
Key Lime
Pie, yum.

WinWais highlights the words in the screen that matched the query. You can save this recipe into a file by clicking the Save button (the one with the diskette); print it by clicking the Print button (next to Save); and do some other document wrangling, which you can find out about easily enough from the help screen, so I won't belabor it here. After you're done looking at the recipe (and saving it if you want to), return to the main screen by selecting File⇨Done from the menu.

Relevantly speaking

Having saved a copy of the Key Lime Pie recipe, scroll down through the list of documents to look for other interesting ones. A recipe for Pumpkin Cake looks interesting. Are other similar recipes available? That's where *relevance searching* comes in. Click once on the interesting recipe (clicking once selects it without going out to the server to retrieve the whole thing) and drag it into the middle window. That action adds it to the *Similar to* list of relevant documents. Click on Search again, and WAIS now looks for more recipes like Pumpkin Cake, as in Figure 21-6.

As you might expect, the Pumpkin Cake recipe itself is the most relevant here, although some other possibilities look interesting.

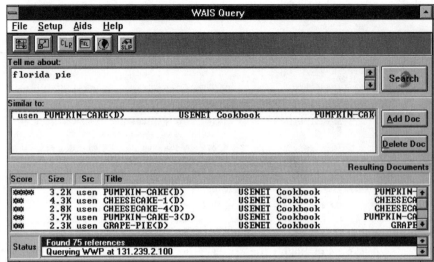

Figure 21-6:
Seeking
pumpkin
cakes.

WAISing into the Sunset

With a decent client program, WAIS is an extremely powerful way to search through databases. Several hundred free WAIS sources are available on the Internet, and many more proprietary ones are coming on-line. Dow Jones, for example, participated in the WAIS work to use for their on-line news service, which contains the text of many years of the *Wall Street Journal* and other magazines. WAIS is probably the future of information retrieval and library searching, so it's worth learning now.

Chapter 22
It's More Than Super, It's Hyper: the World Wide Web

● ●

● ●

*I*f you're beginning to think there's got to be an easier way, there is. One giant leap forward in making computers useful for ordinary mortals has been the attempt to improve the *interaction* between computers and ordinary mortals. The efforts that have been put forth toward making computers do what humans would do seem to be much more fruitful than the typical approach of making humans act like computers.

The *World Wide Web* — or *WWW* or the *Web* to its friends — is a major step forward in making the process of looking for information fast, powerful, and intuitive. WWW is based on a technology called *hypertext* (or now, more accurately, *hypermedia,* because it can handle graphics and sounds as well as text). Hypertext was first described almost twenty years ago but only now is it finding its way into widely-used software.

Although the hypertext concepts have been around for a while, creating the technology to bring them to life has been a challenge. So, even though hypertext may be the *coolest* way to retrieve data, it's not necessarily the *quickest.* Setting up information for hypertext retrieval is still very cumbersome and that's one more reason why information isn't already available in hypertext form.

Hypertext: a reminiscence

The term and concept of *hypertext* were invented around 1969 by Ted Nelson, a famous computer visionary who's been thinking about the relationship between computers and literature for at least 25 years now — starting back when most people would have considered it stupid to think that such a relationship could *exist*. Twenty years ago, he claimed that people would have computers in their pockets with leatherette cases and racing stripes. (I haven't seen any racing stripes yet, but otherwise he was dead on.)

Back in 1970, Ted Nelson told me that we'd all have little computers with inexpensive screens on our desks with super whizzo graphical hypertext systems. "Naah," I said. "For hypertext, you'll want a mainframe with gobs of memory and a high-resolution screen." We were both right, of course, because what we have on our desks in 1993 are little computers that are faster than 1970s mainframes and have more memory and better screens.

Various hypertext projects have come and gone over the years, including one at Brown University (of which Ted was a part) and one at the Stanford Research Institute (which was arguably the most influential project in computing history because it invented screen windows and mice).

Ted's own hypertext system, Project Xanadu, has been in the works for about 15 years, under a variety of financing and management setups, but with many of the same people slogging along making it work. The project addresses many issues that other systems don't. In particular, Ted figured out how to pay authors for their work in a hypertext system, even when one document has pieces linked from others and the ensuing document consists almost entirely of a compendium of pieces of other documents. For a decade, I've been hearing every year that Xanadu will hit the streets the next year. This year I hope they're right.

What's the Big Deal?

If you've ever done research in an area you know little about, you found yourself in a library, staring at the card catalog. You begin with one bit of information, such as a subject or a name. You look up one subject and begin reading the cards. All kinds of new ideas flash into your mind about ways you could continue your search with other subjects or other names. Even if you write down all the ideas, you inevitably have to pick one of them to follow and have to leave your current drawer and find the next. Here you begin again, and again your search may send you in an entirely different direction.

As you follow more and more leads, you may need to back up, look at choices you made earlier, and see what trying a different tack would bring. If you take careful notes, this may be relatively easy, but chances are you have to retrace many of your steps.

Hypertext organizes data to help this kind of information retrieval. It keeps one finger in one drawer and another finger in another drawer and so on to help you to go down one path and then go back and try a different one. And hypertext can have a hundred or more fingers in drawers all over the *planet*. (You might think of it as an extremely large but friendly alien centipede made of information.)

In traditional libraries (both the kinds with books and the kinds in computers), information is organized hierarchically yet somewhat arbitrarily, in the order it's found or in alphabetical order. These orders reflect nothing of the relationships among different pieces of information. In the world of hypertext, information is organized in relationship to other information. In fact, the relationships between different pieces of information are often much more valuable than the pieces themselves.

Hypertext also allows the same set of information to be arranged in multiple ways at the same time. In a conventional library, a book can only be on one shelf at a time, so a book on mental health, for example, is shelved under Medicine or under Psychology, but it can't be in both places at once. Hypertext is not so limited, and it's no problem to have links from both medical topics and psychological topics to the same document.

For example, let's say that you are interested in what influenced a particular historical person. You can begin by looking at the basic biographical information: where and when she was born, the names of her parents, her religion, and other basic stuff like that. Then you can expand on each fact by learning what else was happening at that time in her part of the world, what was happening in other parts of the world, and what influence her religion may have had on her. You draw a picture by pulling together all of these aspects and understanding their connections — a picture that's hard to draw from just lists of names and dates.

A hypertext system creates the connections between pieces of information that allow you to easily find related information. As you draw the connections between the pieces of information, you can start to envision the web created by the links between the pieces. What's so remarkable about WWW (the Web) is that it connects pieces of information from all around the world, on different machines, in different databases, all pretty much seamlessly (a feat you'd be hard pressed to match with a card catalog).

My Spider Sense Is Tingling

Different WWW servers have implemented hypertext *browsing* programs differently. (They're called *browsers* rather than *readers* partly because you usually spend more time puttering about the links than reading any individual document, and also because they all potentially give you the ability to add links and comments of your own.) If you understand what hypertext is about, you more easily understand how it works through any particular browser. Furthermore, if you find that the browser you're using is particularly difficult, you can try another. Different browsing programs make different assumptions about their output and your machine, and a different one may be more suitable for you. It's like underwear — you like what you like, and nobody's going to persuade you any differently.

Very few Internet hosts have their own WWW browsers installed yet, so you begin by telnetting to a WWW server (see Chapter 14 for more details about telnet). Three public servers are

> ✔ *info.cern.ch* (Switzerland)
> ✔ *www.njit.edu* (New Jersey)
> ✔ *hnsource.cc.ukans.edu* (Kansas)

Each server has a different hypertext browsing program, so it's worth trying all three to see which one you prefer.

Using the University of Kansas machine, log in as **www**:

```
           Welcome to WWW at the University of Kansas

     You are using a new WWW Product called Lynx.  For more
           information about obtaining and installing Lynx
           please choose About Lynx

           The current version of Lynx is 2.0.10.  If you are
running
           an earlier version PLEASE UPGRADE!

                        WWW sources
           For a description of WWW choose Web Overview
           About the WWW Information Sharing project
           WWW Information By Subject
           WWW Information By Type

                        Lynx sources
                 University of Kansas CWIS
                 History Net Archives

                        Gopher sources
           University of Minnesota Gopher Server (Home of the
Gopher)
           All the Gopher servers in the world
```

In this WWW system, the hypertext links are highlighted. Use the arrow keys to navigate to the area that interests you and press Enter. In other systems, such as *www.njit.edu*, hypertext links are indicated by numbers enclosed in square brackets, and you choose by number the link that interests you:

```
     NJIT WWW entry point[1]
     gopher://chronicle.merit.edu/[2]
     Overview of the Web[3]
     NJIT Information Technology and World Wide Web Help[4]
```

The information the WWW systems have available is largely the same because at this point not all that much WWW data is available, and it's all linked together. I use the University of Kansas server in my example because from my machine it behaves the best. I want to see what topics are available, so I choose **By Subject** by positioning the cursor there and pressing Enter. Here's part of what it shows:

Mathematics	**CIRM library** (french).The **International Journal** of Analytical and Experimental Modal Analysis. Complex systems
Meteorology	**US weather,** state by state. **Satelite Images. Weather index. ANU weather services**
Movies	Movie database browser.
Music	**MIDI interfacing, Song lyrics** (apparently disabled for copyright reasons), **UK Independant Music.**

I love the movies, so I move the cursor to Movie database browser and press Enter again.

[IMAGE]A Hypertext move the Movie

[IMAGE]

   Aug 25th.. **Images Soon ?**

    [IMAGE]

Select the type of search you'd like to perform:-

      Movie people.....(multi Oscar winners) or

      Movie titles .....(multi Oscar winners)

Searches the "rec.arts.movies" movie database system, maintained by Col Needham et-al, using a mixture of **Col Needham's movie database package v2.6,** and specially written scripts and programs to search the databases.

Here is some information on list maintainers.
Local users can access the database from the command line. See the **Movie** Database directory in /well/lot.

If you have a comment or suggestion, it can be recorded **here**

    [IMAGE]

HERE is a pre-1986 movie information gopher server. (at Manchester UK)

rec.arts.**movies.reviews** can be found here

This is just a taste of the wonderful things WWW can do. Not only can it connect you to all the databases that it highlights, but it can even send Gopher on a search for you. The [IMAGE] blocks show where links to pictures are; telnet only handles text rather than pictures, so it can't show these links. (If you're fortunate enough to have a WWW browser on your own computer, it pops up a window with the appropriate picture if you select an [IMAGE] block.)

The Gopher server I have selected contains information about movies dated before 1986. It asks me for a string to search. I type in **Nicholson**, and it responds with

```
HERE:   Nicholson

(FILE) THE BRIDGE ON THE RIVER KWAI
(FILE) CHINATOWN
(FILE) THE LAST DETAIL
(FILE) ONE FLEW OVER THE CUCKOO'S NEST
(FILE) EASY RIDER
(FILE) THE SHINING
(FILE) THE POSTMAN ALWAYS RINGS TWICE
(FILE) FIVE EASY PIECES
(FILE) TERMS OF ENDEARMENT
(FILE) REDS
(FILE) CARNAL KNOWLEDGE
(FILE) THE LAST TYCOON
```

and pages more, with each movie title linked to more information about the movie. In other instances, WWW happily launches WAIS for you if the links happen to lead in that direction (see Chapter 21 for more on WAIS).

Fame and Fortune

Another wonderful feature of WWW is that the network is ever-expanding, and *you* can add to it. While viewing the information from the Gopher server, WWW prompted me for my comments. WWW solicits comments at different levels so that you can really be involved in its growth. You can comment on the topic you're reading about, a new topic you want to discus, WWW in general, this version of WWW, or whatever. You can enter your comments with your name or anonymously. WWW even lets you request a response from subsequent readers.

Another Way around the Web

The material that WWW displays resides on many different servers all around the world; WWW automatically contacts servers as needed when you move to materials that they contain. As well as providing a subject list as a starting point for *Web-walking*, WWW also provides access to many other network services, such as WAIS (see Chapter 21), telnet (Chapter 15), anonymous FTP (Chapter 16), Network News (Chapter 11), Gopher (Chapter 20), WHOIS, and X.500 (the last two are white pages directory services mentioned in Chapter 9). The Web provides lists of all of these kinds of servers (and indexes into these servers) so that you can literally go from machine to machine and look at all that's available. For example, here is part of the WAIS index provided by WWW:

```
WAIS INDEXES BY NET DOMAIN

Generated automatically at CERN from the TMC directory of serv-
ers. See also: by index name, by Subject.

ariel.its.unimelb.EDU.AU       unimelb-research,
orion.lib.Virginia.EDU         bryn-mawr-clasical-review,
wais.wu-wien.ac.at             cerro-l, earlym-l, rec.music.early,
archie.au                      aarnet-resource-guide,
                               archie.au-amiga-readmes,
                               archie.au-ls-lRt,
                               archie.au-mac-readmes,
                               archie.au-pc-readmes,
                               au-directory-of-servers,
services.canberra.edu.adir     sun-fixes,
wraith.cs.uow.edu.au           acronyms, netlib-index,
uniwa.uwa.oz.au                netinfo-biblio, netinfo-docs,
                               s-archive, sas-archive,
                               spss-archive, stats-archive,
alfred.ccs.carleton.ca         amiga-slip, ocunix-faq,
qusuna.qucis.queensu.ca        software-eng,
```

After you select a server, WWW connects you to it and allows you to search. Again, you can start up WAIS yourself, but WWW integrates it all into one big Web. WWW is a uniquely powerful way to look for and retrieve information, and I'm sure we'll be seeing more of it in the future. If you can only persuade your system manager to install one of the new services (such as Archie, Gopher, WAIS), WWW is definitely the way to go.

NAVIGATE

Battle of the titans: Gopher vs. WAIS vs. WWW

OK, I've told you that you can use Gopher to search Archie and WAIS, you can use WWW to search Gopher, and you can use WWW to search WAIS. If you can use any of them to search anything, which one should you use and when? Confusion reigns! You need guidance.

Well, you're in luck: *Guidance* is my middle name. (Actually, it's *Robert*, but I've been thinking of changing it.) Here are some rules of thumb.

- Use Archie if you're trying to locate software or files available for FTP.

- Use Gopher if you're looking for something for which you suspect someone has built a Gopher menu. (After Gophering around for a while, you learn what to suspect.)

- Use WAIS to search documents by content.

- Use WWW if you're not sure what you're looking for because it subsumes all of the previous ones.

- Archie servers are all overloaded, so it's slow no matter how you use it. Use a local Archie client, telnet, or e-mail as the mood strikes you.

- If you have a local Gopher, WAIS, or WWW client (that is, a program on your own machine), use it rather than telnetting to some other system, because your client is faster and easier to use than telnet. Local Gopher clients can retrieve files directly to your disk, screen, and (if you have one) loud-speaker, whereas telnet versions have to e-mail them to you or download them using *Kermit* or *zmodem* (PC telecommunication software).

- If at all possible, avoid the standard-text WAIS program (the one you get if you telnet to *quake.think.com*) because it's very hard to use. Use a local, graphical WAIS, like WinWais or xwais, if available; otherwise use Gopher or WWW to get to WAIS. ***Note:*** Relevance feedback is only available with the local WAIS clients, and not via telnet, Gopher, or WWW.

- If you're not sure which to use, start with WWW. If you find that what you want is actually provided by Gopher or WAIS, switch.

Part V
The Part of Tens

The 5th Wave   By Rich Tennant

"I DON'T THINK OUR NEWEST NETWORK CONFIGURATION IS GOING TO WORK. ALL OF OUR TRANSMISSIONS FROM OHIO SEEM TO BE COMING IN OVER MY ELECTRIC PENCIL SHARPENER."

In this part...

Some things just don't fit anywhere else in the book, so they are grouped into lists. By the strangest coincidence, exactly *ten* facts happen to be in each list. (*Note to the literal-minded:* You may have to cut off and/or glue on some fingers to make your version of ten match up with mine. Perhaps it would be easier just to take my word for it.)

Chapter 23

Ten Common Problems and How to Avoid Them

The Network's Dead!

Well, actually, it's probably not. For example, let's say that you try to use a service on some remote computer and you can't get to it. You know that you didn't change anything on *your* computer, so the network and/or the remote computer must be kaput, right? Not so fast.

Many moving parts (conceptually speaking) lie between your computer and a computer on the other side of the country (or world). The Internet is a bunch of interconnected networks, so your data probably traverses a dozen different networks between here and there. In theory, then, a failure could come from any one of them. In practice, the networks in the middle are *high-speed, shared* networks with *multiple redundant paths, automatic rerouting, 24/7 monitoring,* and many other buzzword features that mean: A.) they're not likely to break, and B.) even if they *do* break, bells start ringing in less than a second, network connections are rerouted, and people fix things.

Consider this: In more than 20 years, the Internet has experienced only one major backbone failure, and that was due to a software glitch, not to cable failures. On the other hand, if you accidentally kick your computer's network connection out of the wall, who's going to notice but you? So here's a list of things to check.

Is your computer working?

Does your computer act normally when you tell it to do nonnetwork things? Yes, I know it's obvious, but it never hurts to check. (True story: "Hello, help desk? My computer won't boot up." "Is it plugged into the wall correctly?" "I can't tell, the power failed and all the lights are out.")

Is your computer connected to its local network?

The next step is to see if you have any connection to the outside world at all. If you do, the best command to use is *ping,* which sends packets to another host that is supposed to echo them back. The ping command depends only on the very lowest level of networking software. So if ping can't reach another computer, that strongly suggests either a network break or that the other computer is dead. For some reason, the ping command is often hidden away, so you have to type something like **/etc/ping** or **/usr/ucb/ping** to run it. (Find out what the correct incantation is and make a note of it.) When you run ping, its output looks something like this:

```
% ping nearbyhost
PING nearbyhost: 56 data bytes
64 bytes from 127.186.80.3: icmp_seq=0. time=9. ms
64 bytes from 127.186.80.3: icmp_seq=1. time=9. ms
64 bytes from 127.186.80.3: icmp_seq=2. time=9. ms
64 bytes from 127.186.80.3: icmp_seq=3. time=9. ms
^C
—nearbyhost PING Statistics—
4 packets transmitted, 4 packets received, 0% packet loss
round-trip (ms)  min/avg/max = 9/9/9
```

The ping command usually runs until you interrupt it with Ctrl-C or the equivalent. The times it reports are the approximate times it took for each message to reach the other computer and come back, measured in milliseconds (1/1,000 of a second, abbreviated *ms*). For computers on the same Ethernet, the time should be in the vicinity of 10 ms. For computers on the other side of the world, it can be as much as 2,000 or 3,000 ms — two or three seconds. Now and then a ping can get lost in the network. If it only happens now and then, it's no problem. But if it happens frequently (more than ten percent of the time) you have either severe network congestion or, more likely, a flaky network connection with one of the computers.

If you don't have ping, any other network command like *finger* or *telnet* will do. First, see if you can contact a nearby computer — ideally one on the same physical network cable. (The closer another computer is to you, the more likely it's on the same cable. One in the next office is ideal.) Three results are possible:

- Your computer can't even find the other computer.

- Your computer can find the other computer, but the other computer doesn't answer.

- It works.

If it works, you know that your computer and local network are OK, so you can go on to the next step.

If your computer claims that no such computer as the one you're trying to contact exists, you may have lost contact with your *name server* — the computer whose job it is to translate host names to four-part numeric addresses. Assuming that you know the numeric address of your neighboring machine, try contacting it using the numeric address, typed as four numbers separated by periods. (If you don't know the other machine's number, try going to that machine and telling it to ping itself, which should — among other things — report its address. Failing that, ask a local expert where the list of addresses can be found.)

If your computer can contact the neighbor using the numeric address but not the name, you have name server trouble. Contact an expert (politely) and ask for help. If you can report that a numeric address works but the corresponding name doesn't, you narrow down the possibilities considerably. If you want to do some more sleuthing and you know which computer on your local network is the name server (usually the same one that has the big disk, if you use remote files), try pinging it both by name and number to see if the route to that machine is broken.

If your computer tries to contact the other computer and can't, the most likely problem is that your computer has come unhooked from the network. Other than checking whether you've accidentally knocked the network cable out, you can't do much about this. You have to ask for help.

Note to users with computers on Token Rings: If your local network uses a Token Ring (the cable looks like phone wire and uses big square connectors — see Chapter 3), and you unhook your computer by mistake, just plugging the connector back in isn't enough to get you back on the network. Your computer has to do a *network insertion,* a special processing step that reintroduces itself to its neighbors. The insertion requires at least restarting your computer's network software and may require a complete reboot. Check locally. And put the cable someplace where people are less likely to trip over it.

Is the other end OK?

If you can get in touch with a neighboring computer, that pretty much proves that your computer is OK. The next thing to think about is whether the computer at the other end is on. In particular, what are its scheduled hours? Some services are only available part-time. The United States Library of Congress LOCIS system, for example, is only available during library hours. Or maybe they're doing some maintenance at the other end. In what time zone is the other computer? If you're in Los Angeles, it may be 5 p.m. there, but if the other computer is in France, it's 2 a.m. there — a prime time for hardware and software maintenance.

Things to know before your network breaks

It's much easier to diagnose network foul-ups if you gather a few important facts before it breaks. Here's a minimal set.

Your computer's host name _____

Its numeric address _____._____._____._____

Your name server _____

Name server's numeric address
_____._____._____._____

A nearby computer _____
_____

Its numeric address _____._____._____._____

A remote computer _____
_____

Its numeric address _____._____._____._____

Your ping command _____
_____

Also, some companies use low-cost, dial-up access to connect their local network to the Internet, which means that they're on the Net only when someone at that company is using some outside network resource. Otherwise, they're off the Net.

If you've determined that the other computer is indeed supposed to be available, maybe it's just broken. Try some other computers several network hops away from you. (The various network information centers such as *is.internic.net* are good candidates.) If you can get to them, the network is probably OK. If you know someone where the computer you're trying to use is located, call on the phone and ask if there is a problem.

Maybe it's the network, after all

If you can get in touch with a neighboring computer, that proves that your computer is OK. But if you can't contact any computers in the outside world, it sounds like a network problem. At this point, it's often quite informative to wander down the hall and peer into the closet where the network routing equipment lives to see if perhaps someone is working on it. Remember: local network failures are the most likely. It may also help to try pinging computers in the same department, on different floors, in different buildings, and so forth, to get an idea of how far away you can contact because that helps to pinpoint where the failing network-to-network connection is.

What's My Address?

Before you start sending out a great deal of e-mail and news articles, make sure that you know your electronic mailing address. Keep in mind that your address relative to the Internet as a whole may be different from your address within your company. For example, your in-company address may be

```
tom@calmari
```

but your address from the outside may be one of these:

```
tom@calmari.mktg.nebraska.plexxcal.com
Thomas.A.Hendricks@plexxcal.com
```

or even

```
tom%calmari@mktg-gateway.plexxcal.com
```

One easy and nonembarrassing way to make sure you have your address right is to send a message to an automated mail server (see Chapter 9). When the server sends you a response, look at the To: line in the response's message header to see what your address is. If you're at a loss for a mail server to use, send a message right here to *The Internet For Dummies* Central Headquarters, where the address is:

```
dummies@iecc.com
```

While you're at it, add a few words about whether you like this book, because messages go to both an automatic mail responder and to a mailbox where the authors can read your comments.

Also, find out the numeric Internet address of your computer (a four-part number, something like 127.99.88.77). It can come in handy when someone needs to track down a network problem between your computer and the rest of the Internet world.

Real Network-Type Problems

If you attempt to contact another host and get a response like no route to host or connection refused, that usually means a network problem has arisen. See the next chapter for details.

How to Make Enemies via E-Mail and News

By far the quickest way to make a bad name for yourself is to send obnoxious e-mail or news. This is discussed to death in Chapters 8 and 11, but here's a quick list of things not to do:

- Don't send junk mail. Just because it's easy to send e-mail to 10,000 people doesn't mean it's a good idea.

- Don't send advertisements. Traditionally, Internet e-mail is used for noncommercial purposes. It's perfectly OK to talk about work-related topics, but don't send out unsolicited ads to drum up business. If you do, expect to receive buckets of hate mail and for your system manager to boot you off the system.

- Don't send any messages about dying boys, modem taxes, or chain letters. Internet users have heard them all and don't want to hear them again. (See Chapter 8 for the sorry details.)

- DON'T SEND MESSAGES IN ALL UPPERCASE LIKE THIS BECAUSE PEOPLE ASSUME THAT YOU'RE TOO DIM TO FIND AND TURN OFF THE CAPS LOCK KEY ON YOUR KEYBOARD. Use upper- and lowercase, just like on a real typewriter. Some e-mail users evidently feel that neatness no longer counts, but they're wrong.

- Don't forget: E-mail always comes across ruder or more obnoxious than you intend. Over and over, people have discovered this important fact the hard way. E-mail is a funny medium, not really like the phone or paper mail. And it's unexpectedly easy to fly off the handle in response; so easy that the term for this is *flaming*. Don't flame. If you do, people assume that you're a flaming . . . um, well, you know what I mean.

Mailing List and USENET News Etiquette

This is discussed in greater length in Chapter 10, but here's a brief review:

- Know the difference between the address you use to get on or off a mailing list and the address you use to send messages to the list itself.

- Read a mailing list or newsgroup for at least a week before you try to send anything to it, so that you understand what topics it covers and grasp the level of discussion. (For example, a USENET group called *comp.arch* is about computer architecture. But every month or so some clueless newcomer who's never looked at the contents sends in a question about archiving programs. I'm sure you'll never make that kind of mistake now.)

✔ Most lists have an introductory message, and most news groups periodically post a *FAQs (frequently asked questions)* message that introduces the topic and answers the most commonly asked introductory questions. Before you send in your first question, make sure that it's not already answered for you.

✔ When responding to a message, if you include a copy of the original message, trim it down to the minimum needed.

Don't Be a Pig

Because most Internet services are free (after you've paid for the network connection), the popular ones can become slow and overloaded. Don't be a pig. Use what you need, but don't FTP megabytes of junk just because you think you might need it someday.

Help, I've Telnetted and I Can't Get Out

You can use telnet and rlogin to connect to services on other computers all over the world. Amazingly, some of the programs and systems that you telnet to contain *bugs* (computerese for *errors*). Some even *hang* (freeze up) and become catatonic.

Right up there in the top ten embarrassing moments is the one in which your computer is working flawlessly, but your console has gone dead because you're telnetted to something that's hung and you can't make telnet go away. There's always some way to escape, but you have to know what it is, preferably *before* you get stuck. *Note:* On UNIX systems, you usually escape with Ctrl-]. Then when it says telnet>, you type **quit**. If you're logged in through a terminal server, the escape may be two or more letters, like Ctrl-^ followed by X. If you're using a machine with windows (a Mac, Microsoft Windows, or a UNIX system with the X Windows system), a menu item is probably at the top of the telnet window that enables you to disconnect from the remote system.

The rlogin command is very much like telnet, to the point that it has the same problem. For most versions of rlogin, you disconnect by pressing Enter, then ~. (tilde followed by period), and then Enter again. Your version of telnet or rlogin may be different. The telnet command usually tells you what the escape character is at startup; rlogin is extremely taciturn, and you may have no alternative but to consult an expert or — perish the thought — look it up in the manual.

A Not-So-CAPITAL Idea

Back in the Dark Ages of computing, nobody worried about upper- and lower-case. Keypunches and terminals only had capital letters so EVERYTHING WAS IN UPPERCASE, INCLUDING FILENAMES AND MAIL ADDRESSES. BUT IT SEEMED LIKE AN AWFUL LOT OF SHOUTING, SO AS SOON AS TERMINALS COULD HANDLE LOWERCASE, THEY switched to mixed case like normal people use — at least some of them did.

The problem is that some computers (notably those running UNIX) consider upper- and lowercase to be different, whereas others (running most other systems) consider it to be the same. For example, on a UNIX system, *README,* *ReadMe,* and *readme* are three different files, but on most other systems they're merely three different ways to type the name for the same file. What this means is that when you are retrieving files by FTP or RCP, make sure that you type the name in the same mixture of upper- and lowercase that appears in a directory listing. It can't hurt and it may well help.

Another place where this occasionally causes trouble is in e-mail addresses. According to the official standard for e-mail addressing, case doesn't matter in the *domain* part of the address (the part after the @). But the *local* part (the part before the @), can be handled any way the recipient mail system wants. In theory, this means that a really perverse system could interpret *Fred@perverse.org* and *FRED@perverse.org* to be different mail addresses, although I have never actually seen a mail system that does so. In a few cases, you have to type the local part of the address in the same case as the lower system handles it; so if the recipient's address is *fred,* it doesn't accept *Fred.* (These systems are gradually being stamped out, but a few still exist.)

Fortunately, a reliable rule of thumb is that systems that care about upper- and lowercase addresses want the address in lowercase, so use *fred* to be sure.

If you have to use mixed UUCP and domain addresses like *flipper!fred@ntw.org,* be aware that the UUCP site name (*flipper* in this case), is case sensitive. A few mixed-case UUCP host names used to exist, but they are — as far as I can tell — all gone. So use all lowercase to be sure.

Why FTP Mangled Your Files

Finally, here's a mistake that everyone makes sooner or later: You use FTP to retrieve a program or a compressed file (ZIP, .Z, or the like), and the file is messed up. The program hangs, the ZIP file doesn't unzip, or the compressed file uncompresses to trash. Is the disk broken? Is the network corrupt? Nope.

It's just that you forgot to tell FTP to transfer the file in *binary* mode, so it copied it in *ASCII* mode under the misimpression that the file contained plain text. Just transfer it again, in binary mode this time. (Type the command *binary* or *image* to the FTP program before transferring the file.)

An easy way to check for this problem is to compare the size of the file on your computer to the one from which you retrieved it. In binary mode, the two copies should be exactly the same size. If the size differs by a few percent (say one copy is 87,837 bytes and the other is 88,202), you've been bitten by the ASCII copy gremlin. Oops.

## Chapter 24

Ten Problems That Aren't Your Fault and How to Circumvent Them

In This Chapter
▶ Mysterious network failures
▶ Hostile hosts
▶ Dread version creep

When Networks Go Bad

Actually, networks almost never go bad, as I mentioned in the preceding chapter. But a few messages *do* mean that the network isn't doing what you want.

"Connection refused"

This message means just what it sounds like. Your computer asked to talk to some other host, and it said no. The following are several possible reasons for this:

✔ You've tried to use a service that the host doesn't offer. Not every Internet host offers every service. It's up to a host's manager to decide what services are available and what services aren't.

✔ Some hosts don't offer any services at all. For example, if you try to finger, FTP, telnet, or nearly anything else to *xuxa.iecc.com,* you get Connection Refused. It's nothing personal — xuxa lives in my attic, as I've mentioned, and she won't connect to me either because she's a little old 286 PC that just routes data from one network to another. (She does respond to a *ping,* however, if you want to see that she exists.)

✔ The host may only accept requests from certain addresses. Frequently, for security reasons, a host only accepts telnet and FTP from other FTP hosts on the same network, which means that they're in the same organization.

✔ In a few cases, services are only available during certain hours. Many anonymous FTP servers are only available outside of office hours to avoid slowing them down while local users are trying to get work done.

"No route to host" or "Network unreachable"

Sometimes this message actually means that no network connection exists between where you are and where the other host is. This situation may occur if one of the network routers near you or near the other host fails. More likely explanations are

✔ The numeric address of the host doesn't exist, either because you typed in an address wrong, a hard-coded address in a program changed, or some part of the database that translates host names to host numbers is out of sync. (That database is, like much of the rest of the Internet, largely maintained by volunteers who occasionally goof.)

✔ A firewall system between you and the other host decided that you're not authorized to communicate with systems beyond it; so as far as you're concerned, there really *is* no route from here to there. If the firewall is inside your organization, and you're trying to contact a host outside the organization, a special procedure to persuade the firewall that you're OK may be available. Failing that, unless you have pull with the people who run the firewall, you're probably out of luck.

Total silence

Sometimes you try to contact another host and get no response at all. This silence means that the host has a valid numeric address on an actual network somewhere, but the host itself doesn't exist, at least not at the moment. (Think of a street in a subdivision that has all the addresses assigned, but some of the lots are vacant.) Most often this means that the host is down, so try again later.

Sometimes total silence means that the host exists and is working just fine, but doesn't offer the service that you want. Or a firewall in front of the host has declined to pass on your request. Ideally, a host should send an explicit `refused` message when it receives a request for a service it doesn't offer, but sometimes they just ignore them. Try *pinging* the same address (see Chapter 23). If that works, you're being ignored. If you think that the host is supposed to offer that service, you can send a polite message to its *postmaster* asking whether the host is broken or the service has been moved somewhere else.

The FTP That Wouldn't

As I mentioned in Chapter 23, 90 percent of the time, if you copy a file with FTP, it works. When it doesn't work, 90 percent of the time it's because you copied a file in *ASCII* mode rather than *binary* mode. In a few instances, though, FTP can't do what you want it to do for some other reason.

One reason is that on some computers, notably Macintoshes, filenames can contain spaces. This is a problem for FTP programs on most other kinds of computers, which tend to screw up requests for names that have spaces in them, because in most cases the programs assume that spaces separate one name on the command line from another. (A careful reading of the FTP spec shows that FTP programs are supposed to be capable of handling this, but most FTP programs were written long before Macs appeared on the Net in significant numbers.) The usual symptom is that you try to retrieve a file called *read me,* and FTP complains that there's no file called *read.* The only good way around this is to change the name of the file you want to copy.

A bunch of little-used options are available in FTP (so little-used that many FTP programs don't support them). Many of these options were put in place to support the peculiarities of the DEC-20, the most common machine on the ARPANET (the Internet's predecessor) in the early 1970s, but nearly extinct now. This means that, occasionally, when you need to use one of these older computers from your newer one, your version of FTP may not be up to the task. The most likely scenario is that you try to retrieve MS-DOS programs from the FTP archive at SIMTEL-20 *(wsmr-simtel20.army.mil),* which is probably the last remaining DEC-20 on the Net. You need to give a *tenex* command to FTP to tell it to use a peculiar data transfer format that TOPS-20 uses. Some of the snazzy, windowed versions of FTP don't have a tenex button, so if you use one of these, you're out of luck. Fortunately, the SIMTEL-20 collection is mirrored at many other sites that, not being DEC-20s, don't *need* tenex mode (see Chapter 18). Indeed, by the time you read this, SIMTEL will probably have been scrapped because it's 20 years old.

FTP commands that allow you to transfer files from one computer to another, neither computer being the one you're using, are supposed to be available. (It works like this: You're on A and you have FTP transfer a file from B to C.) I've never come across an FTP program that actually lets you do that, and I expect that if you find one, the features at machines B and C that are supposed to support this won't work, either.

FTP also can have problems with some of the structured file types found on systems such as IBM VM and MVS and DEC's VMS. Usually, local conventions can be used either to tell FTP about the file types or to pack up the files in a way that enables you to transfer them by using regular FTP commands and then unpack them after they arrive. Ask a local expert.

Dread Version Creep

Finally, there is *version creep*. All facilities on the Internet have evolved over the years. The older ones, such as telnet, FTP, and finger, have become quite stable, whereas the newer ones, such as Gopher, WAIS, and WWW are still changing. Any successful facility is implemented dozens of different times on dozens of different kinds of computers. That's why, for example, you can use telnet to log into pretty much any kind of comptuter on the Net. Even though their internal structures are quite different, they all provide compatible telnet servers.

With the more recent services, however, people add new features all the time. This means that if you're using, say, Gopher, you may occasionally get a strange message like the one shown in Figure 24-1. This message means that the remote Gopher has offered your system an item that your system doesn't know how to handle. The only solution for this is to get a more recent version of the program. As services become better understood and settle down, they change less often. For now, the more on the cutting edge something is, the more of a pain it is to keep up-to-date. (But really, are you surprised?)

Figure 24-1:
Gopher
can't handle
an item

I'm Sorry but

The Viewer: yet_to_be_wrtten %i %p
For view type:application/cso
is disabled

OK

The 5th Wave By Rich Tennant

"NO, THE SOLUTION TO OUR SYSTEM BEING DOWN IS _NOT_ FOR US TO WORK ON OUR KNEES."

Chapter 25
Ten Handy Shortcuts for Better Internet Use

In This Chapter
▶ Time-saving tricks
▶ Handy hints
▶ Snazzy shortcuts

Remote Commands for Lazy Typists

If you use the UNIX rsh command very much to run commands on other computers, you soon grow sick and tired of typing such things as

```
rsh lester cat somefile
```

to tell it to run a command, in this case on a computer called *lester.* A clever shortcut (at least it seemed clever at the time) is available: If the name under which rsh is invoked is something *other* than rsh, it assumes *that's* the name of the computer to use. So if you make a copy of rsh and call it *lester,* you can just type

```
lester cat somefile
```

If everyone makes dozens of copies of rsh, considerable space is wasted. Fortunately, you can use UNIX *links* to make a new name for rsh *without* making a new copy.

First, make sure that you have a *bin* directory (see Chapter 14 of *UNIX For Dummies* if you're not familiar with bin directories). Then type

```
ln -s /usr/ucb/rsh bin/lester
```

Note: You probably don't use a host called lester, so substitute the name of a host you to use. The name you use can be a full Internet name if it's a faraway host, like *mobydick.ntw.org,* in which case the linking command is

```
ln -s /usr/ucb/rsh bin/mobydick.ntw.org
```

(On a few systems, the true name of rsh is something other than */usr/ucb/rsh,* in which case you can use the command *whereis rsh* to find the name to use in the ln command.) You can make as many links to rsh as you want, one for each system you want to use.

After you make the links, type **rehash** to tell the *shell* that you've added some new commands; then you can go ahead and use them.

If your office has many computers sharing the same set of accounts, a directory may exist called */usr/hosts,* which has links for all the commonly used computers. If so, you can put it in your program search path by typing the following, if you use the *C shell:*

```
set path=($path /usr/hosts)
```

Or, if you use the *Korn* or *Bourne shell,* type this:

```
PATH=$PATH:/usr/hosts
export PATH
```

Using /usr/hosts doesn't preclude making your own links in bin for names of systems you use that aren't in the local list.

Host Naming for Lazy Typists

You may have noticed that Internet host names, particularly those in large organizations, tend to be pretty long. A system may be named something like *thirdbase.yankees.bronx.nyc.ny.us.* Do you really have to type the entire name every time you want to refer to that host? The answer, as long as the name has something in common with yours, is *no.*

The authors of the Internet naming system assumed that the closer a host is to you, the more likely you are to need to refer to it, and the less typing you should have to do. So, in many cases, you can abbreviate the host name and your system can still figure out what you mean.

The name system uses a *search path* — a list of partial names based on your host name — to figure out what you mean when you use an abbreviated name. For example, if you're living at third base, your search path includes

```
yankees.bronx.nyc.ny.us
bronx.nyc.ny.us
ny.us
```

You can enter just the first few parts of a host name. When the name system discovers that the name you've entered isn't a full host name, it guesses the host you want by trying the name you entered relative to the various names in the search path. For example, to talk to *leftfield.yankees.bronx.nyc.ny.us,* you can abbreviate the name to *leftfield,* and the rest is filled in from the search path. The abbreviations *leftfield.yankees* and *leftfield.yankees.bronx* and *leftfield.yankees.bronx.nyc* work, too, because the name system can fill in the rest from the search path.

If you want to do a little scouting at *homeplate.mets.queens.nyc.ny.us,* the abbreviation *homeplate.mets.queens* is adequate because the rest of the name is in the search path.

In practice, this scheme enables you to abbreviate the host names of computers in your department to a single component and names elsewhere in your organization to the first two or three components.

In theory, each system's search path can be changed to include whatever the system manager wants, not just the trailing parts of the local computer's name — but nobody does that because it would be too confusing.

A Compendium of FTP Tricks

Navigating around FTP and transferring many files can be tedious, particularly if you already know which files you want and you just want to get to the darned things. Here are some hints to make FTP less tedious.

Automate that login

Most versions of FTP let you store a list of the usernames and passwords for your frequent FTP targets in a file called *.netrc* (yes, it starts with a dot). When you start FTP, it consults the file to see whether the system you're FTP-ing to is on the list. If so, FTP uses the name from the file. Here's a typical .netrc:

```
machine shamu.ntw.org login elvis password sinatra
default login anonymous password elvis@ntw.org
```

If you FTP to *shamu.ntw.org,* FTP logs you in as *elvis* with the password *sinatra.* Anywhere else, FTP logs you in as *anonymous* with password *elvis@ntw.org.* (Use your own e-mail address, of course.) Some versions of FTP don't understand the default line, so with them you have to put in individual lines for each of the systems you log into for anonymous FTP, like this:

```
machine ftp.uu.net login anonymous password elvis@ntw.org
machine ftp.internic.net login anonymous password elvis@ntw.org
...
```

How can I keep the blasted directory listing on the screen?

One of the charmingly annoying bad habits of UNIX FTP is that it sends its output to your screen as fast as it can. (The UNIX FTP program was written back in the era of slow typewriter terminals that actually *printed stuff on paper,* if you can imagine such a thing.) When you get a directory listing, the list tends to fly off the screen before you can read it. To avoid this problem, you can take advantage of a heretofore unmentioned feature of the FTP *dir* command. You can type two things after the dir command:

✔ The directory to list

✔ The local file into which you want to store the listing

For example, if you want to get a listing of a remote directory called *virtval,* you can type

```
ftp> dir virtval val-dir
```

This puts the directory into the local file *val-dir.* That's still kind of a pain because you have to interrupt FTP to look at the file (although sometimes files with listings of popular FTP archives can be handy to keep around for reference).

Another obscure feature of dir is that if you give FTP a name that starts with | (vertical bar) instead of a local filename, it treats the rest of the name as a command, as in the following example:

```
ftp> dir virtval |more
```

This command feeds the directory to the *more* command that displays info one page at a time.

You can use the same trick on *get* commands. If you want to look at the remote file *README* but don't want to store it locally, type this:

```
ftp> get README |more
```

Compression is your friend

If you're transferring large files (meaning files that take longer to transfer than you want to wait), *compress* them first. For typical text or executable files, compression programs like *zip* (or *PKZIP*), *compress,* or *gzip* squash down the files to about half their original size, which means that they take half the time to transfer. If you're using a slow link (slower than a megabit per second), telnetting in and doing the compression can take much less time than waiting for the usual transfer. If you are transferring many separate files, you also can save time by using *tar, cpio,* or *zip* to combine them into a single archive file, because a significant amount of network overhead is involved when FTP moves from one file to the next.

This applies at least as much when you're using RCP rather than FTP. Before you use RCP to copy a file, you can use rsh to compress or archive the file on the other machine. For example:

```
rsh lester zip tmpzip file1 file2 file3
... zip does its thing ...
rcp lester:tmpzip.zip tmpzip.zip
unzip tmpzip.zip
```

In this example, I first used rsh to run the zip command on remote host lester and created an archive called *tmpzip.zip.* Then I used RCP to copy that archive to my machine and then I unzippped it locally.

Hopping around in FTP-land

The usual way to move from one directory to another in FTP is to issue a *cd* command, look at a directory listing, do another cd, and so forth. But if you know exactly where you want to go, you can cd there in one swell foop, as follows:

```
cd pub/micro/pc/windows/games/new/prnotopa
```

Most systems — UNIX and DOS, at least — require a / (slash) between components in directory names (DOS takes a \ (backslash) also). On other systems, you have to use whatever the local convention is.

Getting a directory at a time

Note: This particular trick assumes that you have an FTP program similar to the standard UNIX one. If you have a spiffy, graphical, windowed FTP program, it doesn't work. Sorry.

Let's say that you want to use FTP to copy several entire directories from one machine to another. With a little planning, you can arrange to do all this in one uninterrupted command that you can give at, say, 11:59 a.m. so that it does all the work while you're at lunch. For example, let's assume that the files you want are everything in the remote machine in the directories *pc/tools, pc/editors,* and *pc/games* (you don't want to miss that last one).

Before you FTP, create the corresponding lowest level directories on your machine — in this case *tools, editors,* and *games.* Then FTP to the other machine and issue the following commands after you log in:

```
binary
cd pc
prompt off
mget tools/* editors/* games/*
```

The first command, *binary,* sets binary transfer mode, which is essential if you're transferring nontext files. The second command, *cd pc,* changes to the *pc* directory on the host, the parent directory of the ones you want to copy. The third command, *prompt off,* turns off the usual file-by-file prompting that the *mget* command usually uses. (If you forget this, mget asks you about each file before it copies it, which totally defeats the point of doing it all in one command.) The fourth command, *mget . . .,* asks to copy everything in the directories tools, editors, and games.

The mget command copies files using the exact same names on the local machine as they have on the remote machine, which is why you need local directories tools, editors, and games ready to receive the the incoming files from the corresponding remote directories.

As it copies each file, the mget command tells you what it just did, so you can see that it's doing what you want. If many files are to be copied, it can take quite a while, but mget does it all unattended.

Hey, make up your mind

The astute reader (that's you) has noticed that I just said on the one hand that you should zip up or archive a bunch of files and then FTP the archive, and on the other hand that you can use FTP and mget or plain RCP to get them one at a time. Which one is better?

Well, it depends. (The astute reader no doubt sees that I'm waffling. Next time I'll write a book for less astute readers. It's easier.) If the computer you're getting the files from is connected to you by a fast link such as an Ethernet (see Chapter 3), the transfer is fast enough that compressing files isn't worth it. On the other hand, if the other computer is connected by a slow phone line, then compression saves a great deal of time.

The question of whether or not to compress is usually moot if you're retrieving files using anonymous FTP, because you don't have the option of logging in and doing compression yourself. But a few anonymous FTP systems do compression automatically. For example, if a file is called *zorplotz,* and you try to get *zorplotz.Z,* these particular FTP systems understand that you want a compressed version and compress the file for you. This also works the other way, in case their version is compressed and you don't have a copy of uncompress handy. This trick only works in a few places, but it doesn't hurt to try. The worst that can happen is that it tells you that no such file as zorplotz.Z exists.

People who use RCP to copy files should be pleased to learn that this same trick is available to them with considerably less work, as shown in the following command:

```
rcp -r ntw.org:pc/tools ntw.org:pc/editors tw.org:pc/games ntwstuff
```

This single line tells RCP to copy *recursively* (that's what the *-r* is for) the three remote directories into a local directory called *ntwstuff.* Recursive copying means that the directories *and* everything in them are copied. The RCP command even creates the local directories if they don't already exist. Lazy typists that use the UNIX C shell can abbreviate this to:

```
rcp -r ntw.org:pc/tools,editors,games ntwstuff
```

Tricks for Windows Users

If you're using a windowing system like Microsoft Windows, you can usually create Program Manager icons for your most commonly used commands and hosts. For example, let's say you're using Windows and, for lack of a local Archie program, you telnet to a system with a telnet Archie server. You can create an icon that runs telnet and gives the name of the host to telnet to on the command line, which is passed to the program as it starts up, as shown in Figure 25-1.

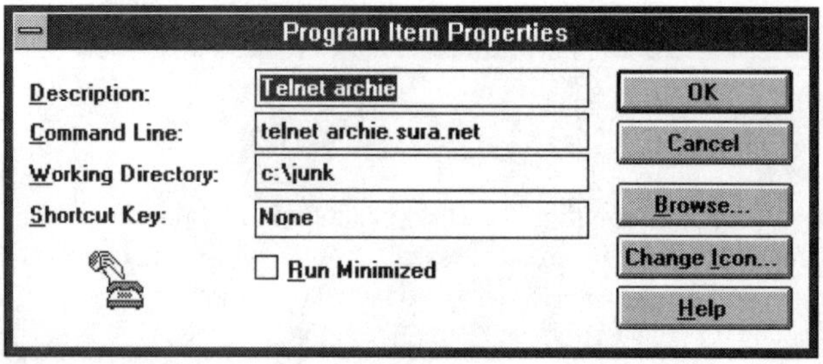

Figure 25-1:
Creating a
specialized
icon in
Windows.

Program Item Properties

Description:	Telnet archie
Command Line:	telnet archie.sura.net
Working Directory:	c:\junk
Shortcut Key:	None
	☐ Run Minimized

OK

Cancel

Browse...

Change Icon...

Help

The details of icon creation vary from one system to another, but it's usually pretty simple. Look at a similar icon (the regular telnet icon is a good choice if you want to make a specialized telnet), copy that, and add some extra text on the command line.

If you're using X Windows, a main menu usually appears whenever you click the mouse outside any window. The entries in that menu come from a file called something like *.twmrc* or *.mwmrc*. Contact a local guru to find out how to add items to the menu. It's not hard once someone shows you where to add them. On my system, the menu lines look like this:

```
"L of C"  !"xterm -name Library -e telnet
locis.loc.gov &"
```

The -**name** is the name to display at the top of the window, and the text after -**e** is the command to run.

Chapter 26
Ten Cool Things You Can Do on the Internet

*T*he Internet is one of the world's best resources for Work Avoidance, the fundamental principle that says when you really, really have to get a report out this afternoon, *first* you must play a game of Tetris. So here are ten ways to use the Internet toward this noble goal.

Learn a New Joke

Everybody needs a new joke now and then, right? USENET has long had a newsgroup called *rec.humor,* in which people post what they consider to be their funniest jokes. Tastes vary, and most of what's there isn't very funny. Indeed, much of what's there consists of complaints that a joke isn't funny, and then more complaints that the complaint isn't funny, and so forth.

Fortunately, a civic-minded USENETTER named Brad Templeton stepped into this disgraceful situation and came up with the improved newsgroup *rec.humor.funny,* in which he selects jokes that he likes from those sent in. The competition is fierce, and probably 95 percent of the putative jokes never make it. Brad has retired to Executive Moderator, but the new person who does the jokes is also pretty good at it. Having carefully followed rec.humor.funny for several years (for research purposes only, of course), I can testify that most of the jokes are indeed pretty funny. So the next time you're reading news, give it a look. You'll be in good company: readership statistics almost always report that rec.humor.funny is the single most widely read group on the Net.

If you like the jokes, you can buy printed *best of* compendia from previous years. See Brad's monthly posts regarding how to order.

Learn a Foreign Language

Well, this at least isn't wasting time — it's self-improvement. Because the Internet spans the world, many languages other than English are spoken on it.

Round the world on USENET

USENET features several dozen *soc.culture* groups for different countries (considerably more groups than there is room to list them in Chapter 12), most of which present discussions partly in the native language. So if you're interested in French, try *soc.culture.french*. For German, try *soc.culture.german* (you get the idea).

Also, Gopher lets you find Gophers all over the world. From the every-Gopher-in-the-world menu at the mother Gopher in Minnesota — which is usually an item on every *other* Gopher menu because it's so useful — you can find Gophers on every continent (well, not on Antarctica yet, but as I mentioned before, Internet hosts are already there, so who knows?).

Everyone's second favorite language

The computing community has always exhibited a quiet but persistent interest in Esperanto, an invented language from the late 1800s. Although nobody is a native speaker of Esperanto, it is designed to be simple, regular, and easy to learn so that it can be a common international language. (Nobody then could foresee that by the late 20th century, the common international language would be broken English, but such are the vagaries of history.)

Mac users can find a Hypercard stack that teaches the rudiments of Esperanto. Use either Archie or Gopher to look for *esperanto* to find a copy near you. Esperanto mailing lists, text editors, and discussion groups are also available. On USENET, the group is *soc.culture.esperanto*.

Write a Letter to the President

Has the government done something lately that you approve of? (Hmm, thought not.) Something that you disapprove of? (More likely.) Don't just gripe about it — write a letter to the President and let him know how you feel. While you're at it, drop a note to the Vice President as well. Their addresses are:

- ✔ president@whitehouse.gov
- ✔ vice.president@whitehouse.gov

Until the White House upgrades its networks, it prints out the messages and handles them with the paper mail. So include your regular mailing address if you want a response. For more info and a sample letter, see last sidebar in Chapter 8.

Learn about the Law

Do you know all the laws that affect your work, home, and hobbies? Surely you know that ignorance of the law is no defense. Better get started now learning about it — you never know when you may need it.

Some experimental Gopher and WWW servers are loaded up with U.S. Supreme Court decisions, which are a good place to start because (unlike most laws) they're written in something resembling English. Also found on these servers: patent and copyright law, the Uniform Commercial Code, and many other things. To find them, you can Gopher to *fatty.law.cornell.edu* or *gopher.law.csuohio.edu.* If you don't have Gopher locally, you can telnet to either of them and log in as *gopher.*

Study History

Is it true that the Articles of Confederation said that Canada could be admitted as a state? (If you paid attention in 7th grade history, you remember that the Articles of Confederation effectively were the Constitution during the American Revolution.) Well, wonder no more about questions such as this — a wealth of historical documents and resources awaits you on the Internet.

Enough documents to put anyone to sleep

Quite a few archives of historical documents are on the Net. They're all pretty new, and their coverage is spotty.

At *ra.msstate.edu* in *pub/docs/history* is a collection of historical documents ranging from the Articles of Confederation (yes, they said that about Canada) to Civil War papers and foreign documents. The archive at *jade.tufts.edu* in *pub/diplomacy* has a slightly different slant: it's not so much historical as it is diplomatic, with many treaties and related documents from this century.

Forward into the past

The University of Kansas has an interactive service for historians, about half of which is history and half of which is the history biz, featuring appointments, grants, and the like. To reach this service, telnet to *hnsource.cc.ukans.edu*, and log in as *history*. What you log into is actually a version of WWW (see Chapter 22), and it has connections all over the place, not just to historical stuff. It even has a connection to the mother Gopher, so you can get to nearly any Gopher resource in the world using WWW commands.

Make New Friends

One of the most ancient (if not exactly honored) of human activities is gossip. The Internet, being largely populated by humans, is as gossipy a place as any. For small-scale gossip, use the *talk* command, which enables you to type back and forth to another person on the Net. But for real, *serious* gossip, *IRC (Internet Relay Chat)* has no substitute. The global on-line gossip network enables people from all over the world to gossip 24 hours a day about nothing in particular. See Chapter 13 for details.

Make New Enemies

IRCs are generally pretty friendly. The same cannot be said of *MUDs (Multi-User Dungeons)*, also known as *MUSEs (Multi-User Shared Environments)*. You may have played an old text mode game called Adventure or Dungeon or Colossal Cave, in which you type commands to travel around a huge multiroom cave, looking for treasure and trying to avoid getting killed. (You may recall responses like "I see no Spam here.")

Well, a MUD is just what it sounds like. It's the same idea, only with many players all over the Net (in other words, all over the world). You interact with other players in ways that range from the extremely hostile to the, uh, highly affectionate. Often, you can create your own rooms and carve out your own part of the cave. Many different MUDs with many different styles are played on the Net.

Because MUDs come and go frequently, listing them here is pointless — the list would be instantly out-of-date. Consult the USENET newsgroup *rec.games.mud.announce* and look for the weekly MUD listing posted every Friday. Send a polite message asking for a list of MUDS to: *mudlist@glia.biostr.washington.edu.* Or you can FTP to *caisr2.caisr.cwru.edu* and look in */pub/mud*.

Visit a Coke Machine

A long-standing tradition is that real hackers drink Coke. And an almost-as-long-standing tradition is that real hackers have an on-line Coke machine. Different Coke machines on the Net are automated to a greater or lesser degree. Some just provide status reports so you can tell whether you can have a cold one if you walk down the hall (or fly several thousand miles, depending on where you are relative to the Coke machine). Others have fancy accounting systems on which users can set up accounts. You can pop up a Coke machine panel on the workstation screen and click on your favorite flavor, and your account is debited as the machine drops a can for you. (A few years back in California, an on-line machine called the Prancing Pony had a double-or-nothing option, in which you had a 50-50 chance of either getting your soda free or at double the regular price.)

Here's the current list of Internet Coke machines. In each case, you can check the status with the *finger* command:

```
drink@csh.rit.edu
graph@drink.csh.rit.edu
coke@cmu.edu
bargraph@coke.elab.cs.cmu.edu
mnm@coke.elab.cs.cmu.edu         (candy machine, actually)
coke@cs.wisc.edu
coke@gu.uwa.edu.au               (Australian hackers drink Coke,
                                  too)
```

Use a Supercomputer

Ever wanted to use a multimillion-dollar, state-of-the-art supercomputer? No? Hmm, well how about being able to impress your geeky friends and coworkers? You can casually tell them that you've been using a state-of-the-art Thinking Machines CM-5 massively parallel supercomputer via a peer-to-peer client/server networked interface. (It doesn't matter whether you know what all those buzzwords mean, only that you can rattle them off without stumbling. You can practice in the shower, perhaps.)

Using the massively parallel blah blah blah is easy. Whenever you use WAIS (see Chapter 21) to search any of the databases at *quake.think.com* at Thinking Machines, you're using a CM-5. They attached it to the Net partly as an experiment, partly as advertising — because many people thought the machine was so exotic that you couldn't do anything useful with it. (The fact that the guy who designed it was already famous for building a tic-tac-toe machine out of Tinker Toys and fishing line — *and* for driving down the middle of the Charles River on sunny days in his 1960s AquaCar — didn't help.)

Read a Book

A book? Pretty retro, eh? A surprising amount of plain old text can be found on the Net, ranging from the works of Shakespeare to the works of Bill Gates. Some files are pretty big, such as a complete copy of *Moby Dick*.

The two main repositories are:

- ✔ The Internet Wiretap at *wiretap.spies.com* (certainly one of the most ominously named machines on the Net)
- ✔ The Online Book Initiative at *obi.std.com* (the *std* stands for Software Tool and Die)

You can get to them by either anonymous FTP or Gopher. If you go by FTP, at wiretap the books are in the directories */Library* and */Etext,* and at obi they're in */obi.* If you go by Gopher, the menus are self-explanatory.

Given a choice, Gopher is easier to use and has better descriptions of what's what — for example, *Mark Twain: A Connecticut Yankee in King Arthur's Court* as opposed to */Library/Classic/yankee.mt* (an actual example at wiretap).

Think of all the money you can save if you use FTP or Gopher to get a copy of that book. You can print it out on your laser printer, which will cost (let's see now, 272 pages at five cents per page, carry the three) around $13.60, whereas a bound copy at your local bookstore easily costs as much as five bucks. Well, maybe it's not that much cheaper if you print it. But it's a steal if you read it on your screen — plus, if you do that it'll look like you're working. Just don't laugh too loud at the jokes.

Lots More Cool Things

Scott Yanoff at the University of Wisconsin keeps a list of special Internet connections with far more cool stuff than this chapter has room for. To find out how to get a current copy, finger *yanoff@csd4.csd.uwm.edu.*

Part VI
Resource Reference

The 5th Wave   By Rich Tennant

"WELL, I NEVER THOUGHT I'D SEE THE DAY I COULD SAY I
TELNETTED TO A BRAZILIAN HOST, THEN USED THE WORLD
WIDE WEB TO GET A GOPHER MENU, ONLY TO FIND OUT I
HAVE TO ANONYMOUS FTP."

In this part...

Now that you're an Internet expert, only one tiny detail remains: How do you get on in the first place? These last three chapters list places that provide access, places that provide software you need to use that access, and finally, some points of departure for continuing on your Internet journey.

Chapter 27
Public Internet Service Providers

In This Chapter

▶ Types of access

▶ A bunch of places that can provide you Internet access

▶ Some places that can even provide access for free

What's in This List?

This chapter concentrates on places where an individual can get dial-up Internet access at prices that make sense for individuals. There are also vendors that can supply high-speed dedicated access for organizations; these are not listed here on the theory that it's probably not your job to get the whole company on the Net.

If it *is* your job to attach your company's network to the Internet and you have a dial-up account somewhere, telnet to the INTERNIC Info Server at *is.internic.net*. Log in as *gopher* and from the first menu select Getting Connected to the Internet. There you'll find an up-to-date list of regional and national networks to contact. Connecting networks together is still a major technical challenge, so you're going to need lots of help from your local network weenies.

All the systems listed in this chapter provide at least interactive telnet and FTP as well as e-mail and USENET news, or they provide on-demand dial-up network connections so you can run any Internet program you want on your own computer. I've excluded systems that only provide access to e-mail because there are thousands of them, ranging from international providers like MCI Mail and AT&T Easylink down to local hobbyist bulletin board systems. Pretty much any BBS that exchanges mail with other BBSs can exchange mail with the Internet via FIDO (a dial-up network of PC BBSs) and other gateways.

Two Kinds of Access

Two basic varieties of dial-up access are available: dialing in as a *terminal* or dialing in as a *network host*. In the first case, you dial into a system using either a regular terminal or, more likely, a computer running a terminal program such as Procomm or Crosstalk. You can use whatever network programs the system you've dialed into provides. If you want to transfer files to or from your computer, use Kermit, zmodem, or something similar (see Chapter 3), just like you would upload or download files to or from a BBS.

If you dial in as a network host, your computer becomes an Internet host for the duration of your call and acts as any other Internet host (except, perhaps, a little smaller and slower, but nobody besides you needs to know that). The advantage of dialing in as a host is that you can run any network application on your computer that you want. If you have a multitasking system like Microsoft Windows or Macintosh System 7, you can even run several programs at once, so you can telnet to one system while retrieving files by FTP in the background. As new services are introduced, you can use them as soon as you can get client software (most often by downloading the client from the Net) instead of having to wait for your dial-up provider to install the software on its machine.

The disadvantage of dialing in as a host is that you need more software than a terminal emulator on your end, and it's considerably harder to set up. (You need to know about things like host numbers, subnet masks, and other network voodoo.) ***Note:*** If you're dialing in as a host, you should have a modem that runs at *at least* 9600 bps (bits per second). Slower modems work, but they they make the network transactions so slow that only the extraordinarily patient find them usable.

It probably makes sense to try a dial-up terminal service first and then try trading up to being a host if you get really hooked. Two variants of host service are called SLIP and PPP. They both work, but, given a choice, PPP is a little faster and more reliable. (See Chapters 3 and 5 for more info.)

Signing Up

Most of the dial-in services allow you to sign up on-line. If there is a modem number listed, you can dial in on that number. Log in using the password provided or follow the prompts after you connect.

Sign-up generally involves providing your name, address, and telephone number, along with billing information, such as a credit card number. Often, access is granted immediately, or the service may call you on the phone to verify that you are who you said you were.

Where to find your provider

An important topic to consider when choosing your provider is the cost of the phone call, because calls to on-line systems tend to be long. Ideally, you want to find a provider who has a dial-in number that's a local call for you — either a direct number or via a network such as Tymnet, Sprintnet, or CompuServe's network.

Failing that, if you can find a Sprintnet dial-in that's local for you, consider using Sprintnet's PC Pursuit service. This service lets you dial in locally and then dial out to any modem in one of over a dozen cities. Off-peak use is about $30 per month for 30 hours. Contact Sprint at 800-736-1130 (voice) or 800-877-2006 (modem) for details.

If no provider is local to you, consider using Speedway, an Internet service in Oregon that charges nothing beyond the cost of the phone call.

A few providers have 800 numbers, but their hourly rates have to be high enough to cover the cost of the 800 call. It's invariably cheaper to dial direct and pay for the call yourself rather than using an 800 access number. (800 access is attractive to people who travel frequently or who don't have to pay their own phone bills.)

Your secret decoder ring

This chapter includes a listing of national providers, and within each listing entry are some code letters you need to know. The following gives what the code letters mean:

Code Letter	What It Means
D	Dial-in interactive service providing at least telnet, FTP, e-mail, and USENET news
T	Dial-in telnet access to other systems
S	SLIP or PPP host access
F	System available for free (except perhaps for the cost of the phone call)
R	Flat rate plan available with no hourly charge (800 or network access usually costs extra)
8	Toll-free 800 access
N	Dial-up network access via Tymnet, Sprintnet, CompuServe, or other network
H	High-speed modem number (faster than 2400 bps)
M	Medium-speed modem number (1200 or 2400 bps)

National Providers

The national providers have 800 access, dial-in numbers in many cities, or provisions for access via a national network such as Tymnet, Sprintnet, or CompuServe's network.

Cooperative Library Agency for Systems and Services
D8

Phone: 800-488-4559
E-mail: class@class.org

Note: Available only to libraries and similar organizations

General Videotex DELPHI
DN

Phone: 800-544-4005
Modem: 800-365-4636 (for sign-up only)
            Log in as *JOINDELPHI,* password *INTERNETSIG*
E-mail: info@delphi.com

Note: Free five-hour test drive usually available when you sign up.

Speedway
DSFT

Modem: 10288-1-503-520-2222
E-mail: info@speedway.net

Note: You must call via AT&T, but there is no charge beyond the cost of the call. Telnet access available without sign-up.

HoloNet
DN

Phone: 510-704-0160
Modem: 510-704-1058
E-mail: info@holonet.net

Netcom Online Communication Services
DSR

Phone: 408-554-UNIX
Modem: 206-547-5992, 310-842-8835, 408-241-9760, 408-459-9851, 415-328-9940,
            415-985-5650, 503-626-6833, 510-426-6610, 510-865-9004, 619-234-0524,
            916-965-1371, 404-303-9765, 617-237-8600, 703-255-5951, 214-753-0045,
            714-708-3800
E-mail: info@netcom.com

Novalink
DN

Phone: 800-274-2814
Modem: 800-825-8852 for access, dial-ups in major U.S. cities
E-mail: info@novalink.com

The Portal System
DNR

Phone: 408-973-9111
Modem: 408-973-8091H, 408-725-0561M
           Log in as *info*
E-mail: cs@cup.portal.com, info@portal.com

PSI's Global Dialup Service
DTNR

Phone: 703-620-6651
E-mail: all-info@psi.com, gds-info@psi.com

UUNET Communications
SR

Phone: 800-4-UUNET-3, 703-204-8000
Modem: Major U.S. and Canadian cities
E-mail: info@uunet.uu.net

The WELL (Whole Earth 'Lectronic Link)
DN

Phone: 415-332-4335
Modem: 415-332-6106
           Log in as *newuser*
E-mail: info@well.sf.ca.us

The World
DSN

Phone: 617-739-0202
Modem: 617-739-9753
           Log in as *new*
E-mail: office@world.std.com

Northeast Providers

Anomaly
DSR

Phone: 401-273-4669
Modem: 401-331-3706M, 401-455-0347 (Telebit)
E-mail: info@anomaly.sbs.risc.net

DMConnection
DSR

Phone: 508-568-1618
Modem: dial-ups available in Boston and Hudson, MA
E-mail: info@dmc.com

The IDS World Network
DSR

Phone: 401-884-7856
Modem: 401-884-9002, 401-785-1067
E-mail: sysadmin@ids.net

MindVOX
DR

Phone: 212-989-2418
Modem: 212-989-4141
         Log in as *mindvox,* password *guest*
E-mail: info@phantom.com

MV Communications, Inc.
DS

Phone: 603-429-2223
Modem: Dial-ups available in Southern New Hampshire
E-mail: info@mv.com

NEARnet
SR

Phone: 617-873-8730
Modem: Dial-ups available in Boston, MA and Nashua, NH
E-mail: nearnet-join@nic.near.net

NYSERnet
SR

Phone: 315-443-4120
Modem: Dial-ups available throughout New York state
E-mail: luckett@nysernet.org

PANIX Public Access UNIX
DR

Phone: 212-877-4854 Alexis Rosen
         212-691-1526 Jim Baumbach
Modem: 212-787-3100
         Log in as *newuser*
E-mail: alexis@panix.com, jsb@panix.com

Middle Atlantic Providers

Express Access — Online Communications Service
DRS

Phone: 800-969-9090, 301-220-2020
Modem: 301-220-0462M, 301-220-0258H, 410-766-1855M, 410-768-8774H,
         714-377-9784, 908-937-9481, 215-836-4832
         Log in as *new*
E-mail: info@digex.net

Grebyn Corporation
DR

Phone: 703-281-2194
Modem: 703-281-7997
         Log in as *apply*
E-mail: info@grebyn.com

The John von Neumann Computer Network — Dialin' Tiger
DSR8

Phone: 800-35-TIGER, 609-258-2400
Modem: Dial-ups available in Princeton and Newark, NJ;
         Philadelphia, PA; Garden City, NY; Bridgeport, New
         Haven, and Storrs, CT; Providence, RI
E-mail: info@jvnc.net

PREPnet
TSR

Phone:	412-268-7870
Modem:	Dial-ups available in Philadelphia, Pittsburgh, and Harrisburg, PA
E-mail:	prepnet@cmu.edu

Telerama BBS
D

Phone:	412-481-3505
Modem:	412-481-5302
	Log in as *new*
E-mail:	info@telerama.pgh.pa.us

Southern Providers

Texas Metronet
SDR

Phone:	214-401-2800
Modem:	214-705-2902H, 214-705-2917M
	Log in as *info*, password *info*;
	or log in as *signup*, password *signup*
E-mail:	srl@metronet.com, 73157.1323@compuserve.com

Vnet Internet Access
DR

Phone:	704-374-0779
Modem:	Dial-ups available in major cities in North Carolina

NeoSoft's Sugar Land Unix
DR

Phone:	713-438-4964
Modem:	713-684-5900
E-mail:	info@NeoSoft.com

Midwestern Providers

APK — Public Access UNI* Site
DR

Phone:	216-481-9428
Modem:	216-481-9436M, 216-481-9425H
E-mail:	zbig@wariat.org

InterAccess
DSRH

Phone:	800-967-1580
Modem:	708-671-0237
	Log in as *guest*
E-mail:	help@interaccess.com

GENESIS/MCSNet
DR

Phone:	312-248-8649
Modem:	312-248-0900H, 312-248-0970H, 312-248-6295 (Telebit)
E-mail:	info@genesis.mcs.com

Merit Network, Inc. — MichNet Project
TSNR

Phone:	313-764-9430
Modem:	Michigan; Boston, MA; Washington, DC
E-mail:	info@merit.edu

MSen
DSR

Phone:	313-998-4562
Modem:	Detroit area
E-mail:	info@msen.com

OARnet
D8

Phone:	614-292-8100
Modem:	Dial-ups avilable in major cities in Ohio
E-mail:	nic@oar.net

Mountain States Providers

Community News Service
D8

Phone:	719-579-9120
Modem:	719-520-1700
	Log in as *new,* password *newuser*
E-mail:	klaus@cscns.com

Colorado SuperNet, Inc.
DS8

Phone: 303-273-3471
Modem: Dial-ups available throughout Colorado: Alamosa, Boulder/Denver, Colorado Springs, Durango, Fort Collins, Frisco, Glenwood Springs/Aspen, Grand Junction, Greeley, Gunnison, Pueblo, Telluride
E-mail: info@csn.org

Old Colorado City Communications
DR

Phone: 719-632-4848, 719-593-7575, 719-636-2040
Modem: 719-632-4111
Log in as *newuser*
E-mail: dave@oldcolo.com or thefox@oldcolo.com

Western Providers

a2i communications
DR

Phone: 408-293-8078
Modem: 408-293-9010H, 408-293-9020 (Telebit)
Log in as *guest*
E-mail: info@rahul.net

Sublight SRW
DR

Modem: 408-866-0262
Log in as *guest*
E-mail: info@sunlight.com

CR Laboratories Dialup Internet Access
DS8R

Phone: 415-381-2800
Modem: 415-389-UNIX
E-mail: info@crl.com

RainDrop Laboratories
D

Modem: 503-293-1772M, 503-293-2059H
         Log in as *apply*
E-mail: info@agora.rain.com

The Cyberspace Station
DR

Modem: 619-634-1376
         Log in as *guest*
E-mail: help@cyber.net

DIAL n' CERF
DS8

Phone: 800-876-2373, 619-455-3900
Modem: Dial-ups available in major cities in California
E-mail: help@cerf.net

Eskimo North
DR

Phone: 206-367-7457
Modem: 206-367-3837M, 206-362-6731H, 206-742-1150 (Telebit)
E-mail: nanook@eskimo.com

Halcyon
DR

Phone: 206-955-1050
Modem: 206-382-6245
          Log in as *new*
E-mail: info@halcyon.com

Northwest Nexus Inc.
S

Phone: 206-455-3505
Modem: Seattle area
E-mail: info@nwnexus.wa.com

Canadian Providers

Communications Accessibles Montreal
DSR

Phone:	514-923-2102
Modem:	514-281-5601H, 514-466-0592H, 514-738-3664 (Telebit)
E-mail:	info@cam.org

Internex Online Toronto
DRF

Phone:	416-363-8676
Modem:	416-363-3783
	Log in as *new*
E-mail:	vid@io.org

Australian Providers

connect.com.au pty ltd
DS

Phone:	+61-3-528-2239
E-mail:	connect@connect.com.au

U.K. Providers

Demon Internet Systems
DSR

Phone:	+44-81-349-0063
Modem:	+44-81-343-4848
E-mail:	internet@demon.co.uk

UK PC User Group
DR

Phone:	+44-81-863-6646
E-mail:	info@ibmpcug.co.uk

TIP

Don't touch that dial

As we were writing this book, our local cable company in Boston announced that it would start providing high-speed Internet connections via cable TV wiring. These connections were much faster than dial-up connections and cost only about $100 per month. (It'd been rumored for nearly a year, but they were just now announcing it.) This is a fraction of what any other vendor charges for a comparable service. If you want a fast connection, try calling your local cable company and ask when and if they'll be getting in on the Internet action.

It's FREE!

A year or so ago, a bunch of civic-minded people at a university in Cleveland got together and created what they called a *freenet*. This is a free system that people in the community use to share information and to take advantage of the Internet. It was quite successful (the Cleveland Freenet now consists of three machines, each supporting many users), and freenets have appeared all over the United States and Canada.

Freenets provide lots of local community information and offer limited telnet and FTP, which allows general access to libraries and other public-interest kinds of hosts. It's not full Internet access by any means but it's interesting in its own right. And, after all, it's *free*. One thing you can do is telnet from one freenet to another, so if you can get to one of them, you can get to all of them.

Freenets really are free, but to get full access you have to register so they have some idea of who's using the system. They all allow registration on-line.

Freenets all allow incoming telnet access, so if you have Internet access elsewhere, drop into a freenet and look around.

How can freenets really be free?

Most freenets are run by unpaid volunteers who borrow facilities from a local college or university. Many of them have managed to acquire charitable foundation money, too, because they're community based and educational. Most of them welcome contributions from users, although they aren't pushy about it.

Cleveland Freenet
Cleveland, OH

Modem: 216-368-3888
Log in as *fnguest*
Telnet: freenet-in-a.cwru.edu
freenet-in-b.cwru.edu
freenet-in-c.cwru.edu

Youngstown Freenet
Youngstown, OH

Modem: 216-742-3072
Log in as *visitor*
Telnet: yfn.ysu.edu

Heartland Freenet
Peoria, IL

Modem: 309-674-1100
Log in as *bbguest*
Telnet: heartland.bradley.edu

Lorain County Freenet
Lorain County, OH

Modem: 216-277-2359 (Lorain)
216-366-9753 (Elyria)
Log in as *guest*

Medina County Freenet
Medina County, OH

Modem: 216-723-6732

Tri-State Online
Cincinnati, OH

Modem: 513-579-1990
Log in as *visitor*
Telnet: cbos.uc.edu

Denver Freenet
Denver, CO

Modem: 303-270-4865
Log in as *guest*
Telnet: freenet.hsc.colorado.edu

Tallahassee Freenet
Tallahassee, FL

Modem: 904-488-5056, 904-488-6313
          Log in as *visitor*
Telnet: freenet.fsu.edu

Victoria Freenet
British Columbia, Canada

Modem: 604-595-2300
Telnet: freenet.victoria.bc.ca

National Capital Freenet
Ottawa, Ontario, Canada

Modem: 613-780-3733
          Terminals in Ottawa and Nepean public libraries
          Log in as *guest*
Telnet: freenet.carleton.ca

Big Sky Telegraph
Dillon, MT

Modem: 406-683-7680
          Log in as *bbs*

Buffalo Free-Net
Buffalo, NY

Modem: 716-645-6128
          Log in as *freeport*
Telnet: freenet.buffalo.edu

Columbia Online Information Network (COIN)
Columbia, MS

Modem: 314-884-7000
          Log in as *guest*
Telnet: bigcat.missouri.edu

Wellington Citynet
Wellington, New Zealand

Modem: +64-4-801-3060
Telnet: kosmos.wcc.govt.nz

Coming Soon

Freenets are under construction or have been proposed in Boston, Washington D.C., and the Silicon Valley.

Chapter 28
Sources of Internet Software

In This Chapter

▶ Software for your PC

▶ Software for your Mac

▶ Other odds and ends

What Kind of Nerds Do You Take Us For?

When it comes to installing software, there are two kinds of people: those who dislike doing it, and those who just plain won't. I expect you're probably in the latter category, unless you're a PC or a Mac user. If you use a different kind of computer or a workstation, it's somebody else's job to acquire software, negotiate contracts, handle installation and maintenance, and otherwise keep things going smoothly. But for a PC or a Mac, who knows? With luck, someone is supposed to handle all that, but maybe not. This is particularly true in an office with a bunch of workstations, all of which are on the Internet as a matter of divine right, except you have a PC that you'd like to connect — even if only to avoid running around with floppies.

This chapter gives sources of Internet software for PCs and Macs. This listing isn't exhaustive — particularly for the PC, new vendors of TCP/IP software appear practically every month, and new applications appear on the Net weekly.

MS-DOS and Windows TCP/IP Software

 All of these packages include the underlying network software and a set of the traditional applications, including telnet and FTP. Much of the information in this section is adapted from an on-line list compiled by C. J. Sacksteder at the Pennsylvania State University and is used with his permission. That list is posted to the USENET newsgroup *comp.protocols.tcp-ip.ibmpc* whenever it has major changes. You can FTP it from *ftp.cac.psu.edu* in *pub/dos/info/ tcpip.packages*.

Table 28-1 lists the names and sources of the TCP/IP packages listed. Most are commercial; a few are free or shareware. *Note:* The first column is an abbreviated name that is used in later tables in this chapter. Table 28-2 gives contact information for these sources.

Table 28-1 TCP/IP Packages for DOS and Windows

ID	Package	Version[1]	Publisher/Vendor	Phone
PCTCP	PC/TCP	2.2	FTP Software, Inc.	800-282-4387
Chameleon	Chameleon	3.10	NetManage, Inc.	408-973-7171
Super-TCP	Super-TCP	3.00r	Frontier Technologies	414-241-4555
IBM/DOS	TCP/IP for DOS	2.10	IBM	800-IBM-CALL
BW	BW-TCP DOS	3.0a	Beame & Whiteside Ltd.	416-765-0822
Distinct	Distinct TCP	3.02	Distinct Corp.	408-741-0781
Pathway	Pathway Access	2.0	The Wollongong Group	800-962-8649
PC-NFS	PC-NFS	5.0	SunSelect	508-442-0000
LWPD	LAN Workplace	4.1r8	Novell, Inc.	800-772-UNIX
HP	NS & ARPA Services	2.5	Hewlett-Packard	408-725-8111
NCSATel	NCSA Telnet	2.3.0	Nat'l Center for Super-computing App.	
CUTCP	CUTCP/CUTE	2.2d	Clarkson University	
QVT/Net	QVT/Net	3.4	QPC Software	716-377-8305 (fax)
Ka9q	Ka9q	[3]		
WATTCP	WATTCP	Aug 3 1993	Werick Engelke	
3Com	3Com TCP w/ DPA	2.0	3Com	800-638-3266

ID	Package	Version[1]	Publisher/ Vendor	Phone
Fusion	Fusion		Pacific Software	800-541-9508
MSLanMan	TCP/IP Util. for LanManager	1.0	Microsoft	
	TCP/2 for DOS		Essex Systems	508-532-5511
ICE/TCP	ICE/TCP		James River Group	612-339-2521
AIR	AIR for Windows		Spry, Inc.	206-286-1412
TTCP	TTCP	1.2r2	Turbosoft Pty Ltd.	+61 2 552 1266
PC-LINKD	PC-LINK for DOS	?	X LINK Technology	408-263-8201
PC-LINKW	PC-LINK for Windows	?	X LINK Technology	408-263-8203 (fax)
Lanera	TCPOppen/ Standard	2.2	Lanera Corporation	408-956-8344
Piper	Piper/IP		Ipswitch, Inc.	617-942-0621
WinNT	Windows NT	3.1[2]	Microsoft	206-882-8080

[1]The version that information here applies to. There may be a newer version.

[2]Although not a separate package, Windows NT includes TCP/IP and some utilities, so is listed for comparison purposes.

[3]Subscribe to mailing list *tcp-group@ucsd.edu* by sending mail to *tcp-group-request@ucsd.edu.*

NAVIGATE

Table 28-2	Contact Information and FTP Addresses	
ID	Address	E-mail address
PCTCP	2 High St. North Andover, MA 01845	sales@ftp.com
Chameleon	20823 Stevens Creek Blvd. Cupertino, CA 95014	support@netmanage.com

(continued)

Table 28-2 *(continued)*

ID	Address	E-Mail Address
Super-TCP	10201 N. Port Washington Rd. Mequon, WS 53092	tcp@frontiertech.com
IBM/DOS	Dept. E15 P.O. Box 12195 Research Triangle Park, NC 27709	
BW	P.O. Box 8130 Dundas, Ontario CA L9H 5E7	sales@bws.com
Distinct	P.O. Box 3410 Saratoga, CA 95070-1410	mktg@distinct.com
Pathway	1129 San Antonia Rd. Palo Alto, CA 94303	sales@twg.com
PC-NFS	2 Elizabeth Drive Chelmsford, MA 01824	
LWPD	122 East 1700 South Provo, UT 84606	
HP	19420 Homestead Rd. Cupertino, CA 94014	
NCSATel		anon FTP simtel20 or mirrors pub/msdos/ncsaelnet
CUTCP		anon FTP sun.soe.clarkson.edu cutcp@omnigate.clarkson.edu
QVT/Net		anon FTP ftp.cica.indiana.edu or mirrors djp@troi.cc.rochester.edu
Ka9q		anon FTP ucsd.edu pub/ham-radio/packet/tcpoip/ka9q
WATTCP		anon FTP dorm.rutgers.edu pub/msdos/wattcp
MSLanMan	One Microsoft Way Redmond, WA 95052-6399	
ICE/TCP	125 North First St. Minneapolis, MN 55401	jriver@jriver.com

ID	Address	E-Mail Address
AIR	1319 Dexter Ave. North Seattle, WA 98109	sales@spry.com
TTCP	248 Johnston St. Annandale, NSW Aus. 2038	info@abccomp.oz.au
PC-LINKx	741 Ames Avenue Milpitas, CA 95035	tom@xlink.com
Lanera	516 Valley Way Milpitas, CA 95035	lanera@netcom.com
Piper	580 Main St. Reading, MA 01867	ub@ipswitch.com
WinNT	One Microsoft Way Redmond, WA 95052-6399	

Table 28-3 contains the following codes, and here is what they mean:

✔ **Y:** Yes, feature included

✔ **N:** No, feature not included

✔ **M:** Requires this feature

✔ **S:** Feature supported via *shim* that simulates a different software interface

Also, the column *Stack Provided* indicates whether libraries are provided to support new or third-party applications. *Ethernet, Token Ring,* and *FDDI* are kinds of physical network connection. *Packet Drivers* are a standard way to handle many different brands of Ethernet card. *NDIS* allows sharing cards with LAN Manager. *ODI* shares with Novell. *SLIP* and *PPP* handle serial (modem) communications.

Table 28-3   Hardware Supported

ID	Drivers Included					Interfaces Supported			
	Stack Provided	Ethernet	Token Ring	FDDI	Packet Drivers	NDIS	SLIP	PPP	ODI
PCTCP	Y	Y	Y		Y	Y	Y	Y	Y
Chameleon	Y	Y	Y	Y	N	Y	Y	N	
Super-TCP	Y	Y	Y	N	Y	Y	Y	X	Y
IBM/DOS	Y	Y	Y		S	Y	Y	N	N

(continued)

Table 28-3 *(continued)*

ID	Drivers Included					Interfaces Supported			
	Stack Provided	Ethernet	Token Ring	FDDI	Packet Drivers	NDIS	SLIP	PPP	ODI
BW	Y	Y	Y		Y	Y	Y	N	Y
Distinct	Y	Y	Y	Y	Y	Y	Y	Y	Y
Pathway	Y	Y	Y		Y	Y	Y		Y
PC-NFS	Y	Y	Y		S	Y	Y	N	Y
LWPD	Y	Y	Y		S	S	Y	Y	Y
HP	Y	Y	Y		Y	Y	N	N	S
NCSATel	N	N	N		M				
CUTCP	N	N	N						
QVT/Net	N	N	N		M		Y		
Ka9q[3]	N	N	N	N	Y	N	Y	Y	N
WATTCP	Y	N	N	N	Y	N	N	N	N
3Com		Y	Y		N	Y			
Fusion		Y			N	Y			
MSLanMan [1]		Y	Y	Y		Y			
ICE/YCP					Y				
AIR	N					Y			Y
TTCP		Y	Y		Y	S	N	N	S
PC-LINKD		Y			Y	Y	Y		Y
Lanera	Y	Y	N	N	Y	Y	Y	N	Y
Piper	Y	Y	Y	?	?	Y	Y	?	Y
WinNT	Y	Y	Y	Y	N	Y[2]	N	N	

Note: Most packages include more drivers than are listed here. Any package that supports packet drivers also supports NDIS and ODI using compatibility software.

[1]The stack is provided with LAN Manager

[2]Supports NDIS 3.0 (others are all 2.0)

[3]Ka9q comes with C language source code so that a nerdy friend can adapt it to whatever hardware you have.

Table 28-4 contains some abbreviations that require some illuminating. *All Apps:* All applications are Windows based. *Some Apps:* Some are Windows, some are DOS or character. *All DLL:* Stack is implemented as "100 percent Windows DLL" code. *WINSOCK:* Supports Windows Socket API (1.1) for add-on applications. *VDev:* Includes a virtual device drive to support DOS apps running under Windows. *Network Driver:* A Windows driver that allows connecting and disconnecting drives and remote printing.

Table 28-4	Microsoft Windows Applications and Support					
ID	All Apps	Some Apps	All DLL	WINSOCK	VDev	Network Driver
PCTCP	N	Y	N	Y	Y	Y
Chameleon	Y	N	Y	Y		
Super-TCP	Y	[1]	Y[1]	Y	Y	Y
IBM/DOS	N	Y	N[2]	Y		
BW	N	Y	N	N[3]		
Distinct	Y	N	Y	Y		
Pathway	Y					
PC-NFS	N	Y	N	Y	Y	Y
LWPD	N	Y	N	N[3]		
HP	N	N	N	N		
NCSATel	N	N	N	N		
CUTCP	N	N	N	N		
QVT/Net	Y	N	N	N	N	N
Ka9q	N	N	N	N	N	N
WATTCP	N	N	N	Y	N	N
3Com						
Fusion						
MSLanMan	N	N	N	[5]		
AIR						
TTCP	N	Y	N	N[3]		
PC-LINKW						

(continued)

Table 28-4 *(continued)*

ID	All Apps	Some Apps	All DLL	WINSOCK	VDev	Network Driver
Lanera	N	Y	N	Y		
Piper	?	?	N	Y	?	N
WinNT	N[4]	N[4]	N[4]	Y		

[1]Super-TCP/NFS includes DOS-based applications and an optional TSR.

[2]The stack is protected mode code that sits entirely in extended memory except for a small interface TSR.

[3]WINSOCK is scheduled soon, as an update or in the next version.

[4]Windows NT doesn't run on top of DOS, and TCP/IP is part of the system. Some of the applications are graphical, many utilities are character based.

[5]As of May 1993, you can find a beta version of WINSOCK for FTP on *rhino.microsoft.com.*

Table 28-5 contains two codes you should know:

- ✔ **D:** DOS or character-based application
- ✔ **W:** Windows-based application

Also: *SMTP* is outgoing e-mail. *POP* is incoming e-mail. *NNTP* is USENET news. *SNMP* is a network monitoring facility. *NFS* are remote disk files.

Table 28-5 — Major Applications

ID	Telnet	TN3270	FTP Client	FTP Server	SMTP	POP[2]	NNTP Client	SNMP Agent	NFS Client
PCTCP	DW	D	DW	D	D	D2 D3	D	Y	DW
Chameleon	W	W	W	W	W	W2	N	W	X
Super-TCP	W	W	W	W	W	W2 W3	W	W	DX WX
IBM/DOS	DW	DW	DW	D	DW	D2	N	Y	X
BW	DW	DW	DW	DW	W	W2 W3	N	Y	X
Distinct	W	N	W	W					
Pathway	DW	DW	DW	D				D	DW

ID	Telnet	TN3270	FTP Client	FTP Server	SMTP	POP[2]	NNTP Client	SNMP Agent	NFS Client
PC-NFS	DW	X	DW	D	DW	D23 W23	N	Y	DW
LWPD	DW	DWX	DW	DW	N	N	N	Y	X
HP	D		D						
NCSATel	D	[4]	D		N	N	N	N	N
CUTCP	D	D	D	D	N	N	N	N	N
QVT/Net	W	N	W	W	N	W	W	N	N
Ka9q	D	N	D	D	D CS	D23	D	N	N
WATTCP	N	N	N	N	N	?	N	N	N
3Com									
Fusion									
MSLanMan	D		D						
AIR	W	W	Y						X
TTCP v2.0	[1]		DW						
PC-LINKD	D		D						Y
PC-LINKW									Y
Lanera	DW	DW	D	D	N	N	N	N	X
Piper	Y	Y	Y	Y	CS	?	Y	Y	Y
WinNT	W	N	D[3]	[5]	N	N	N	y	

[1]Terminal emulation products sold separately.

[2]POP: 2 is version 2, 3 is version 3 and implies an SMTP client to send mail.

[3]D means *character based.*

[4]Get *TN3270* (*CUTCP*) package from Clarkson University.

[5]Server for NT will be in production version.

DOS and Windows Network Applications

The following are Internet network applications. Most of them require one of the TCP/IP packages in the preceding tables or, for Windows applications, any package that supports WINSOCK. This list omits gateways between TCP/IP and other networks such as Novell; see the on-line list (mentioned previously) which you can FTP from *ftp.cac.psu.edu* in *pub/dos/info/tcpip.packages*.

FTP Nuz

Shareware DOS USENET client for PC/TCP. Find via FTP to *calvin.sfasu.edu* in */pub/dos/network/ftp-pctcp*.

HGopher (beta 2.2)

WINSOCK Gopher client (see Chapter 20). FTP at *lister.cc.ic.ac.uk* directory *pub/wingopher* or at *sunsite.unc.edu: /pub/micro/pc-stuff/ms-windows/winsock/apps*. Get files *readme.txt* and *hgopher.exe* (WINSOCK Version) or *hngopher.exe* (PC NFS Only Version).

Microsoft TCP/IP for Windows for Workgroups

It has only a ping utility, but has a WINSOCK.DLL and provides NetBIOS over TCP/IP. It works, but takes a lot of low addressed memory.

NUPop

Primarily a POP3 mail client, but 2.0 (in beta as of 5/93), includes a Gopher client, telnet, FTP, and other built-in utilities. Works with packet drivers and PC/TCP kernels. Find via anonymous FTP to *ftp.acns.nwu.edu* in */pub/nupop*.

OS Mail

Open Systems Mail is a commercial Windows POP3 client for various stacks (PC-NFS, PC/TCP, Wollongong Pathway). Send to *pinesoft@netcom.com* for information.

PC Eudora

This is a Windows POP3 client that works with WINSOCK. Anonymous FTP to *ftp.qualcomm.com*. Formerly free, now a commercial product sold by Qualcomm.

PC Gopher

DOS Gopher clients (II and III) are for packet drivers. Find via anonymous FTP to *boombox.micro.umn.edu*. The University of Michigan has a version of PC Gopher II for PC/TCP kernel. Anonymous FTP to *ftp.msu.edu*. See also UTGopher at that site. PC Gopher III now works with PC/TCP, too.

Trumpet

Trumpet is a news reader. Find in MS-DOS archives. It works with packet drivers and LWPD; there is interface code for PC/TCP kernels. New Windows version in beta test comes in several flavors to work with different TCP/IP packages, including one for WINSOCK. FTP from *ftp.utas.edu.au* or *biochemistry.cwru.edu.*

Cello

This is a full-featured World Wide Web browser for Windows. It needs the Distinct TCP/IP package (limited version included) or WINSOCK. It's available by FTP from *fatty.law.cornell.edu,* in */pub/LII/Cello.*

WINSOCK applications

A variety of applications that use the WINSOCK API are found via anonymous FTP to *microdyne.com* or *sunsite.unc.edu, /pub/micro/pc-stuff/ms-windows/ winsock.* Most of these are still in development. Various documents related to the Windows Sockets API can be found there, too.

Macintosh TCP/IP Software

Nearly every Mac Internet application requrires MacTCP, which is sold by APDA (phone 800-282-2732 or 716-871-6555). You want at least version 2.0.2. Generally, you should have your Macintosh dealer order it from APDA. The order numbers and list prices are as follows:

- ✔ M8113Z/A   TCP/IP Connection for Macintosh ($59.00)
- ✔ M8114Z/A   TCP/IP Administration for Macintosh ($199.00)

Many universities and large corporations have inexpensive site licenses; check before you shell out for your own copy. E-mail to *apda@applelink.apple.com.*

MacSLIP

This is a commercial SLIP (dial-up Internet connections) as a MacTCP extension from TriSoft. E-mail to *info@hydepark.com* or call 800-531-5170.

InterSLIP

This is a SLIP extension to MacTCP from InterCon. It's available as part of the TCP/Connect II package or at no charge via FTP from *ftp.intercon.com* in *InterCon/sales.*

Macintosh Network Applications

MacTCP provides only low-level support and a control panel. If you actually want to do anything, you need applications. Many applications are free or shareware and can be retrieved by FTP. The major Mac FTP archives are:

- ✔ mac.archive.umich.edu (Also provides files by e-mail. Send a message containing *help* to *mac@mac.archive.umich.edu.*)

- ✔ ftp.apple.com (This is the official Apple archive for free Apple-provided software.)

- ✔ microlib.cc.utexas.edu

- ✔ sumex-aim.stanford.edu (It's the best-known archive, hence it's badly overloaded — so try others first.)

- ✔ wuarchive.wustl.edu (Copies of *sumex* files are in *mirrors/infomac* and of *umich* files in *mirrors/archive.umich.edu.*)

NCSA Telnet

NCSA Telnet is the oldest and most widely used Mac telnet program. It also provides incoming and outgoing FTP. Available via FTP. Unlike every other application listed, it runs with or without MacTCP. While running without MacTCP, it contains its own SLIP (dial-up) package.

Comet (Cornell Macintosh Terminal Emulator)

Features telnet and TN3270. Available via FTP from *comet.cit.cornell.edu* in *pub/comet.*

Hytelnet

Hytelnet is a Hypercard version of telnet. E-mail to Charles Burchill at *burchil@ccu.umanitoba.ca.*

Eudora

Eudora is the most widely used mail package: flexible, complete, and free. What more could you ask? FTP from *ftp.cso.uiuc.edu* in *mac/eudora,* or inquire by e-mail to *eudora-info@qualcomm.com.*

LeeMail

This is an inexpensive shareware mail program. Available by FTP or from the author Lee Fyock at *<laf@mitre.org>.*

NewsWatcher

NewsWatcher is a free USENET news program. Available by FTP. Nerds can get the source code by FTP from *ftp.apple.com.*

Nuntius

This is a graphical USENET reader. Contact the author, Peter Speck, at *speck@dat.ruc.dk.*

TCP/Connect II

This is a full-featured commercial suite (telnet, FTP, news, and more) of Internet applications. Available from InterCon Systems. Phone 703-709-9890 or e-mail to *sales@intercon.com.*

SU-Mac/IP

This suite of network applications (telnet, FTP, remote printing, and more) is from Stanford University. It's available only to "degree-granting institutions of higher education," at little or no cost. Call 415-723-3909 or e-mail *macip@jessica.stanford.edu.*

VersaTerm

VersaTerm is a commercial package from Synergy Software providing flexible versions of telnet and FTP. SLIP (dial-up) also available. Call 215-779-0522.

Chapter 29
I Want to Learn More

The Internet is growing so fast that no single human can keep up with it all. Here are a few resources to help keep abreast of what's new.

Publications

Note that two of these are available either on paper or in electronic versions over the Net.

Internet World

This is a new, bi-monthly, glossy magazine for Internet users. Articles include tips, case histories, interviews with notable Internauts, product and service reviews, and so on. Contact:

Internet World
Meckler Corp.
11 Ferry Lane West
Westport, CT 06880

Phone: 203-226-6967
E-mail: meckler@jvnc.net or 70373.616@compuserve.com

Matrix News

A monthly newsletter about networks, including but not limited to the Internet. Available on paper or by e-mail. Contact:

Matrix Information and Directory Services
1106 Clayton Lane, Suite 500W
Austin, TX 78723

Phone: 512-451-7602
Email: mids@tic.com

Internet Business Journal

Covers business issues on nascent commercial Internet. Case histories, studies, and the like. Available both on-line and on paper. Contact:

Michael Strangelove, Publisher
The Internet/NREN Business Journal
1-60 Springfield Road
Ottawa, Ontario, CANADA, K1M 1C7

Phone: 613-747-0642
FAX: 613-564-6641
E-mail: 441495@acadvm1.uottawa.ca

Organizations

Each of the following organizations also publishes a magazine.

The Internet Society

The Internet Society is dedicated to supporting the growth and evolution of the Internet. Supports development and evolution of Internet standards to keep the Net working as it grows. Publishes a magazine, holds conferences, and has many on-line resources. Both individual and organizational memberships are available. Contact:

Internet Society
Suite 100
1895 Preston White Drive
Reston, VA 22091

Fax: 703-620-0913
Email: isoc@isoc.org

The Electronic Frontier Foundation (EFF)

The EFF works at the electronic frontier on issues of free speech, equitable access, and education in a networked context. It offers legal services in cases where users' on-line civil liberties have been violated.

It publishes a magazine, has a USENET group, keeps on-line files, and maintains human resources. Contact:

Electronic Frontier Foundation
1001 G Street, NW
Suite 950 East
Washington, DC 20001

Phone: 202-347-5400
Fax: 202-393-5509
Email: eff@eff.org
USENET: comp.org.eff.news and comp.org.eff.talk

The Society for Electronic Access (SEA)

The SEA works to promote civil rights and civilization in the networked digital world, primarily through research and education. Contact:

The Society for Electronic Access
Post Office Box 3131
Church Street Station
New York, NY 10008-3131

E-mail: sea-member@sea.org

Appendix A
Internet Geographic Zones

This list is correct as of April 1993, and will certainly be out of date by the time you read it. But at least the country codes don't change too often.

How to Read This Table

The letters in the *How* field describe what connections to the Net the country has. An uppercase *I* means that it's on the Internet. A lowercase *i* means that it has an internet-type network, but it isn't connected to the rest of the world. The other letters refer to other kinds of networks that aren't really part of the Internet but can exchange electronic mail with it. The networks are *B* for *BITNET*, *F* for *FIDONET*, *U* for *UUCP*, and *O* for *OSI*. An uppercase letter means that there are more than five sites of that type; lowercase means one to five.

Table A-1		Two-Letter Zone Names
Zone	*How*	*Country*
AF	——	Afghanistan (Democratic Republic of)
AL	——	Albania (Republic of)
DZ	——	Algeria (People's Democratic Republic of)
AS	——	American Samoa
AD	——	Andorra (Principality of)
AO	——	Angola (People's Republic of)
AI	——	Anguilla
AQ	-I—	Antarctica
AG	——	Antigua and Barbuda
AR	BIUF-	Argentina (Argentine Republic)
AM	—u—	Armenia
AW	——	Aruba
AU	-IUFo	Australia
AT	BIUFO	Austria (Republic of)
AZ	—U—	Azerbaijan
BS	——	Bahamas (Commonwealth of the)

(continued)

Table A-1 *(continued)*

Zone	How	Country
BH	b——	Bahrain (State of)
BD	——	Bangladesh (People's Republic of)
BB	——	Barbados
BY	—UF-	Belarus
BE	BIUFO	Belgium (Kingdom of)
BZ	——	Belize
BJ	——	Benin (People's Republic of)
BM	—uf-	Bermuda
BT	——	Bhutan (Kingdom of)
BO	—U—	Bolivia (Republic of)
BA	——	Bosnia-Hercegovina
BW	—f-	Botswana (Republic of)
BV	——	Bouvet Island
BR	BIUFO	Brazil (Federative Republic of)
IO	——	British Indian Ocean Territory
BN	——	Brunei Darussalam
BG	biUF-	Bulgaria (Republic of)
BF	—u—	Burkina Faso (formerly Upper Volta)
BI	——	Burundi (Republic of)
KH	——	Cambodia
CM	—u—	Cameroon (Republic of)
CA	BIUFO	Canada
CV	——	Cape Verde (Republic of)
KY	——	Cayman Islands
CF	——	Central African Republic
TD	——	Chad (Republic of)
CL	BIUF-	Chile (Republic of)
CN	—ufO	China (People's Republic of)
CX	——	Christmas Island (Indian Ocean)
CC	——	Cocos (Keeling) Islands

(continued)

Zone	How	Country
CO	B-u—	Colombia (Republic of)
KM	——	Comoros (Islamic Federal Republic of the)
CG	—u—	Congo (Republic of the)
CK	——	Cook Islands
CR	blu—	Costa Rica (Republic of)
CI	—u—	Cote d'Ivoire (Republic of)
HR	-lufo	Croatia
CU	—U—	Cuba (Republic of)
CY	bl—	Cyprus (Republic of)
CZ	BIUF-	Czech Republic
DK	BIUFO	Denmark (Kingdom of)
DJ	——	Djibouti (Republic of)
DM	——	Dominica (Commonwealth of)
DO	—Uf-	Dominican Republic
TP	——	East Timor
EC	blu—	Ecuador (Republic of)
EG	b-U—	Egypt (Arab Republic of)
SV	——	El Salvador (Republic of)
GQ	——	Equatorial Guinea (Republic of)
EE	-IUF-	Estonia (Republic of)
ET	—F-	Ethiopia (People's Democratic Republic of)
FK	——	Falkland Islands (Malvinas)
FO	——	Faroe Islands
FJ	—u—	Fiji (Republic of)
FI	BIUFO	Finland (Republic of)
FR	BIUFO	France (French Republic)
GF	—u—	French Guiana
PF	—u—	French Polynesia
TF	——	French Southern Territories
GA	——	Gabon (Gabonese Republic)
GM	——	Gambia (Republic of the)

(continued)

Table A-1 *(continued)*

Zone	How	Country
GE	—UF-	Georgia (Republic of)
DE	BIUFO	Germany (Federal Republic of)
GH	—F-	Ghana (Republic of)
GI	——	Gibraltar
GR	BIUFO	Greece (Hellenic Republic)
GL	-I-f-	Greenland
GD	—u—	Grenada
GP	b-u—	Guadeloupe (French Department of)
GU	—F-	Guam
GT	—u—	Guatemala (Republic of)
GN	——	Guinea (Republic of)
GW	——	Guinea-Bissau (Republic of)
GY	——	Guyana (Republic of)
HT	——	Haiti (Republic of)
HM	——	Heard and McDonald Islands
HN	——	Honduras (Republic of)
HK	BI-F-	Hong Kong (Hisiangkang, Xianggang)
HU	BIUFo	Hungary (Republic of)
IS	-IUFo	Iceland (Republic of)
IN	bIUfO	India (Republic of)
ID	—u—	Indonesia (Republic of)
IR	b———	Iran (Islamic Republic of)
IQ	——	Iraq (Republic of)
IE	BIUFO	Ireland
IL	BIUF-	Israel (State of)
IT	BIUFO	Italy (Italian Republic)
JM	—u—	Jamaica
JP	BIUF-	Japan
JO	——	Jordan (Hashemite Kingdom of)
KZ	—Uf-	Kazakhstan

(continued)

Zone	How	Country
KE	—f-	Kenya (Republic of)
KI	—u—	Kiribati (Republic of)
KP	——	Korea (Democratic People's Republic of)
KR	BIUFO	Korea (Republic of)
KW	-I—	Kuwait (State of)
KG	—U—	Kyrgyzstan
LA	——	Lao People's Democratic Republic
LV	-IUF-	Latvia (Republic of)
LB	——	Lebanon (Lebanese Republic)
LS	—u—	Lesotho (Kingdom of)
LR	——	Liberia (Republic of)
LY	——	Libyan Arab Jamahiriya
LI	——	Liechtenstein (Principality of)
LT	—UFo	Lithuania
LU	bIUFo	Luxembourg (Grand Duchy of)
MO	—F-	Macau (Ao-me'n)
??	——	Macedonia (Former Yugoslav Republic of)
MG	——	Madagascar (Democratic Republic of)
MW	——	Malawi (Republic of)
MY	bIUF-	Malaysia
MV	——	Maldives (Republic of)
ML	—u—	Mali (Republic of)
MT	—u—	Malta (Republic of)
MH	——	Marshall Islands (Republic of the)
MQ	——	Martinique (French Department of)
MR	——	Mauritania (Islamic Republic of)
MU	—f-	Mauritius
MX	BIuF-	Mexico (United Mexican States)
FM	——	Micronesia (Federated States of)
MD	—UF-	Moldova (Republic of)
MC	——	Monaco (Principality of)

(continued)

Table A-1 *(continued)*

Zone	How	Country
MN	——	Mongolia (Mongolian People's Republic)
MS	——	Montserrat
MA	——	Morocco (Kingdom of)
MZ	—u—	Mozambique (People's Republic of)
MM	——	Myanmar (Union of)
NA	—u—	Namibia (Republic of)
NR	——	Nauru (Republic of)
NP	——	Nepal (Kingdom of)
NL	BIUFO	Netherlands (Kingdom of the)
AN	——	Netherlands Antilles
NT	——	Neutral Zone (between Saudi Arabia and Iraq)
NC	—U—	New Caledonia
NZ	-IUF-	New Zealand
NI	—u—	Nicaragua (Republic of)
NE	—u—	Niger (Republic of the)
NG	——	Nigeria (Federal Republic of)
NU	——	Niue
NF	——	Norfolk Island
MP	——	Northern Mariana Islands (Commonwealth of the)
NO	BIUFO	Norway (Kingdom of)
OM	——	Oman (Sultanate of)
PK	—U—	Pakistan (Islamic Republic of)
PW	——	Palau (Republic of)
PA	b-uF-	Panama (Republic of)
PG	—u—	Papua New Guinea
PY	—u—	Paraguay (Republic of)
PE	—Uf-	Peru (Republic of)
PH	—uF-	Philippines (Republic of the)
PN	——	Pitcairn
PL	BIUF-	Poland (Republic of)

(continued)

Zone	How	Country
PT	bIUFO	Portugal (Portuguese Republic)
PR	bIUF-	Puerto Rico (uses U.S. names)
QA	——	Qatar (State of)
RE	—u—	Re'union (French Department of)
RO	B—f-	Romania
RU	BiUF-	Russian Federation
RW	——	Rwanda (Rwandese Republic)
SH	——	Saint Helena
KN	——	Saint Kitts and Nevis
LC	——	Saint Lucia
PM	——	Saint Pierre and Miquelon (French Department of)
VC	——	Saint Vincent and the Grenadines
WS	——	Samoa (Independent State of)
SM	——	San Marino (Republic of)
ST	——	Sao Tome and Principe (Democratic Republic of)
SA	B——	Saudi Arabia (Kingdom of)
SN	—Uf-	Senegal (Republic of)
SC	—u—	Seychelles (Republic of)
SL	——	Sierra Leone (Republic of)
SG	bIuF-	Singapore (Republic of)
SK	bIUF-	Slovakia
SI	-IUFO	Slovenia
SB	——	Solomon Islands
SO	——	Somalia (Somali Democratic Republic)
ZA	-IUFO	South Africa (Republic of)
SU	BiUF-	Former Soviet Union (officially obsolete but still in use)
ES	BIUFO	Spain (Kingdom of)
LK	—U—	Sri Lanka (Democratic Socialist Republic of)
SD	——	Sudan (Democratic Republic of the)
SR	—u—	Suriname (Republic of)
SJ	——	Svalbard and Jan Mayen Islands

(continued)

Table A-1 *(continued)*

Zone	How	Country
SZ	———	Swaziland (Kingdom of)
SE	BIUFo	Sweden (Kingdom of)
CH	BIUFO	Switzerland (Swiss Confederation)
SY	———	Syria (Syrian Arab Republic)
TW	BIuF-	Taiwan, Province of China
TJ	—uf-	Tajikistan
TZ	—f-	Tanzania (United Republic of)
TH	-IUF-	Thailand (Kingdom of)
TG	—u—	Togo (Togolese Republic)
TK	———	Tokelau
TO	———	Tonga (Kingdom of)
TT	—u—	Trinidad and Tobago (Republic of)
TN	bIUfo	Tunisia
TR	BI-F-	Turkey (Republic of)
TM	—U—	Turkmenistan
TC	———	Turks and Caicos Islands
TV	———	Tuvalu
UG	—f-	Uganda (Republic of)
UA	—UF-	Ukraine
AE	———	United Arab Emirates
UK	bIUFO	United Kingdom (official code is GB)
US	BIUFO	United States (United States of America)
UM	———	United States Minor Outlying Islands
UY	—UF-	Uruguay (Eastern Republic of)
UZ	—UF-	Uzbekistan
VU	—u—	Vanuatu (Republic of, formerly New Hebrides)
VA	———	Vatican City State (Holy See)
VE	-IU—	Venezuela (Republic of)
VN	———	Vietnam (Socialist Republic of)
VG	———	Virgin Islands (British)

(continued)

Zone	How	Country
VI	—f-	Virgin Islands (U.S.)
WF	——	Wallis and Futuna Islands
EH	——	Western Sahara
YE	——	Yemen (Republic of)
YU	——	Yugoslavia (Socialist Federal Republic of)
ZR	——	Zaire (Republic of)
ZM	—uf-	Zambia (Republic of)
ZW	—uf-	Zimbabwe (Republic of)

Index

Order Form

Order Center: (800) 762-2974 (8 a.m.–5 p.m., PST, weekdays) or (415) 312-0650

For Fastest Service: Photocopy This Order Form and FAX it to: (415) 358-1260

Quantity	ISBN	Title	Price	Total

Shipping & Handling Charges

Subtotal	U.S.	Canada & International	International Air Mail
Up to $20.00	Add $3.00	Add $4.00	Add $10.00
$20.01-40.00	$4.00	$5.00	$20.00
$40.01-60.00	$5.00	$6.00	$25.00
$60.01-80.00	$6.00	$8.00	$35.00
Over $80.00	$7.00	$10.00	$50.00

In U.S. and Canada, shipping is UPS ground or equivalent.
For Rush shipping call (800) 762-2974.

Subtotal _____

CA residents add
applicable sales tax _____

IN and MA residents add
5% sales tax _____

IL residents add
6.25% sales tax _____

RI residents add
7% sales tax _____

Shipping _____

Total _____

Ship to:

Name _____

Company _____

Address _____

City/State/Zip _____

Daytime Phone _____

Payment: ❑ Check to IDG Books (US Funds Only) ❑ Visa ❑ Mastercard ❑ American Express

Card# _____ Exp. _____ Signature _____

62   60

Please send this order form to: IDG Books, 155 Bovet Road, Suite 310, San Mateo, CA 94402.

Allow up to 3 weeks for delivery. Thank you!